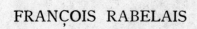

FRANÇOIS RABELAIS

FRⁱ RABELAIS.

RABELAIS
REPRODUCTION DU PORTRAIT
conservé à la Bibliothèque de Genève

FRANÇOIS RABELAIS

BY

ARTHUR TILLEY, M.A.

KENNIKAT PRESS
Port Washington, N. Y./London

FRANÇOIS RABELAIS

First published in 1907
Reissued in 1970 by Kennikat Press
Library of Congress Catalog Card No: 79-113326
ISBN 0-8046-1002-9

Manufactured by Taylor Publishing Company   Dallas, Texas

PREFACE

THE publication of Des Marets's and Rathery's edition of Rabelais's works, in 1857, marked a new epoch in the study of Rabelais. To this edition was prefixed a *Life*, by Rathery, in which, for the first time, all the legendary matter was carefully pruned away, and no fact was admitted that was not based upon trustworthy evidence. During the last fifty years this biography has held the field, and except for one or two important discoveries made by M. Heulhard in connection with Rabelais's visit to Italy, and embodied in his book, *Rabelais, his Travels in Italy, his Exile at Metz* (*Rabelais, ses Voyages en Italie, son Exil à Metz*) (1891), little addition has been made to our knowledge of Rabelais until very recently.

But at the close of 1902 a fresh impetus was given to Rabelaisian studies by the foundation of the Société des Études Rabelaisiennes, with M. Abel Lefranc as its first President. The organ of the Society, the *Revue des Études rabelaisiennes*, made its first appearance in January, 1903, and already, during its short existence, has added very considerably to our

5

knowledge of the subject, especially as regards
Rabelais's life. Notably, M. Lefranc has made
important discoveries in regard to his family,
while other links in the chain have been sup-
plied by other writers, especially by M. Clouzot,
the Treasurer of the Society. An important
step has also been taken by the publication
of a reprint of *The Ringing Island* (*L'Isle
sonnante*), from the unique copy in the possession of a private owner. M. Boulenger has
shown in his admirable introduction that this
represents the original and most authoritative
state of the text of this part of the Fifth Book,
and that it ought to form the basis of a critical
edition. Meanwhile it is greatly to be desired
that the manuscript of the whole Fifth Book
in the Bibliothèque Nationale should be reprinted, for Montaiglon's edition (1868–1872),
the only one which reproduces this text, is
out of print, and is rare and expensive.

As regards the text generally of Rabelais's
works, there is still considerable room for improvement. The worst text is Des Marets's,
for it is a purely arbitrary one, convenient perhaps for the general reader, but quite unsuited
to the demands of scholarship. The best is
that of Marty-Laveaux, which comprises volumes I–III of his edition, and which appeared
from 1868 to 1873; for it gives the whole of

PREFACE

Rabelais's writings, is based on original and authoritative editions, and is the work of a careful and competent editor. But it was certainly a mistake to make the edition of 1564 the basis of the Fifth Book, and as regards Books I, II, and IV, it is a question whether absolutely the most authoritative editions have been chosen for reproduction.

The commentary is still in a very incomplete condition. The best, on the whole, is that of Des Marets and Rathery, which is conveniently placed below the text, and is terse and to the point. Similar praise may be given to the commentary in Mr. W. F. Smith's English translation, while that of the German translator, Gottlob Regis, though far too bulky, is enriched by much learning and wealth of illustration. But there are still numerous passages in Rabelais's work which remain unexplained, or of which the explanation is wholly inadequate. It is to be hoped that the labours of the Société des Études Rabelaisiennes will eventually produce an edition of Rabelais worthy of the great writer and of the great country which gave him birth.

The above outline gives some indication of the authorities which have helped me in writing this account of Rabelais and his work. In the narrative of his life I have tried to avail

PREFACE

myself of all the existing information; but as hardly a number of the *Revue des Études rabelaisiennes* appears without adding something to our knowledge, it is evident that no biography, for some little time to come, can hope to be complete. For there can be little doubt that for the last twenty years of Rabelais's life, when he had become a well-known man, having relations with many of the leading personages in France, there must be scraps of interesting information lurking in unpublished letters and other documents.

In my discussion of Rabelais's work I have assumed less knowledge on the part of my readers than I should have done if I had been writing for Frenchmen, and accordingly I have given a more or less detailed analysis of *Gargantua* and *Pantagruel*. I have also quoted from the text here and there at considerable length, using for this purpose the admirable translation of Mr. W. F. Smith, which adheres much more closely to the original than does Urquhart's classical work. In some of the shorter passages quoted the translation is my own.

ARTHUR TILLEY.

CAMBRIDGE UNIVERSITY, October 16, 1906.

8

CONTENTS

FRANÇOIS RABELAIS

CHAPTER I

CHILDHOOD AND EDUCATION

It is a characteristic of the very greatest writers that they sum up, with more or less completeness, the thought, the aspirations, and the temper of their age, and this not only for their own country, but for the whole civilised world. Of this select band is Rabelais. He is the embodiment not only of the early French Renaissance, but of the whole Renaissance in its earlier and fresher manifestations, in its devotion to humanism, in its restless and many-sided curiosity, in its robust enthusiasm, in its belief in the future of the human race.

It seems fitting that he should have been born in Touraine, for Touraine, though one of the smallest of French provinces, has produced some of the most illustrious names in France: Richelieu, her greatest statesman, Balzac, her greatest novelist, Descartes, her greatest philosopher, and André Duchesne, one of her greatest men of learning. Moreover, Touraine, "the garden of France", as Rabelais calls it,

and as it is still called at the present day, is
blessed with a soil of remarkable fertility,
especially in that rich alluvial land watered
by the Loire and its tributaries, which gave
birth to Rabelais—a vigorous mother of a vigorous offspring. It was in Touraine, too, that
the kings of France from Charles VII. to
Louis XII. chiefly resided, whether at Tours,
or Loches, or Chinon, or Plessis, or Amboise,
or Blois; and, as a natural result of this royal
sunshine, it was in Touraine that the art of
the French Renaissance put forth its earliest
blossoms. That excellent illuminator, Jean
Fouquet, painter to Louis XI., was a native
of Tours, and there worked his successors,
Jean Bourdichon and Jean Poyet. It was at
Tours that Michel Colombe founded an important school of sculpture, which flourished till
his death, when he was over eighty, about the
year 1512. Tours, too, was one of the first
towns in France to feel the influence of the
Renaissance spirit in architecture. The beautiful cloister of the abbey church of St. Martin, of which only the eastern side remains,
was begun in 1508, and about the same time
Jacques de Beaune de Semblançay completed
his magnificent hôtel, which still stands at the
corner of the market-place. Here, too, is the
beautiful Fontaine de Beaune, executed in

white marble from the designs of Michel Colombe. Further up the Loire Charles VIII. rebuilt Amboise, and Louis XII. built the eastern front of Blois. Finally, Touraine was as celebrated in Rabelais's day as it is now for the purity with which all classes spoke their native language. Thus if Warwickshire, the home of Shakespeare, is "the heart of England", Touraine, when it gave birth to Rabelais, was, in an even more vital sense, "the heart of France".

Fifty years ago the story of Rabelais's life was still in the legendary stage. Rathery was the first to cut away the overgrowth of legend, and to write a critical biography, which was prefixed to the edition of Rabelais's works edited by him and Burgaud des Marets, and published in 1857–1858. But there still remained many dark places, and it is only in recent years that patient research has begun to shed a partial light on the obscurity which veils Rabelais's career down to the day on which he matriculated as a student of medicine in the University of Montpellier. One source of information, hitherto more or less neglected, is beginning to occupy more and more the attention of investigators; for it is now generally recognised that Rabelais's writings contain a considerable amount of autobiographical statement, and that especially in the book of *Gargantua* he has introduced many recollections of his childhood and early manhood. It is needless to say that this is a source of information which must be used with prudence and caution.

Our difficulties begin with the date of Rabelais's birth. The traditional date, which is based only on vague statements that he was seventy at the time of his death, in 1553 or 1554, is 1483, the year in which Louis XI. died and Luther and Raphael were born. If this date is correct, then Rabelais must have been forty-nine when he began his literary career, forty-seven when he matriculated at Montpellier, forty-one when his friend Tiraqueau described him as a man learned beyond his years, and thirty-nine when in a letter to Budé he speaks of himself as a young man. On these grounds it seems, on the whole, reasonable to abandon the traditional date, and, in default of any positive evidence on the subject, to adopt the view now generally prevalent, that François Rabelais was born about the year 1495.

Even as regards the place of his birth there is room for doubt. On his admission to the University of Montpellier, he described himself as *Chinonensis*, or a native of Chinon, "the famous, noble, and ancient town of Chinon, the first town in the world". It is situated on the river Vienne, about eight and a half miles from its confluence with the Loire. Above the town, on a rock three hundred feet high, rises the castle, now a ruin, but formerly the favourite residence of Henry II. of England when he visited his French dominions. There he was brought to die, and there lying in the delirium of fever he cursed himself and his sons (except the faithful Geoffrey, who watched over him to the end), and muttered, "Shame on a beaten king!" On the third day of the fever came the calm which announced the end, and twenty-four hours later he was borne upon the shoulders of his barons down the hill and across the Vienne to the great abbey church of Fontevrault, where his recumbent statue, with those of Eleanor, his wife, Richard Cœur de Lion, and Isabel of Angoulême, the wife of John, may be seen at the present day. A hundred and forty years later another memorable scene took place at the castle of Chinon: it was there that the Maid of Orleans had her celebrated interview with the Dauphin, the future Charles VII. In the time of Rabelais it had ceased to be a royal residence.

At Chinon Rabelais's father possessed a

house which bore the sign of "The Lamprey",
now numbered 15 in the street of that name,
and it is here that the majority of his biographers place his birth. But his description
of himself as *Chinonensis* does not necessarily
imply that he was born in Chinon itself, and
there is a long-established local tradition that
his actual birthplace was La Devinière, about
three miles to the southwest of Chinon, where
his father had also a property. "Rabelais's
house", as it is called, the construction of
which is said to date from the fifteenth century,
stands at the end of the present hamlet, which
forms part of the commune of Seuilly. This
local tradition is strongly supported by the
testimony of Rabelais's book, for while Chinon
is only mentioned here and there, and never
at any length, La Devinière, Seuilly, and the
surrounding district play an important part,
especially in the account of the birth of Gargantua, and in that of the war between Grandgousier and Picrochole. The neighbours from
Ciné, Seuilly, La Roche-Clermaud, Vaugaudry,
Coudray, and Montpensier, who come to feast
with Grandgousier, dance after dinner to the
sound of the flageolets and the bagpipes in a
meadow which still bears the name of La
Saulsaye, "the willow-plantation". It borders
the left bank of the little river Négron, about

a mile from La Devinière. In the same neighbourhood are conducted all the operations of the Lilliputian war between Picrochole and Grandgousier. The abbey of Seuilly is the scene of Brother John's heroic resistance. Lerné, two and a half miles to the west of Seuilly, is Picrochole's capital. La Roche-Clermaud, on the main road from Chinon to Loudun (it has a station on the modern railway), is taken by Picrochole and retaken by Gargantua, while the bridge over the Négron figures in the narrative as the Ford of Vedé.

It is true that La Devinière did not become the property of Rabelais's father till the year 1505, on the death of Rabelais's grandmother; but it is quite possible that he lived there in her lifetime, for after the death of Rabelais's grandfather she married again, and she had another property at Chavigny-en-Vallée, on the north bank of the Loire. Even if Rabelais was not born at La Devinière, the whole neighbourhood must have been familiar to him from his childhood. The charming picture of Grandgousier, "warming himself after supper by a good, clear, and great fire, and, while his chestnuts are roasting, writing on the hearth with a stick burnt at one end, wherewith they poke the fire, and telling to his wife and family pleasant stories of times gone by", is surely a reminiscence of this childhood. Does not Grandgousier here stand for Rabelais's father?

It is only recently that the name and profession of Rabelais's father have been discovered. His name was Antoine, and not Thomas, as is generally stated, and he was neither an innkeeper nor an apothecary, but an advocate and a licentiate in law. This last information is due to M. Abel Lefranc, who has discovered a document of the year 1527, in which the Parliament of Paris orders that Antoine Rabelais, as the senior advocate of the district, shall continue to act as deputy, in the absence of the general and particular lieutenants, until the election of a regular deputy. It thus appears that Rabelais's father was a person of consideration in the neighbourhood, a member of a distinguished profession, and possessed of a considerable amount of property. The tradition that he was an innkeeper doubtless arose from a circumstance which absolutely disproves it: namely, that his house at Chinon was afterwards turned into an inn —a fact recorded by the historian De Thou in some Latin verses. The name of Thomas and the other profession, that of apothecary, attributed to him may be accounted for by the existence of a Thomas Rabelais who was an

apothecary, and whose son Antoine and grand-
son Thomas successively owned La Devinière.
But this Thomas was a younger man than
François Rabelais, possibly his nephew.

We do not know the name of Rabelais's
mother, but he had two brothers, Jamet and
Antoine—of whom the latter inherited La
Devinière—and one sister, Françoise.

The country round La Devinière is undu-
lating and woody, and must once have formed
part of the forest of Fontevrault. The abbey
of that name, which lies between seven and
eight miles from La Devinière, was founded
in 1099 by the crusader Robert d'Arbrissel;
and its church, with its fine apsidal choir,
in spite of the baser uses to which it has been
put—the nave has been converted into dormi-
tories for the prisoners—still stands to testify
to its former greatness. Two and a half miles
north of Fontevrault, just above the junction
of the Vienne with the Loire, is Candes, where
St. Martin of Tours died, and a little west
of Candes is Montsoreau, with its castle, the
remains of which, including a fine staircase,
are now turned into modest dwelling-houses.

Such were the surroundings, rich in historical associations, amid which François Rabelais spent his childhood. The tradition that
he received his first schooling at the abbey of

Seuilly, a Benedictine foundation, is rendered probable by the conspicuous part which that abbey plays in the war between Picrochole and Grandgousier. But the boy was soon to be taken from these scenes. "He had barely attained his tenth year," says Antoine Le Roy, in the long rigmarole account of Rabelais which he wrote at Meudon during the Fronde, "when his father determined to make him a Franciscan." "I marvel," says the author of the *Isle sonnante*, and it is surely Rabelais himself who is speaking, "that mothers bear their children nine months in their bodies, seeing that they cannot bear them nor brook them in their houses nine years, nay, most often not seven, but put a shirt over their dress, and cut a few hairs on the top of their heads." According to fairly good evidence, it was in the Franciscan convent of La Baumette, near Angers, that the young François became a novice and received his education. There is a tradition that among his schoolfellows were Guillaume and Jean du Bellay and Geoffroy d'Estissac, all three his friends and patrons in later years, and the tradition receives some support from the fact that the Du Bellay arms are in one of the chapel windows; but it is doubtful whether the Du Bellay brothers or Estissac would have been sent to a purely conventual school such as La Baumette was. The Du Bellays, however, were at the neighbouring University of Angers, and it is possible that Rabelais may have come across them there. La Baumette is mentioned only once in Rabelais's book, where it is cited as an instance of the stables being at the top of the house. The explanation of this is that the park and gardens laid out by King René, the last Duke of Anjou, were built on terraces.

We do not know where or in what year Rabelais completed his novitiate and took the vows of a Franciscan. But in a document dated April 5, 1519, his signature is appended to a purchase of land made by the Franciscan convent of Fontenay-le-Comte, and he is qualified as *frère mineur*. At some time or other, therefore, before 1519 he went from La Baumette to Fontenay-le-Comte, the capital of Lower Poitou. Among the other signatures to this document is that of Pierre Amy, who was Rabelais's chief friend in the convent. He was evidently an older man than Rabelais, and had already attained considerable distinction as a scholar, especially in Greek. Whether Rabelais had begun the study of Greek while he was still at La Baumette we do not know. It is possible that he may have profited by the presence of some teacher of Greek in the neighbouring University of Angers, but no such teacher is known to us. At any rate, under the guidance of Pierre Amy he became a competent Greek scholar.

Greek, it must be remembered, was at this date more or less of a new study in France. Though from 1458 there had been a few stray and incompetent teachers of the subject in Paris, it was not till the arrival of the learned Greek, Janus Lascaris, in 1495 that the study can be said really to have taken root in that city. For Lascaris, though his duties at Court allowed him little leisure for regular teaching, was always ready with help and encouragement, and under his benignant influence a little circle of Greek scholars was gradually formed. Its chief members were Jacques Lefèvre d'Étaples, Guillaume Budé and his two intimate friends Louis de Ruzé and François de Luines, both holding high judicial office, Germain de Brie, better known as Germanus Brixius, Nicolas Berauld, the two physicians Guillaume Cop and Jean Ruel, and the printer Josse Bade (Badius). The *doyen* of the group was Jacques Lefèvre, but though he had studied Greek in Italy for six years and was an indefatigable lecturer and writer of commentaries on Aristotle, he was far inferior in scholarship to Budé, who ranked

with Erasmus as the leading scholar in Europe.
Budé's reputation had first been made by his
treatise *De Asse*, published in 1514, which,
while nominally an account of the Roman *as*,
contained not only a thorough investigation of
the money, weights, and measures of the ancients, but embraced in numerous digressions
a wide field of classical learning. A collection
of Budé's letters, including several written in
Greek, published by Badius in 1520, set the seal
on his reputation.

But in the year 1520, though a man like
Budé, thanks to his indomitable perseverance
and his lavish expenditure on books and manuscripts, had forced his way to the forefront
of European scholars, the study of Greek in
Paris was attended with many difficulties.
There were as yet few manuscripts, and books
had to be imported from beyond the Alps.
The first Greek book printed in France had
appeared only as recently as 1507, from the
press of Gilles Gourmont, and in 1512 we find
Girolamo Aleandro complaining, in the preface
to his Greek-Latin dictionary, of the wretched
condition of Greek printing at Paris, and
especially of the scanty supply of Greek type.
In spite of the diligent labours of Gourmont,
the editions of Greek books for the next fifteen
years barely averaged one a year.

FRANÇOIS RABELAIS

If these were the difficulties which beset a student of Greek at Paris, what must have been those which Rabelais and his friend had to encounter in a Franciscan convent, the brethren of which, according to Colletet, "took vows of ignorance as well as religious vows"? But they were encouraged by the support and friendship of a humanist circle, consisting chiefly of lawyers and ecclesiastics, which had formed itself in Poitou. At Fontenay itself were Arthus Cailler, lieutenant of the bailiwick, his son-in-law and successor André Tiraqueau, "the good, the learned, the wise, the most humane, the most kindly and just Tiraqueau", Jean Brisson, king's advocate, and another advocate, Hilaire Goguet.

About six miles off was L'Hermenault, where Geoffroy d'Estissac, the Bishop of Maillezais, had a château. He was a young man of about Rabelais's age, a member of an illustrious family of the neighbouring province of Aunis. In full sympathy with the Renaissance movement, a lover of books and every form of culture, and one of the most active builders of his day, he was a man after François I.'s own heart; and his appointment (1518), at an early age, to the see of Maillezais was one of the first-fruits of the Concordat (1516).

He seems to have been specially useful to Amy and Rabelais in procuring them books, particularly Greek books. We learn this from an extant receipt, which sets forth that one of the agents of Henri Estienne the elder had received from Pierre Amy the sum of seven gold crowns for books sold to the Bishop of Maillezais. Among these books were an Aristotle, a Homer, and a Cicero. At a considerably greater distance from Fontenay, but not out of reach, were Aymery Bouchard, president of the seneschal's court at Saintes, to whom Rabelais, as we shall see later, dedicated an edition of some Latin documents, and Briand de Vallée, president of the court at Poitiers, who is mentioned in eulogistic terms by Rabelais in his Fourth Book.

We must not, therefore, picture to ourselves Rabelais and his friend Amy as confined to the society of stupid and unsympathetic monks, nor even as always residing in the convent. We hear of Amy paying a visit to Bouchard at Saintes, and Rabelais himself speaks of Saintes as if he had been there. There may also have been visits to the Bishop of Maillezais, either at L'Hermenault or at his château of Ligugé, near Poitiers.

But the two Greek students found another sympathiser in no less a person than Budé

himself. It appears from a Latin letter which
he wrote to Amy early in 1521 that the latter,
who was already known to Budé's friend,
François de Luines, had already begun a correspondence with the great scholar. Then
Rabelais, encouraged by his friend, also wrote
to Budé, but waited five months in vain for
an answer. A second letter was more fortunate. The answer, which is dated April 12
(1522), though chiefly composed of rhetorical
commonplace and pedantic pleasantry, is thoroughly cordial in tone.

Rabelais's Greek studies thus progressed,
and before long he accomplished a translation
of one of the books of Herodotus. But further
letters from Budé, one to Amy, dated February 23 (1523), and one to Rabelais, dated
January 27, and probably to be assigned to the
year 1524, inform us that the two friends
were subjected to a petty persecution at the
hands of their fellow-monks on account of
their studies, and that the superior deprived
them for a time of their cherished Greek
books. Budé expresses warm sympathy and
indignation, and ends his letter to Rabelais
with a long tirade against the obscurantist
party in general, "who have," he says, "all
but succeeded in banishing as guilty of heresy
those who are devoted to Greek literature".

For heresy was already in the air. Towards the close of 1520 Guillaume Briçonnet, another native of Touraine, had summoned to Meaux, of which see he was Bishop, his old tutor Lefèvre d'Étaples, with some of his friends and pupils, to carry on the work of "preaching Christ from the sources". In the spring of 1521 the Sorbonne had formally condemned Luther's writings, which for the last two years had been eagerly read at Paris by "the whole band of the learned".

As the result of the persecution to which the two monks of Fontenay-le-Comte were subjected, Amy escaped from the convent, and took refuge in the Benedictine monastery of Saint-Mesmin. Rabelais, however, acted with greater prudence. He addressed a petition to the new Pope, Clement VII., asking permission to leave not only the convent of Fontenay, but the Franciscan order, and to enter the neighbouring Benedictine abbey of Maillezais, the abbot of which was Rabelais's friend the Bishop of Maillezais, the abbey church being used as the cathedral, and the abbey buildings as the episcopal palace. The Bishop doubtless backed the petition, and the required permission having been granted, Rabelais became a Benedictine monk instead of a Franciscan friar.

FRANÇOIS RABELAIS

Though a nominal inmate of the abbey of Maillezais, Rabelais seems to have resided generally with the Bishop-abbot at his priory of Ligugé, near Poitiers. Here the Bishop had built himself a princely château, surrounded with splendid gardens. Poitiers, which was only five miles distant, was something of a literary centre. Among its ornaments was Jean Bouchet, a relic of the *rhétoriqueur* school, who had retired to Poitiers at the beginning of the reign of François I.; and here, during such leisure as his business of a hardworking lawyer allowed him, he continued to produce reams of jog-trot verse. It is possible that Rabelais may have made his acquaintance at Fontenay, but at any rate they now became friends, and Bouchet's published work includes a rhymed epistle addressed to him by Rabelais, together with his own answer. From these we learn that the Bishop had taken Rabelais into his service, possibly as domestic chaplain, and that a little room was set apart for him in the château. The two epistles are dated respectively the 6th and the 8th of September, but unfortunately the year is not given. Except for this momentary glimpse, we have no direct record of Rabelais's life from the time he left Fontenay-le-Comte to the day on which he matriculated at the University of Montpellier, more than six years later. To fill up the blank we must resort more or less to conjecture.

Our first help comes from the fact that Rabelais was admitted to the degree of bachelor of medicine only two and a half months after his matriculation. It is generally said that this was owing solely to his proficiency in medical studies. But, in the first place, where could he have acquired this proficiency except at Paris, at the only university in France which had a medical school of any account? Secondly, the medical school of Montpellier had enacted, as recently as 1526, that they would recognise no course of study for their own degrees save that of the University of Paris. It follows almost as a necessity that Rabelais must have studied medicine at Paris. The next question is, for how long? The Montpellier statutes required that a candidate for the degree of bachelor of medicine should have attended "ordinary" lectures for twenty-four months—that is to say, three academic years. But, as we shall see presently, Rabelais can hardly have come to Paris before the beginning of July, 1528, and this would only give him time for sixteen months of "ordinary" lectures at that university. We must, therefore, suppose that the University of Montpellier allowed him to count attendance at "extraordinary" lectures as part of the twenty-four months' course. Now, "ordinary" lectures were only given in term-time, but "extraordinary" lectures might be delivered in the long vacation, so that with the help of three long vacations and a certain amount of attendance at lectures at Montpellier Rabelais could just have made out his full time. In his case there was very good reason for allowing him to count attendance at "extraordinary" lectures, for among the bachelors of medicine who were lecturing at Paris during his period of residence were Jean Günther of Andernach and Jean Fernel, both of whom took their doctor's degree in 1530.*

The year 1530, the second, probably, of Rabelais's residence at Paris, was marked by an important event in the history of humanism. At the beginning of 1530 the long-promised Regius professorships were established, and on the 24th of March the new professors entered

* A year before Rabelais took his degree of bachelor of medicine, the celebrated physician, Jacques Dubois, better known as Sylvius, was admitted to the same degree at Montpellier (November 29, 1529), only three days after his matriculation. He was at this time fifty-one and of great eminence, but, as he had studied at Paris, it is not necessary to suppose that the degree was conferred on him as a mark of special distinction.

on their duties. This partial fulfilment of the King's promise to found a royal college was in a large measure due to Budé, who in the preface to his *Commentarii Linguæ Græcæ* (1529), addressed to the King, had amidst a good deal of courtier-like flattery spoken plainly on the subject. One wonders whether Rabelais followed up his former correspondence with the leader of French humanism by making his personal acquaintance. Possibly, too, he became acquainted with some of the other members of the humanist circle, with the physicians Cop and Ruel, or with Germain de Brie (Brixius), whose name has found a place in his book. He also mentions Janus Lascaris, speaking of him as "my good friend", but as Lascaris left Paris in 1528, it is more likely that Rabelais did not make acquaintance with him till a later period, probably during his first visit to Rome.

Another event which took place at Paris probably during his residence there was of a nature to make a deep and unpleasant impression upon him. On April 17, 1529, Louis de Berquin, a gentleman of Picardy noted for his learning and a friend of Erasmus, who had on more than one occasion been in trouble with the authorities for sympathy with the Lutheran doctrines, was burnt for heresy.

FRANÇOIS RABELAIS

"He might have been the Luther of France," says Beza, "had François been a Frederick of Saxony." But François, who had ordered his release from prison three years earlier, now left him to his fate. Was it the price paid to the Sorbonne for the withdrawal of their opposition to the Regius professorships? It was possibly the impression caused by Berquin's death which inspired Rabelais with a dread of being "burned alive like red-herrings", and to say, in his favourite phrase, that he would maintain his opinions "to the fire exclusively".

For the rest of the period between 1524 and 1530 we must resort to conjecture of a more uncertain kind. But we get a valuable hint from Le Roy's statement that "Rabelais visited all French universities under the name of Pantagruel", or, in other words, that the amusing and graphic account which he gives of Pantagruel's experiences at various provincial universities is a piece of autobiography. This account, with a few unimportant omissions, runs as follows:

"So he came to Poitiers to study, and there profited much; at this place, seeing that the scholars were sometimes at leisure and did not know how to bestow their time, he took compassion on them, and one day took from a great ridge, called Passe-Lourdin, a huge rock of about twelve fathoms square and fourteen spans thick, and with great ease put it on four pillars in the middle of a field, to the end that the said scholars, when they had nothing else to do, might pass their time in getting up on the said stone and there feasting with store of flagons, hams, and pasties, and carving their names upon it with a knife. It is now called the Lifted Stone. And in memory of this, no one is entered in the matriculation book of the said University of Poitiers unless he have drunk in the Caballine Fountain of Croustelles, passed at Passe-Lourdin, and got up on the Lifted Stone. . . .

"And going from Poitiers with some of his companions, they passed by Ligugé, visiting the noble Abbot Ardillon; then by Lusignan, Sansay, Celles, Colonges, Fontenay-le-Comte, saluting the learned Tiraqueau; and from there arrived at Maillezais. . . .

"Then he returned not to Poitiers, but determined to visit the other universities of France, so, passing on to La Rochelle, he took shipping and came to Bordeaux, in which place he found no great diversion, excepting the bargees playing cockall on the strand.

"Thence he came to Toulouse, where he learned to dance well, and to play with the two-handed sword, as is the custom of the scholars at that university; but he did not stay there long when he saw that they caused their regents to be burned alive like red-herrings, for he said: 'Now God forbid that I should die this death, for I am by nature sufficiently dry already, without being further heated.'

"Next he came to Montpellier, where he found very good wines of Mirevaux and jovial company, and he thought to set himself to study medicine; but he considered that calling was much too troublesome and melancholy. Wherefore he would study law; but seeing there were only three scald-pates and one bald-pate who were legists of the said place, he departed thence, and on the road constructed the Pont du Gard and the Amphitheatre at Nismes in less than three hours, which, notwithstanding, appears to be a work rather divine than human; and so he came to Avignon, where he was not

33

three days before he was in love. Seeing this, his tutor Epistemon took him from there and brought him to Valence in Dauphiné; but he saw that there was not much recreation, and that the louts of the town did beat the scholars, at which he took offence; and one fine Sunday, when all the world was at the public dancing, a scholar wished to take his place in the dance but the bumkins would not allow it. Seeing this, Pantagruel drove them all before him with blows right to the banks of the Rhône, and would have made them all drown, but they did skulk underground like moles, for a good half league under the Rhône. The hole is still to be seen there.

"After that he departed thence, and in three steps and a jump came to Angers, where he found himself in good quarters, and would have stayed there some time, had it not been that the plague drove them away.

"And so he came to Bourges, where he studied a very long time and profited much in the faculty of the laws. And he said sometimes that the law-books seemed to him like a fine robe of cloth of gold, marvellously pompous and precious, but trimmed with dung; for, said he, there are no books in the world so fine, so ornate, so elegant, as the texts of the Pandects, but the bordering of them, to wit, the Gloss of Accursius, is so filthy, scandalous, and foul, that it is nothing but dirt and villainy.

"Leaving Bourges, he came to Orléans, and there found a lot of clownish scholars who made him great entertainment at his coming; in a little time he learnt to play tennis with them so well that he was a master at the game; for the students of that place are good in practice of it; and they took him sometimes to the islands to recreate himself at the game of poussavant [ninepins]. And as for breaking his head overmuch with study, he would none on't, for fear of his eyes spoiling; especially as a certain one of the regents often said in his lectures that there was nothing so hurtful to the sight as disease of the eyes.

"And one day when one of the scholars of his acquaintance passed as licentiate in law, one who in learning had but little more than the rest of his set, but as a set-off was well skilled in dancing and playing tennis, he thus made the blazon and device of the licentiates in that university:

> " 'Tennis-ball in his placket,
> His hand on a racquet,
> A law in his tippet,
> At a jig he would trip it:
> And there you are hooded.' " *

A glance at the map will show that except for the long circuit from Valence to Bourges by way of Angers, which Pantagruel made in "three steps and a jump", the itinerary is a perfectly natural one. Further, it will be noticed that the only two universities at which Pantagruel is said to have "profited much", or indeed to have spent any considerable time, are Poitiers and Bourges, though it appears from a subsequent chapter that he spent some time at Orléans. As regards Poitiers, nothing is more natural than that Rabelais should have obtained from his friend the Bishop of Maillezais leave to become a student there, for such leave for the purpose of university study was frequently given. He may either have continued to live with the Bishop, for in those days of enthusiastic learning a man of

---

* *Pantagruel*, II, v.

Rabelais's robust physique would have thought nothing of trudging five miles into lecture and back again; or it is possible that he spent only his vacations at Ligugé, for it will be recollected that the only record we possess of his residence there, the rhymed epistle to Bouchet, bears the date of September.

The University of Poitiers, founded by Charles VII. in 1432, during the English occupation of Paris, was of considerable repute at this time, especially as a law-school; and Andrea Navagero, the well-known Latin poet and diplomatist, writing in 1528, says that it had four thousand students, a number which we must divide by at least five for the purpose of comparison with modern universities. The students had the reputation of being the best dancers in France, and the *bransle* (English "brawl") *de Poitou* was as celebrated as the Irish jig. The town was one of the strongest and largest in France, and Rabelais elsewhere speaks of it as comparable with Lyons. It stood in a commanding position, occupying the summit and flanks of a considerable eminence, and almost entirely surrounded by the river Clain and its tributary the Boivre. Its aspect must have been much the same as it is now, for many of the old houses and most of the old churches—Notre-Dame, with its splendid Romanesque façade of the twelfth century, the cathedral of St. Pierre, begun by Henry II. of England, St. Radegonde and St. Porchaire with their Romanesque towers, St. Hilaire the Great, where Richard Cœur de Lion was enthroned as Duke of Aquitaine—are still standing. But the great Clock-tower, one hundred and twenty-eight feet in height, facing Notre-Dame, the bell of which Pantagruel wished he had on his chin when he and his friends were feasting after the discomfiture of the Dipsodes, has long vanished.

That delightful person, Mr. Justice Bridlegoose, who decided lawsuits by means of the dice, tells Pantagruel and his friends that when he was a student of law at Poitiers, a certain labourer named Perrin Dandin settled more actions than were disposed of in the whole Palace of Poitiers. This refers to the ancient palace of the Counts of Poïtou, which in Rabelais's day was used as a *palais de justice*. The great hall, called *la Salle des Pas Perdus*, which dates from the twelfth century and is said to have been built by Eleanor of Aquitaine, and the adjoining keep of the thirteenth century still testify to its former magnificence. There Charles VII., in spite of the Treaty of Troyes, was proclaimed King of France; and there, seven years later, Joan of Arc, after her

37

interview with Charles at Chinon, was examined for two months by a commission of learned theologians, who reported that they found "nothing but good in her".

Whether Rabelais was a student at the University of Poitiers or not, the intimate knowledge which he shows of the neighbourhood, and indeed of the whole of Upper Poitou, makes it certain that he must have spent a considerable time either at Poitiers itself or at Ligugé. At what period he committed the irregularity of laying aside the Benedictine habit and assuming that of a secular priest is not clear. In the first petition to Pope Paul III. he implies that it was just before he began to study medicine, in the second that it was just before he matriculated at the University of Montpellier, but he is naturally not very precise with regard to this delicate point. It is difficult to believe that even so indulgent a superior as Geoffroy d'Estissac would have given him permission to wander from university to university. We must therefore suppose that if in his account of Pantagruel's visits to the various universities he is relating his own experience, he must have abandoned the Benedictine order when he left Poitiers. Further, if we are to accept his statement that he "remained for several years

in that order", we can hardly put his departure from Poitiers before 1527.

The universities which Pantagruel next visited, Bordeaux, Toulouse, Montpellier, Avignon,
Valence, and Angers, were all left after a
brief stay. Bordeaux, small and unendowed,
was at this time at a very low ebb, and it was
not until 1533 that its College of Arts was
transformed into the College of Guyenne, to
become the most flourishing grammar-school
in the kingdom. The law-school at Toulouse
was the most celebrated in France, but it was
the stronghold of mediæval jurisprudence and
religious orthodoxy. The reference in Rabelais's text is to an event which had taken place
only a short time before the words were written.
In June, 1532, Jean de Caturce, a licentiate in
law whose lectures had gained him a considerable reputation, was burnt for Evangelical
opinions. There are only two other references
to Toulouse in Rabelais's book, and in each
case it is in connection with the Moulins du
Bazacle, famous mills in the Garonne which
still exist, and which Rabelais mentions in a
way that suggests a personal impression.

The University of Avignon had been steadily
declining since the departure of the Popes.
Valence was mainly a law-school, but it was
not till a generation later that Cujas and

other illustrious jurists gave it celebrity. At Angers, we are told, Pantagruel "found himself in good quarters, and would have stayed there for some time had not the plague driven them away". "Black Angers" must have been familiar to Rabelais when he was at the neighbouring convent of La Baumette, but there is nothing but a vague tradition to show that he was ever at the University. A manuscript history which goes into considerable detail makes no mention of him.

On the other hand, the indirect evidence in favour of his having been at Bourges is very strong. First, we are told that Pantagruel studied there "a very long time and profited much in the faculty of the laws", and that he contrasted the study of the actual text of the *Pandects* with that of the *Gloss*—in other words, the new jurisprudence of the humanists with the old mediæval methods. Now, it was at the close of 1527, or, at the latest, before the summer of 1528, that the Italian jurist Andrea Alciati came to Bourges on the invitation of Margaret of Navarre, and though he was not appointed a professor with a regular salary till March, 1529, he began to give lectures soon after his arrival, and among those who attended them was almost certainly François Rabelais. For Rabelais was evidently well acquainted with Bourges. He tells us that when Pantagruel was a baby, "his broth was given him in a great basin, which is still at the present day at Bourges, near the palace"; and he frequently refers to the "great tower" or "Butter Tower" of the cathedral, which was so called because, like those at Rouen and Bordeaux, it had been partly paid for out of the moneys received for permission to eat butter in Lent.

Orléans ranked next to Toulouse as a law-school, and Pierre de l'Estoile, grandfather of the diarist, the pioneer of the new jurisprudence in France, as Alciati was its founder, had been lecturing there since 1512. His lectures were attended by Calvin, who entered the University in 1528 as a law-student, and proceeded to his degree of licentiate in law probably in 1530, after the usual two years' course. It would be interesting to think that Rabelais and Calvin, those two great masters of French prose, had sat on the same bench in the lecture-room at Orléans, but history is silent on this point. It is clear, however, that Rabelais knew Orléans well. No town in France, except Paris and Lyons and possibly Montpellier, is so frequently mentioned in his book. Moreover, his knowledge of it is antecedent to the writing of *Pantagruel*, for the references to it in that book are numerous: to its wall, to the bell-tower of Sainte-Croix (now destroyed), and to the great bell of Saint-Aignan, which Pantagruel, at the request of the inhabitants, set up in its tower after it had been lying on the ground for two hundred and forty years. We are also told that Pantagruel had studied there very well, which is a little inconsistent with the passage quoted above. On the whole, it seems a fair inference that Rabelais studied for a short time at the University of Orléans, between leaving Bourges and going to Paris. Possibly he left Bourges at Easter, 1528, and spent the summer term, or, as it was called, the "little ordinary", at Orléans.

This attempt to reconstruct the record of Rabelais's life during the six years from 1524 to 1530 has led, then, to the following conclusion: that after about three years spent either at Ligugé or at the University of Poitiers, during which period he still remained nominally attached to the abbey of Maillezais, he proceeded, without permission from his superior, to visit various universities in the south of France; that towards the close of 1527 he became a student of law, first at Bourges, and then at Orléans; and that at midsummer, 1528, he migrated to Paris, where he remained as a student of medicine for rather more than two years. Much of this is necessarily conjectural, and fresh evidence may at any time turn up to modify the results. But of one thing we may be sure: that during these six years Rabelais was quietly garnering up those stores of encyclopædic knowledge which are displayed so marvellously in his book. A new chapter in his life now opens. Hitherto he has only been known as an eager student to a small circle of friends. At Montpellier he appears before a larger audience. Before long he is recognised as the "honour and glory of the healing art", and as one of the leading humanists of France.

CHAPTER II

WE now come to firmer ground. The records of the University of Montpellier enable us to trace with satisfactory precision Rabelais's progress through its medical school. In the book of matriculations there appears, under the year 1530, the name of François Rabelais, with the date of September 17, written in his own clear and beautiful hand; against it on the margin is "Biij^{lt}", an abbreviation for *solvit tres libras* ("paid three livres"). This note has puzzled M. Dubouchet, the author of *François Rabelais at Montpellier* (*François Rabelais à Montpellier*), who says that though other marginal notes occur in the register, this is the only instance of a sum of money being mentioned. He believes, however, that the proctor's book furnishes a solution of the puzzle. For there under the same year (1530) the proctor, Guillaume Rondelet, the well-known author of the *Natural History of Fishes*, then a young man of five-and-twenty, has recorded the receipt of an *aureus*, or gold crown, from François Rabelais for matriculation. So much of the record is in Rondelet's writing, but another hand, almost certainly Rabelais's, has added the date, September 17, 1530. The explanation which M. Dubouchet has offered is unfortunately based on the supposition that the gold crown at that time was equal to three livres, whereas, as a matter of fact, its real value was two livres. A better explanation may be suggested. The matriculation fee at Montpellier consisted of two livres for the right to become a scholar, and one livre for the customary fee to the proctor. The first of these fees would naturally be entered in the proctor's book; the second would as naturally not be entered, because it went into the proctor's pocket, and not into the University chest. Moreover, it was a customary and not a statutable fee. It may be conjectured that Rabelais at first objected to paying this fee, and did not pay it till after the day of his matriculation. He then insisted, first, on adding in the proctor's book the date on which he paid the gold crown, or two livres, in order to show that at the time of his matriculation he had paid the whole statutable fee, and secondly, on noting in the register of matriculations that he had paid altogether three livres. If this explanation is correct, it furnishes an illustration of the tenacity, not to say pugnacity, which was a decided feature of Rabelais's character.

On December 1, 1530, two months and a half after his matriculation, Rabelais was admitted to the degree of bachelor of medicine. By mistake he has written November instead of December in the book of matriculations, but the true date is given in the proctor's book. He was now required, as a candidate for the license, to give a three months' course of lectures, from the beginning of the following year to Palm Sunday. The subject assigned to him was the *Aphorisms* of Hippocrates, with the *Little Art* of Galen. Hitherto lecturers had been content to lecture from Latin translations of the Greek medical writers, without ever referring to the Greek text. But Rabelais had a "very ancient" Greek manuscript of Hippocrates in his possession, and he accordingly made textual criticism a special feature of his lectures, which attracted a large class. His copy of Galen's complete works, in five volumes, printed at Venice in 1525, with his autograph on the title-page of each volume, is in the library of University College, Sheffield.

But our vision of Rabelais at Montpellier is not confined to these strictly academic pursuits. He tells us in his book that he acted at Montpellier in the moral comedy of *The*

Man Who Had Married a Dumb Wife, and it is doubtless to his first residence there that this event must be referred.

Documentary evidence shows that he was still at Montpellier on October 23, 1531, but on June 3, 1532, we find him dedicating to his friend André Tiraqueau a volume of the Latin letters of Giovanni Manardi, a physician of Ferrara, on medicine, which he had edited for the well-known Lyons publisher, Sebastian Gryphius. He must therefore have moved to Lyons a little before that date, probably about Easter (March 31), after the end of the winter term at Montpellier. Lyons at this time had almost a greater right than Paris to be regarded as the intellectual centre of France. In the number of its scholars and men of letters and in the books which issued from its printing-presses it rivalled, if it did not surpass, the capital. In some respects, indeed, it was a more desirable place of residence for the votaries of the new studies, for it breathed an air of greater intellectual freedom, untainted by the blighting influence of the Sorbonne. Situated on the very borders of Savoy, it lay on the direct road between France and Italy, and between the south of France and Switzerland. Thus it was a natural resting-place alike for the King with his armies and for scholars and reformers with their books. It was half Italian in character, more than half the inhabitants being foreigners, and the greater part of these being Italians.

Among the distinguished men who lived there at the time of Rabelais's arrival were several of his own profession, such as Jean de Canappe, Pierre Tolet, and Symphorien Champier, the latter an eager antiquary, an editor of ancient chronicles and records of chivalry, and a warm sympathiser with the new studies. That remarkable man, Cornelius Agrippa, had also practised medicine there for four years; but he had departed in 1528, after writing his book *On the Uncertainty and Vanity of Knowledge*. The leading scholar of the place was the Hebraist, Santo Pagnino. Among the men of letters was Maurice Scève, then quite young, but shortly to become the centre of an admiring circle, and to be honoured as a poet, a musician, a painter, and an architect, and as an expert in many branches of learning. Nor must we forget Jean Grolier, Vicomte d'Aguizy, the prince of bibliophiles, whose library, containing more than three thousand volumes, must have been the finest private library in France, and whose practice of inscribing on his books the hospitable phrase *I. Grolieri et amicorum* was imitated by Rabelais.

At the head of the printing and publishing profession was Sebastian Gryphius, whose services to humanism were inferior to those of no other French printer. A good Latin scholar, he chiefly devoted himself to the printing of Latin classics, especially in pocket editions. The volume of Manardi's letters which he employed Rabelais to edit had already appeared at Ferrara, and Rabelais's work consisted in little more than writing a Latin dedication. M. Plattard, in an interesting article in the *Revue des Études rabelaisiennes* on Rabelais's learned publications, calls attention to the picturesque images, popular proverbs, and racy expressions which give a certain savour to this first production of his pen, and faintly foreshadow the glories of *Gargantua* and *Pantagruel*.

His next work, also for Gryphius, was an edition of Latin translations of the *Aphorisms* of Hippocrates (with three other treatises of the same writer) and Galen's *Art of Medicine*, the books upon which he had lectured at Montpellier. The Greek text from his own manuscript was appended to the edition, which was furnished with numerous marginal notes consisting largely of references to that text. The notes are of no great value, but the book was successful, and Gryphius published a second edition in 1543.

Rabelais next edited for the same publisher
two Latin legal documents, a will and a con-
tract of sale, "relics", as he calls them, "of
venerable antiquity". Unfortunately, they
turned out to be forgeries by an Italian humanist, but this was not discovered till more than
thirty years after Rabelais's death. The book
was preceded by a dedication, dated September
4, 1532, to his friend Aymery Bouchard.

Meanwhile, in this busy year 1532, Rabelais had been employed by Claude Nourry,
a printer and publisher of popular vernacular
literature, on a very different work. He had
written, or rather revised, for him a burlesque
romance of chivalry entitled *The Great and
Inestimable Chronicles of the Great and Enormous Giant Gargantua* (*Les grandes et inesti-
mables Cronicques du grant et enorme Geant
Gargantua*). It had an immense success. Two
months later Rabelais could say of it that
more copies had been sold than there would
be Bibles in nine years. This he said in the
prologue to what was ostensibly a continuation of the story of Gargantua, and which was
entitled *The Horrible and Terrible Deeds and
Prowesses of the Much Renowned Pantagruel,
King of the Dipsodes, Son of the Great Giant
Gargantua: recently composed by Master Alcofribas Nasier* (*Les horribles et espouventables*

MONTPELLIER: LYONS: ROME

Faictz et Prouesses du tresrenomme Pantagruel, Roy des Dipsodes, Filz du grand Geant Gargantua: composez nouvellement par Maistre Alcofribas Nasier). We may infer from a remark in the last chapter, to which Professor Birch-Hirschfeld has called attention, that the new work was completed in September, 1532, at the time of the vintage, and apparently at Chinon or La Devinière, where the prologue, which would naturally be written last, was composed: "I have come to visit my own country, and to know if any of my kindred are still alive." The book was published by Nourry in the form of a small quarto volume of sixty-four leaves. There is no date of publication, but if the conjecture is correct that it was ready for the press in September, it must almost certainly have appeared before the end of the year, for Rabelais was back at Lyons before the end of October, and the book can hardly have taken more than a month to print.

But we have not yet completed the tale of Rabelais's production for the year 1532. He also composed for Nourry an almanac and a *Pantagrueline Prognostication* for the coming year, 1533. The almanac seems to have been the first of a series which he wrote annually down to 1550. Like the other almanacs of

the day, it not only gave the dominical letter
and other information of this sort, but purported to be a prophecy, founded on astrological science, of the events of the year. But
though Rabelais in his first almanac calls himself professor of astrology, he protests against
the folly of the so-called science and disclaims
all knowledge of the future: "These are secrets
of the close counsel of the Eternal King, who
rules, according to His free will and good pleasure, everything that is and that is done."
All the fragments of his almanacs that have
come down to us are entirely serious in tone.
The *Prognostication*, on the other hand, which
is a prophecy of much greater length than
those contained in the almanacs, is purely
humorous, and is written in the exuberant
style which characterises his great work.
Several editions of it were published in the
author's lifetime, the date being altered to
suit the year, till in 1542 *lan perpetuel* was
substituted for the date of the particular year.

About this time we find Rabelais writing a
Latin letter of singular interest, the original
of which, or possibly only a copy, is preserved
in the town library of Zurich. It is dated
from Lyons, November 30, 1532, but the
name of Rabelais's correspondent has disappeared. The letter was first printed (1702)

with the heading *Bernardo Salignaco*, but M. Ziesing of the University of Zurich has conclusively shown that this heading rests on no authority, and that the letter was really written, not to an unknown Bernard Salignac, but to Erasmus. The contents of the letter, indeed, leave no doubt on this point. Its occasion was a request made by Georges d'Armagnac, Bishop of Rodez (of whom we shall hear again), to Rabelais that he would pass on to Erasmus, if he found a trustworthy person going to Basel, a Greek manuscript of Josephus which Erasmus had lent the Bishop. After addressing Erasmus as his "most humane father", Rabelais adds:

> "I have called you father; I would also say mother, if your indulgence would allow it. . . . You have educated me, although unknown to you in face, unknown also to fame, and have ever nurtured me with the purest milk of your divine learning, so that did I not put down as owing to you alone all that I am and all that I am worth, I should be the most thankless of all men now living or hereafter to live."

And then he addresses him again as "the ornament of his country, the defender and protector of literature, the most invincible champion of the truth". It is an eloquent and well-deserved recognition of the debt which France, and northern Europe generally, owed to the enthusiasm for learning, the hatred of pedantry and narrowness, the tender love for humanity, which glowed within the soul of Erasmus.

Rabelais had now found other work to do besides that of writing books. On November 1, 1532, he was appointed physician to the hospital of Pont-du-Rhône at Lyons, at an annual stipend of forty livres. It has been conjectured that this appointment was due to the influence of Symphorien Champier, who at that time was one of the aldermen (*échevins*) of the city, and that in return for his good offices Rabelais helped him to write certain medical works which he published from 1532 to 1534, and which Scaliger accused him of not having written himself.

In the following year the Lyons printer and publisher, François Juste, brought out a new edition of *Pantagruel*, in the peculiar *format*—about 5 by $2\frac{1}{4}$ inches—characteristic of his press. It is described on the title-page as "augmented and revised", but the alterations are unimportant, and it is carelessly printed. In the same year no less than four pirated editions were issued from other presses. So attractive a book could not fail to come under the notice of the Sorbonne. In October it was put upon the Index.

Before the end of the year an event took place at Paris which made the position of the

author of a condemned book highly dangerous. The customary Latin oration delivered
by Nicolas Cop, the new rector of the University, on November 1, contained a passage
which expressed open approval of the Lutheran
doctrine of justification by faith, and it became known that the whole oration had been
written by Cop's friend Jean Calvin, a young
scholar who had published a commentary on
Seneca's *De Clementia*. The scandal was great,
and the King on hearing of it immediately
wrote to the Parliament, enjoining it to proceed diligently against "the accursed heretic
Lutheran sect". Within a week fifty Luther-
ans were in prison, and an edict was issued
that any one convicted of being a Lutheran
by two witnesses should be burned forthwith.

It was probably from alarm at these proceedings that Rabelais left Lyons, apparently
without leave from the authorities of the hospital, at the beginning of the year 1534, and
went to Rome in the suite of Jean du Bellay,
who had been sent there on a mission in the
matter of Henry VIII.'s divorce. The party
reached Rome on February 2. Jean du Bellay
was one of six brothers, of whom four achieved
considerable distinction. Guillaume, the eldest,
Seigneur de Langey, soldier, diplomatist, and
scholar, was one of the ablest men in the king-

dom; Martin, lieutenant-general of Normandy, was the author, with Guillaume, of the well-known Du Bellay memoirs; René, Bishop of Le Mans, was a zealous horticulturist, and had a garden famous for its rare plants. Jean was not the equal of Guillaume either in practical ability or in solidity of character, but he held enlightened views, and was a constant and liberal patron of art, letters, and learning. It was largely through his influence that the Regius professorships had at last been founded. A pluralist in an age of pluralists, he rivalled Jean de Guise in the number of his bishoprics and abbeys, at one time enjoying the revenues of no less than five sees and fourteen abbeys. But his income did not suffice for his princely expenditure, and he seems to have been continually in debt. In November, 1532, he had been appointed to the important see of Paris. This was the man who took Rabelais with him to Rome at the beginning of 1534, and proved himself his staunch friend and liberal patron for the rest of his life.

On his arrival in Rome Rabelais had three objects in view: first, to confer with learned men, and hear their opinion on doubtful problems which had long perplexed him; secondly, to collect plants, animals, and drugs for the purposes of his profession; thirdly, to write an account of the topography of the city. His last intention he proceeded to carry out with the help of two young men attached to Du Bellay's household—Claude Chappuys, librarian to François I., and Nicolas Le Roy, a rising jurist. So diligently did he set to work that, in Juvenal's phrase, he believed that "no one's house was known to its master better than Rome and all its streets were to him". But before he had begun actually to write his book, he found that a similar work by an Italian named Marliani was already in print. He thereupon renounced his own project, much to his relief, for, as he says, "it did not appear easy to arrange with clearness, aptness, and neatness his cumbrous and undigested mass of material". Marliani's book appeared at the end of May under the title of *The Topography of Ancient Rome*, and a copy was sent to Lyons, to which place Rabelais must have returned, if he travelled with his patron, on April 14. Urged, no doubt, by Rabelais, Gryphius set about preparing a French edition, which appeared in the autumn, with a dedication to Jean du Bellay, dated August 31, from Rabelais's pen. It is from this dedication that we get our information about his first visit to Rome.

In all probability, before setting out for Rome

he had already completed a new volume which was to take the place of *The Great Chronicles* as a history of Gargantua, the father of Pantagruel. In the Bibliothèque Nationale at Paris there is a copy, the only one known, of an edition of *Gargantua* printed in the same *format* as Juste's 1533 edition of *Pantagruel*, and with the same type and the same capitals as the edition of *Gargantua* which Juste published in 1535. But the title-page is unfortunately missing, and in its absence we cannot positively determine the date of its publication. It is, however, certainly earlier than the edition of 1535, for the impression of the type is clearer. Moreover, certain considerations enable us to form at least a conjecture as to when it was written and when it was published.

The first indication of date is given by the Protestant flavour of certain passages in the book. Now, in February, 1534, Protestantism was again in the ascendant. The persecutions which had been set on foot after the scandal caused by Cop's Latin oration had ceased, and Evangelical doctrines were again preached in the Louvre to large congregations. In the spring Guillaume du Bellay was sent on a mission to Germany, with the object of arranging some *via media* with the German theologians, and he returned in the autumn with a paper of suggestions drawn up by Melanchthon. Never before had there seemed so fair a prospect of a peaceful settlement of the religious controversy. Then, like a thunderclap in a clear sky, came the Affair of the Placards. On the morning of October 18, 1534, the inhabitants of Paris awoke to find all the principal thoroughfares placarded with a broadside in which the mass and its celebrants were attacked in the coarsest and most offensive terms. The people were thoroughly roused and frightened by this gross outrage on their religion, and the King was furious. A persecution began in Paris which far exceeded all preceding ones in rigour, and which lasted, though with gradually diminishing fury, till July 16, 1535, when the Edict of Coucy put an end to the prosecutions except in the case of Sacramentarians and relapsed persons.

Now, it is inconceivable that Juste should have published during the persecution a work containing decidedly Protestant passages, even supposing that he suppressed his name on the title-page. The book therefore must have appeared before the Affair of the Placards, or at any rate before the news of it reached Lyons. But it was probably written some time before this, possibly before Rabelais's visit to Rome. For it is noticeable that there is not

FRANÇOIS RABELAIS

a word in the book to suggest such a visit,
and Rabelais, as we know, was fond of record-
ing his personal impressions. On the other
hand, it must be admitted, even in the Third
Book there is only one reference to Rome
that reads like a first-hand impression.

Another possible indication is that Grandgousier's letter in the twenty-ninth chapter
is dated September 20. For there is no obvious
reason why Rabelais should have chosen that
date for the letter, except that he happened to
be writing it on that day. If this is the case,
the year must almost certainly be 1533, for
there would not have been time for the rest
of the book, more than half, to be written and
the whole book to be printed between September 20 and October 18.

On the whole, the most likely supposition
seems to be that Rabelais had completed the
book before he set out for Rome at the beginning
of 1534, having begun it when the scenes of
his childhood, revived by his visit to Chinon
in the autumn of 1532, were still fresh in his
memory, but that owing to the unfavourable
condition of the religious atmosphere during
the winter of 1533–1534, the printing of it was
not put in hand till after his return from
Rome, in April, 1534.

During the persecution which followed the

Affair of the Placards the author of *Gargantua* disappeared from Lyons, and apparently went into hiding. By the middle of February, 1535, he had been so long absent that applications began to be made for his post at the hospital. A meeting of the governors was held on February 23. Some were for proceeding to an election at once; others were for waiting till Easter, to see if Rabelais would return. One elector had heard that he was at Grenoble, but no one knew for certain where he was. The meeting was adjourned to March 5, when Pierre Du Castel was appointed in Rabelais's place. We read in the minutes that this was the second time that Rabelais had been absent without leave. We may conjecture that the first time was when he went to Rome with Du Bellay. In both cases the reason was doubtless the same, the wish to avoid persecution; for at the beginning of 1534 he was known as the author of *Pantagruel*, a book which had been placed on the Index, and now he had added to his offence not only by writing *Gargantua*, with its flavour of Protestantism, but by issuing a new edition of *Pantagruel*, in which he had revenged himself upon the Sorbonne for their treatment of it by introducing a little extra mirth at their expense.

Once more Jean du Bellay came to the

rescue. Having been made a cardinal in May, 1535, he set out for Rome in the following July to receive his cardinal's hat, and he took Rabelais with him as his physician. On their way they stopped at Ferrara, where Clément Marot was now residing at the ducal court as secretary to the Duchess, Renée of France. Here also Rabelais might have met a distinguished triumvirate of humanists, Giovanni Manardi, whose letters on medicine he had edited, Celio Calcagnini, a man of encyclopædic knowledge, whose writings were to supply some material for his book, and Lilio Gregorio Giraldi, the neo-Latin poet and historian of neo-Latin poetry, who had lately returned to his native town to end his days in the company of his two friends. Another Ferrarese humanist, the intimate friend of Calcagnini, was in exile, and did not return till three years later. This was Pellegrino Morato, father of the celebrated Olympia Morata, who in 1536 was only a girl of ten, but who must already have made considerable progress in that knowledge of Greek and Latin which before long was to astound not only Ferrara but the whole of Italy.

At Florence, now groaning under the tyranny of Alessandro de' Medici, the Cardinal and his party visited the beautiful palace of Filippo Strozzi, the wealthy banker, and saw, as Rabe-

lais tells us, his porcupines and ostriches.
Strozzi himself was absent at Rome, plotting
the overthrow of his mortal enemy Alessandro.
Rabelais also notes the beauty of Florence and
its situation, the admirable structure of the
dome of Santa Maria del Fiore, the richness of
the churches, and the magnificence of the palaces. The party reached Rome about the
middle of August.

During his stay in the Eternal City Rabelais
kept up a correspondence with his old friend
Geoffroy d'Estissac, the Bishop of Maillezais,
copies of part of which have come down to us.
They comprise three separate despatches, each
despatch being divided into several parts
written on different occasions. The first despatch is dated December 30, without the year
being given, but it clearly belongs to the year
1535. The dates of the others are January 28,
1536, and February 15, 1536. The letters,
as they have come down to us, show little or
no trace of Rabelais's powers as a writer,
but they have probably been altered in form,
though not in substance. Rabelais keeps his
correspondent posted with the latest political news and gossip, and gives him some interesting information about the Pope's family.
For Alexander Farnese, Paul III., who had
been elected to the papacy in October, 1534,

in more ways than one merited the appella-
tion of "the last of the Renaissance popes",
given to him by a modern historian. He was
a good Greek and Latin scholar, and loved
beauty and magnificence in various forms.
When Rabelais arrived at Rome, the noble
palace of his family, now the home of the
French Embassy, was in process of reconstruc-
tion by Antonio da Sangallo, though it was not
till after that architect's death, eleven years
later, that it received its crowning glory in
the cornice of Michelangelo, who on September 1, 1535, had been appointed chief architect,
painter, and sculptor to the Vatican.

Paul III. showed also, at any rate at the
outset of his pontificate, strong sympathy
with the reforming movement within the
Church, and must therefore have found himself, in ideas as well as in tastes, in close agreement with the new French cardinal, Jean du
Bellay. It was doubtless the favour in which
his patron was held at the Vatican which suggested to Rabelais that it was a good opportunity to set himself right with the Church,
and to furnish himself with a papal absolution
for the irregularities he had committed. Accordingly he deposited in the Papal Chancery
a supplication for apostasy (that is to say, for
apostasy from the rules of the Church), in

which he set forth how without permission
from his superior he had abandoned the habit
of a monk and taken that of a secular priest,
had for a long time travelled about the world,
and during that time had studied medicine,
taken his medical degree, lectured, and practised, occasionally celebrating mass and taking part in other services of the Church. For
all this he expressed deep contrition, and
begged the Holy Father to grant him absolution from the taint of apostasy, and to allow
him to transfer himself from the church at
Maillezais to some other monastery of the order
of St. Benedict and to hold any benefice that
might be canonically conferred on him, and at
the same time be empowered to practise the
art of medicine in the way of charity, without
expectation of lucre or gain, and without the
use of cautery or knife. Thanks to the favour
of Cardinal du Bellay and the French ambassador, the Bishop of Mâcon, and aided by the
good offices of two Italian cardinals, Rabelais
obtained, without any difficulty or delay, a
brief dated January 17, 1536, in which the
Pope granted to his "beloved son" all that he
had demanded of him.

One of Rabelais's letters to the Bishop of
Maillezais contains directions with regard to
certain seeds which he had sent the Bishop, in-

cluding various kinds of salads, melons, pump-
kins, Alexandrian pinks, dame's-violets, and
certain medicinal herbs. For the Bishop was
a great gardener as well as a great builder,
and had celebrated gardens both at Ligugé
and also at L'Hermenault, near Fontenay-le-
Comte. In the same letter Rabelais asks the
Bishop to send him some more money: "For
the thirty crowns which you were pleased to
have paid to me here are all but come to an end;
and yet I have spent nothing for any ill use,
nor yet upon eating, for I eat and drink with
my Lord Cardinal du Bellay or my Lord de
Mâcon. But in those little trumperies of despatches and hiring of chamber-furniture and
keeping up one's dress a great deal of money
goes, although I live as frugally as I possibly
can."

Towards the close of his last despatch,
dated February 15, 1536, he tells his correspondent that the Emperor Charles V. is expected at Rome at the end of the month, and
that great preparations are being made for
his coming. "It is pitiable," he adds, "to see
the ruins of the churches, palaces, and houses
which the Pope has had thrown down to prepare and level the road." But Charles did not
reach Rome till the 5th of April, and before
that date Cardinal du Bellay, having heard

of a plot for his own assassination, had suddenly and secretly escaped from the city. By the 20th of March he was in Paris, and doubtless Rabelais accompanied him as far as Lyons.

At the end of the previous year (1535) Pompone de Trivulce had been succeeded as governor by Cardinal de Tournon, who, though a liberal patron of men of letters, was also a zealous and severe guardian of orthodoxy. When Clément Marot, having at last received permission from the King to return to his native land, reached Lyons, in December, 1536, he was compelled by the Cardinal to make a public recantation of heresy, a ceremony which included the application, at intervals, of a rod to the penitent's shoulders. It is therefore little to be wondered at if Rabelais found Lyons a less desirable place of residence than formerly.

About this time Rabelais took a step which put him under the official protection of his friend Cardinal du Bellay. On receipt of the papal brief authorising him to enter any Benedictine monastery that would receive him, he had asked permission from the Cardinal to enter his abbey of Saint-Maur-des-Fossés, a bull for the secularisation of which had been issued in 1533. The permission was granted, and at some date between his return to France in

the spring of 1536 and August 17 of that year,
when the secularisation was carried into effect,
Rabelais was formally admitted. As usual,
there was a slight irregularity in his situation.
Had he already been admitted at the date of
the bull which authorised the secularisation
of the abbey, he would have become a canon
with the other monks; but he had not been
admitted, and it is for this reason, doubtless,
that his name does not appear among those
of the new canons who were installed on
August 17.

We hear no more of him till March, 1537,
when we find him at Paris, taking part in a
dinner which was given in honour of Étienne
Dolet, to celebrate the royal pardon which
had been granted him for a homicide committed in self-defence, at Lyons, on the last
day of the previous year.

"There were assembled," says Dolet, in a Latin poem
in which he commemorates the event, "those whom we
justly call the luminaries of France: Budé, the first in
every branch of learning; Berauld, fortunate in his natural endowments and in his flowing eloquence; Danès, distinguished in all arts; Toussain, deservedly entitled the
living library; Macrin, to whom Apollo has given empire
over every kind of poetry; Bourbon, likewise rich in
verse; Dampierre; Voulté, who inspires the learned
world with high hopes; Marot, that French Maro, who
shows a divine force in his poems; François Rabelais,
the honour and sure glory of the healing art, who even

from the threshold of Pluto can recall the dead and restore them to the light."

Of the names above mentioned, those of Budé
and Berauld are already familiar to us as
members of the small band which formed the
first generation of Greek scholars at Paris.
Then come the two most distinguished names
of the second generation, Pierre Danès and
Jacques Toussain, the first royal professors of
Greek and both pupils of Budé. The next
four guests were, with Germain de Brie, who
died in the following year, and Dolet himself,
the chief Latin poets of their day in France:
Jean Salmon, whose nickname of Maigret
(given him on account of his thinness) was
Latinised into Macrinus and so became Macrin;
Nicolas Bourbon, of Vandœuvre in Champagne,
who was tutor to Lord Hunsdon and the Dud-
leys, and a friend of Bishop Latimer and Dean
Boston; Jean Dampierre; and Jean Visagier,
called Vulteius, and generally known in French
as Voulté. He had spent some time at Lyons
in 1535 and 1536, and in this very year, 1537,
published a volume of Latin epigrams in which
he expressed his admiration for Rabelais's
writings. But before long he changed his note,
and in his next two volumes, which appeared
in 1538, attacked him as an impious disciple
of Lucian. Nicolas Bourbon was also at Lyons

in 1536, and among his Latin poems is one which he addressed to Rabelais, probably in the same year, on the eve of his leaving that city for Paris. Macrin, who was at this time secretary to the Cardinal du Bellay, was also a friend of Rabelais.

The next name is that of Clément Marot. It is interesting to find him in the company of these ardent humanists, for he himself had little learning. But his presence marks the solidarity of feeling that existed at this time not only between scholars and men of letters, between those who wrote in Latin and those who wrote in the vernacular, but between humanists and Protestants. Marot, who had just returned from the exile to which he had been condemned for his religious opinions, was still regarded as fighting in the same camp as Budé and Rabelais, against the same enemies, against obscurantism and the Sorbonne. Neither humanists nor Protestants had yet realised how great a breach had been made between the two religions ‑by the Affair of the Placards, or how it had been widened by the publication of Calvin's *Institution of the Christian Religion*. It was to be made quite clear to them when François I., after his interview with Charles V. at Aigues-Mortes, in July, 1538, began to put into execution the policy of repression which he had long been nursing in secret. Meanwhile Rabelais and his friends feasted together in harmony.

It will be noticed that Dolet describes Rabelais, not as a man of great learning, nor as the author of *Pantagruel* and *Gargantua*, but as the "honour and glory of the healing art". Similarly, Salmon Macrin, in a Latin ode of about the same date, addressed to "Rabelais, the most skilful physician", says that "Paris, Narbonne, the banks of the Aude, and Lyons, where your home is, are witnesses to your skill". We may infer from this that since his return from Rome with the Pope's permission in his pocket he had devoted himself chiefly to medical practice. In the month following the dinner in honour of Dolet we find him again at Montpellier, paying his fees for the degree of licentiate in medicine (April 3, 1537). He probably took his degree on the same day, and on the 22d of May following he proceeded to the degree of doctor. It was probably in this summer, rather than during his residence at Montpellier six years earlier, that he visited the Islands of Hyères, for it is not till the publication of his Third Book, in 1546, that he describes himself as Patriarch (*Calloier*) of these islands. In the body of the same book he speaks of them as "my islands", and as they were renowned for medicinal plants, in which he took great interest, we may infer that he made a thorough exploration of them.

In August we find him at Lyons, for in a letter dated August 10, which M. Bourrilly has shown must be assigned to this year (1537), the Cardinal de Tournon informs the Chancellor, Antoine Du Bourg, that he is enclosing a letter written by Rabelais to Rome, "by which you will see what sort of news he sends to one of the greatest rascals in Rome. I have ordered him not to stir from this town until I know your pleasure. And if he had not spoken of me in the letter, and been, too, under the protection of the King and Queen of Navarre, I should have had him clapped into prison as an example to all these newsmongers."

At some date before September 27 of this year, Rabelais was appointed one of the four "ordinary professors" of the faculty of medicine, so called to distinguish them from the royal professors. He then had to choose a subject for his lectures during the ensuing term, from October 18 to the eve of Palm Sunday. It is noticeable that in the minutes of the proceedings the minute which refers to his choice of a subject is written in his own hand. Apparently he was absent from the congregation which was held on September 27, 1537—probably he was still at Lyons—and it was not then known whether he would accept his appointment. His friend Jean Esquiron, therefore, provisionally chose a subject for him. Then Rabelais arrived, accepted the post, selected his subject, and was authorised to alter the minutes, striking out the minute about Esquiron, and inserting one about himself. The proceeding seems irregular, but it is characteristic of Rabelais, who was fond of committing irregular acts under the sanction of authority. It should be further noticed that the minute ends with the words *Græce interpretatus est*, meaning that Rabelais, as he had done before, used a Greek text for his lectures by the side of the Latin translation. The subject was a book of the *Prognostics* of Hippocrates, and we learn from a letter written by Jean de Boyssonné to Maurice Scève that the lectures again attracted a large audience.

The next recorded fact about Rabelais is that on November 17, 1537, a gold crown was paid to the proctor on his behalf for an "anatomy", or demonstration on a human body, in the medical theatre at Montpellier. A similar demonstration which he gave at Lyons in the following year was commemorated by Dolet in a Latin poem. It must be remembered that the dissection of the human body, though it had been practised in Italy for two centuries, was still a rare event in France. At Paris, in accordance with an immemorial custom, four bodies a year were allowed to be dissected. At Montpellier the statutes of 1340 provided for an "anatomy" at least every two years, and the faculty of medicine was entitled to the body of one criminal a year. But these rare dissections were performed in a perfunctory and ignorant manner, being left entirely to the barber-surgeon who acted as prosector to the professor. The professor himself seldom, if ever, handled the knife, and he was generally less competent to do so than even the barber-surgeon. Vesalius, who attended Sylvius's lectures at Paris between 1533 and 1536, and for part of this time acted as prosector to Jean Günther of Andernach, records the difficulties which surrounded a student of human anatomy in this early dawn of the science. He says that he never saw a knife in Günther's hands except at meals. Sylvius, it is true, made certain discoveries which he could only have arrived at by practical work, but Vesalius speaks of the unsatisfactory nature of the dissecting work at his demonstrations, the anatomical preparations being confined to the bones of dogs. Vesalius himself used

to prowl round the gibbet at Montfaucon, and
fight with the dogs for the arm or leg of a criminal. There is no reason for supposing that
Rabelais's knowledge of anatomy was superior
to that of Günther or Sylvius, and doubtless
his regard for his orders went so far as to prevent him from actually using the knife himself
at his demonstrations; but the fact of his lecturing on the human body at all stamps him
as one of the more advanced men of science
of his time.

Probably during his earlier residence at
Montpellier, if not later, he had actually dissected, and he would have found fellow-workers
in Jean Esquiron, whom he had chosen as his
"father" (*pater*), or patron, on entering the
University, and Guillaume Rondelet, who tells
us that he was the first person at Montpellier,
he believed, to dissect the human muscles, and
that he meditated publishing a treatise on dissection, but gave up the idea on the appearance of Vesalius's work. That Rabelais had at
any rate a thorough knowledge of human
anatomy is shown by his wonderful description
of the anatomy of Lent (*Quaresmeprenant*) in
the Fourth Book. It was formerly supposed
that the comparisons which he uses to illustrate
the various parts of the human body were
more or less fanciful, but the distinguished

anatomist and compatriot of Rabelais, Dr. Le
Double, with the help of M. Danty-Collas's
admirable illustrations, has made it clear
that all the comparisons are extraordinarily
apt and vivid. He has also pointed out that
the descriptions of Friar John's death-dealing
exploits in defence of the abbey of Seuilly
and of how, when he was afterwards taken prisoner, he killed his guards, as well as other
notices of fatal blows in the account of the
war between Grandgousier and Picrochole,
and elsewhere in the book, testify to a competent knowledge of surgical anatomy. Rabelais also invented two surgical instruments,
one for the reduction of fractures of the thigh-
bone, and the other for operating in cases of
strangulated hernia.

As regards his knowledge of physiology,
the chief passage bearing on the subject is
the celebrated one on the function of the blood,
which occurs in the middle of Panurge's panegyric on debtors. Some commentators have
seen in this passage a premonition of Harvey's great discovery of the circulation of the
blood, and possibly Rabelais, whose scientific
imagination was very strong, may have had a
dim vision of it. His knowledge, though
somewhat confused, shows an advance beyond
the Galenic doctrine of two kinds of blood,

which was prevalent in his day, but it stops far short of that of his younger contemporary, Servetus. It is, however, interesting to note that Rabelais begins his account with the same Scriptural statement, that "life consists in blood", which formed the basis of Servetus's theory.

We have already seen in what high repute Rabelais stood as a practising physician. This is easy to understand, for he had not only knowledge and skill, but the cheerful and joyous manner which he rightly believed to be of great importance to the patient. His views on this point are set forth in the original prologue to the Fourth Book, and repeated in the letter to Cardinal de Châtillon which he prefixed to the complete edition of this book. He cites from Hippocrates a dictum that "there should be nothing in the physician to offend the patient; face, gestures, clothing, words, looks, and touch should all please and delight him". He also refers to another passage of the same author, where it is pointed out that a sour, morose, downhearted, and frowning countenance depresses the patient, while a joyous, serene, pleasant, and smiling one elates him. There are, no doubt, some people who think laughter unbecoming to a doctor, and prefer him to wear a long face and make the worst of their maladies, but the majority agree with Rabelais. According to his own account, his chief reason for writing his book, next to his own recreation, was that it might beguile the weariness of sick persons, and so give them in his absence "that little relief which he willingly gave to those who sought the help of his art and service".

After this digression on Rabelais's medical skill, we may return to him at Montpellier. His lectures would naturally have come to an end on the eve of Palm Sunday (April 14), 1538, but between this date and July, 1540, when we find him at Turin, the record is again almost a blank. Not, however, completely. From a letter written to Étienne Dolet by a Provençal magistrate named Antoine Arlier, and recently discovered by M. Émile Picot, we learn that Rabelais formed one of the French King's suite on the occasion of his interview with Charles V. at Aigues-Mortes (July 14–16, 1538), and that he returned with the Court to Lyons (July 30). We do not know where he first joined the King, who had been in the south since the first of April, nor in what capacity he was attached to the Court. Arlier's letter implies that he left Lyons in attendance on the King, who turned his steps by way of Romorantin to the Loire, and

finally reached Saint-Germain on September 7.
In any case, it is interesting to come upon
this record of Rabelais's first introduction to
the Court. We know now that this was the
occasion on which he saw the lighthouse of
Aigues-Mortes, and the "little man quite
crippled with gout" who dominated Europe.
We also know, thanks to M. Revillout, that
Rabelais was at Montpellier on August 13 of
the next year (1539), for on that date a
matriculating student chose him as "father".

Possibly Rabelais next took up his abode
in Jean du Bellay's abbey of Saint-Maur-des-
Fossés, for it was about this time that he addressed a petition to Pope Paul III., in which
he says that he is "tortured by a conscientious
scruple" about the irregularity in connection
with his canonry, and prays that it may be
condoned. There is no date to the petition
in the copy which has come down to us, but
as it especially refers to Rabelais's degree
of doctor in medicine, it must have been
drawn up after he had taken that degree.
It was particularly desirable at this period
that Rabelais should be in safe protection,
and that his relations to his protector should
be on a regular official footing. For, since
the interview at Aigues-Mortes, François I.
had begun to take severe measures for the

repression of heresy, and in December, 1538, and June, 1539, had issued edicts in pursuance of his new policy. The Pope's answer to Rabelais's petition has not been preserved, but it was doubtless as favourable as that to his former one had been.

CHAPTER III

DURING the war of 1536–1537, between François I. and Charles V., the French troops had conquered the whole of Savoy and two thirds of Piedmont, occupying among other places Turin. Accordingly, after the armistice of November 28, 1537, Guillaume du Bellay, Seigneur de Langey, was appointed governor of the Piedmontese capital. Two years later he became the governor of the whole of Piedmont, for Marshal d'Annebault, the titular governor, was summoned to the Court in the spring of 1540, and henceforth only made short visits to his government. It is in July, 1540, that we first hear of Rabelais at Turin, as physician in ordinary to the governor. As his absences from France generally coincided with periods of religious persecution, it is possible that the severe Edict of Fontainebleau, issued on June 1, 1540, was the cause of his entering Guillaume du Bellay's service. On the other hand, he may have accompanied Du Bellay to Piedmont at the close of 1539.

Our information as to his movements comes

from three letters written to him by Guillaume
Pellicier, Bishop of Montpellier (where the see
had been transferred from Maguelonne as
recently as 1536) and at this time French ambassador at Venice. Pellicier, like Jean du
Bellay, was a typical Concordat bishop. His
see provided him with a salary, but he divided his time between diplomacy and the
collection of manuscripts, serving his master
with equal zeal and ability in both employ-
ments. He also collected largely on his own
account, and his library at the time of his
death could boast of Greek manuscripts alone
to the number of eleven hundred and four.
Furthermore, he was a student of natural
history, and contemplated an edition of Pliny.
With such a man Rabelais had naturally
many interests in common, and the Bishop's
letters deal with such congenial topics as
Greek manuscripts which he was having copied
for the King, the forthcoming second volume
of the edition of Cicero's *Orations* by Paulus
Manutius (the first complete edition), which
appeared in 1541, with a dedication to Guillaume du Bellay, and two plants, a yellow
monkshood (*Aconitum Anthora*) and a valerian
(*Valeriana Celtica*), natives of Savoy and
Piedmont respectively, which Rabelais was
to send him.

TURIN: METZ: ROME

The three letters which have been preserved are dated July 23, 1540, October 17, 1540, and May 20, 1541, but Rabelais was not at Turin during the whole of this period. At the beginning of January, 1541, we hear of him passing through Chambéry from Turin, with the intention of shortly returning there. This piece of information comes from a letter of Jean de Boyssonné, the distinguished jurist who had introduced the new methods of jurisprudence into the conservative stronghold of Toulouse, and had narrowly escaped the fate of Jean de Caturce. Recently appointed a councillor of the newly constituted Parliament of Chambéry, he was on friendly terms with various members of Guillaume du Bellay's staff and household, and expressed great devotion to the governor himself.

It is from Boyssonné, too, that we hear of a somewhat mysterious episode in Rabelais's life. In various short Latin poems he refers to the death of a child of two, named Théodule Rabelais:

"Lyons is his country, Rabelais is his father; he who does not know either of these does not know the two greatest things in the world."

And again:

"Small though he is in his body, he is great in his father, learned, erudite, versed in all arts which it becomes a man who is good, pious, and honourable to know. He whom you see reposing in this little tomb had when he lived Roman prelates for his attendants."

There can be little doubt that the father of this little boy, whom cardinals had dandled, was François Rabelais, but of the mother nothing is known. Nor can we determine with any certainty the date of his death. But the fact that he was born at Lyons, the mention of the "Roman prelates", and the places where the various Latin verses occur in Boyssonné's manuscript all support M. Heulhard's conjecture that his death took place while Rabelais was in Guillaume du Bellay's service and his friend Boyssonné was at Chambéry. He may, indeed, have died at Turin.

The task of organising the French acquisitions in Piedmont and of putting Turin and other places in an efficient state of defence was no light one, and Langey, in spite of ill health, gave to it his whole mind and energies. He had already done much for the fortification of Turin in 1530, but the work had been stopped for want of funds. He now completed it, demolishing the extensive suburbs and even reducing the limits of the ancient walls. He spared neither the amphitheatre nor the other Roman remains, humanist though he was;

hence at the present day few Italian towns show less trace of their Roman origin. But the work was thoroughly done. The Venetian ambassador could report that he believed there was not a stronger place in Italy.

In the work of fortification Rabelais evidently took a great interest. In one place he refers to the "four bastions of Turin", and the prologue to the Third Book bristles with ravelins and casemates and counter-scarps and barbicans.

Another work in which he seems to have shared was that of exploring, partly from a military and partly from an antiquarian point of view, the passes between France and Italy. In the last chapter of the Third Book he mentions the larch-trees which grow on the mountains of Briançon and Embrun, Briançon being at the foot of the Pass of Mont Genèvre, and Embrun, which is lower down on the Durance, being connected by roads with the next two passes, the Col de la Traversette and the Col d'Argentière. It was doubtless on one of these expeditions that he found the valerian and the yellow monkshood.

It may, however, have been other than military or antiquarian motives which took him into the valley of the Durance. It was along the Durance, though nearer its junction with the Rhône than Embrun, that the Waldenses dwelt, and it was in the winter of 1540–1541 that Guillaume du Bellay made an inquiry into their character and religious opinions. It is of course pure conjecture that Rabelais took some part in this inquiry. There is no specific reference to the Waldenses in his book, but it has been suggested, with some probability, that the unfortunate Popefigs of the Fourth Book, whose island had been surprised, sacked, and wasted by the Papimanes, may stand for the Waldenses.

In November, 1541, Langey took a well-earned holiday, and did not return to his post till May, 1542. It is very probable that Rabelais accompanied him to France, for there are various facts pointing to his presence in France in the early part of 1542. First, there was issued in this year from Juste's press at Lyons a new edition of *Gargantua* and *Pantagruel*. It was a work which required considerable care and discretion, for the times were highly dangerous. The Edict of Fontainebleau was still in force, and Guillaume Poyet, a fanatical upholder of orthodoxy who had succeeded the moderate Antoine Du Bourg in November, 1538, was Chancellor. The first half of the year 1541 had been a period of great distress for the Reformers, and constant additions were still being made to the roll of their martyrs. Rabelais, therefore, who was a martyr *jusques au feu exclusivement*, went carefully through his two books, expurgating all dangerous words and phrases, and especially all references to the Sorbonne. Judge, then, of his disgust when, almost immediately after the publication of Juste's revised edition, there appeared another, from the press of his friend Dolet, which, while it purported to be revised and largely augmented by the author, was in fact a mere reproduction of the old text. He was naturally furious, and in a reissue of Juste's edition by his successor in business, Pierre de Tours, there appeared a notice from the printer to the reader, in which not only Dolet's special offence against Rabelais, but his whole character as a scholar and a printer was dealt with in lively and expressive language. The style of this notice, which is carelessly printed, makes it difficult to believe that it is by Rabelais, but certain touches both in form and in substance warrant the supposition that he had a hand in it.

There was also published at Lyons in this same year, 1542, a work entitled *Military Manœuvres, that is to say, Valiant Deeds and Artifices of War Performed by the Pious and*

FRANÇOIS RABELAIS

Greatly Celebrated Knight of Langey at the Beginning of the Third War with the Emperor (Stratagèmes, c'est-à-dire Prouesses et Ruses de Guerre du preux et trescélèbre Chevalier Langey au Commencement de la tierce Guerre césariane). It was a translation by Claude Massuau from the Latin of Rabelais, who had written this account of his patron's exploits, after the model of Frontinus, the Roman writer on strategy. The title of the translation has been preserved by the bibliographer Du Verdier, but unfortunately neither the book itself nor the Latin original is in existence.

We may also, in all probability, refer to the year 1542 a letter written by Rabelais from Saint-Ay, near Orléans, and dated March 1, but without the addition of the year. As it is the only letter we have that is characteristic of his joyous humour, it may be given, with a few unimportant omissions, *in extenso.* After a quotation from the immortal farce of *Patelin*, it goes on as follows:

"These words set before your reverence, translated from Patelin language into our vernacular of Orléans, mean much as if I were to say, 'Sir, you are very welcome on your return from the wedding, from the festival, from Paris.' If the goodness of God should inspire your paternity to transport yourself so far as to this hermitage, you would have fine stories to tell us; moreover, the lord of the place would give you certain carp-like

88

fish which pull one another by the hair. But you will
do this, not when it pleases you, but when you shall be
brought hither by the will of the great, good, and merciful God, who never created Lent, but rather salads,
herrings, codfish, carp, pike, dace, graylings, bleak,
sticklebacks, etc.; *item*, the good wines, especially that
which is kept here against your coming as a Holy Graal,
and as a second, nay, a fifth essence. Therefore come,
my lord, and do not delay, I mean without inconvenien-
cing yourself or leaving your more urgent affairs. Sir,
after having most heartily commended myself to your
kind favour, I will pray our Lord to keep you in perfect
health. From Saint-Ay, this first day of March.

"Your humble ruler of the feast, and friend,

"FRANC⁵ RABELAIS, Physician.

"The Sheriff, Monsieur Pailleron, will find here my humble recommendations to his kind favour, as also to my
lady his wife, and to the Bailie, Monsieur Daniel, and to
all your other good friends and yourself. I beg the holder
of the seals to send me the Plato which he had lent me.
I will send it back soon."

The letter is addressed to "the Bailie of the
Bailies of the Bailies, Monsieur Antoine Hullot,
at Orléans", of whom we know only that he
was an advocate of that city. The Bailie
Daniel is no doubt François Daniel, well known
as a fellow-student and friend of Calvin.
Étienne Lorens, Seigneur of Saint-Ay, with
whom Rabelais was staying, had for some years
been closely attached to Guillaume du Bellay,
who had employed him in 1541 to put Mirandola in a state of defence, and had given him
the command of the citadel at Turin. We

know from documentary evidence that he was at his own home on March 21, 1542, so that doubtless he returned with his chief to France; and we may accept M. Henri Clouzot's conjecture that Rabelais's letter, the tone of which implies a visit of considerable length, is to be referred to the same year.*

In May, 1542, Du Bellay returned to Turin, doubtless accompanied by his physician. Two months later a fresh war was proclaimed against the Emperor, and at the close of the year Du Bellay, finding his plans for the conduct of the war thwarted by Marshal d'Annebault, whom the King had sent to Piedmont, set out to return to France. He was carried in a litter, his limbs being so crippled with gout that he could not mount a horse. Midwinter though it was, he accomplished the journey across the Alps in safety, but on the other side of Lyons he became very ill. The little band had to stop at the village of Saint-Symphorien, at the foot of Mont Tarare, ten miles short of Roanne, and there on January 9, 1543, Guillaume du Bellay, surrounded by his faithful friends and servants, breathed his last. His death seems to have made a great

---

* *Revue des Études rabelaisiennes*, III, 156 (where the letter is for the first time correctly printed, from a sixteenth-century copy) and 351 ff.

impression on Rabelais, who in two places
(III, xxi, and IV, xxvi, xxvii) refers to the
prodigies which announced it, so "diverse and
terrible" that "all in dismay looked at one
another in silence, without uttering a single
word, but assuredly all thinking and foresee-
ing in their minds that shortly France would
be deprived of a knight so accomplished and
so necessary for her glory and protection, and
that the heavens were claiming him again as
due to them by their own natural right".

The funeral was celebrated with great pomp
on the 5th of March in the cathedral of Le
Mans. We know from a letter written by the
Bishop of Le Mans, René du Bellay, to his
brother the Cardinal, that Rabelais, who with
the assistance of another physician had em-
balmed the body, accompanied it as far as
Saint-Ay, and we may be sure that he was
also present at the final ceremony on the 5th
of March, when his patron's mortal remains
were deposited in their resting-place in the
Lady-chapel of Le Mans cathedral.

He was not forgotten in Du Bellay's will,
receiving a bequest of one hundred and fifty
livres a year until the heirs should have provided him with church preferment of the
annual value of three hundred livres. Du
Bellay's debts, however, chiefly owing to the

expenses which he had incurred as governor
of Piedmont, were so large (three hundred
thousand livres) that it is doubtful whether
Rabelais ever received the money.*

Our knowledge of Rabelais during the years
1543–1545 is again almost a blank. He was almost certainly in the neighbourhood of Paris,
and probably he resided at Saint-Maur-des-
Fossés, either in the monastery or in Jean du
Bellay's château. Wherever he was, one of
his occupations must have been the continuation of his great work, with which he had made
little progress since the publication of *Gargantua*, in 1534. The first five chapters of
the Third Book, which are connected in subject-matter with the close of the Second Book,
were probably written considerably earlier
than the rest of the book, and the reference
by Panurge in the third chapter to St. Babolin, the first abbot of Saint-Maur-des-Fossés,
may be taken as an indication that when Rabelais was writing this* chapter he was residing
within the walls of that monastery. As we
have seen, he probably did reside there for
a time in 1539–1540.

The prologue to the Third Book must have

* For G. du Bellay, see V. L. Bourrilly, *Guillaume du
Bellay* (1905).

been written during the first seven or eight
months of the year 1544, for its highly patriotic
note is inspired by the military preparations
which were going on throughout the kingdom,
in view of the expected attack on Paris by the
combined forces of Charles V. and Henry
VIII. The rest of the book, which, as we shall
see later, clearly shows the influence of André
Tiraqueau, must have been added during the
years 1544 and 1545. In the autumn of the
latter year Rabelais applied for a privilege.

The times were more dangerous than ever.
The Peace of Crépy (September 18, 1544),
which had ended the war with the Emperor,
though not with the King of England, contained vague but alarming provisions for the
reunion of religion and for "the prevention
of the extreme danger that threatened it".
Rabelais's friend François Errault, Sieur de
Chemant, who in June, 1543, had been promoted
from the post of President of the Parliament
of Turin to that of Chancellor of France, had
died in the very year of the peace.

The spring of the following year, 1545, was
made hideous by the massacre of the Waldenses. Of the men who had taken part in the
banquet in honour of Dolet, Marot had recently
died in exile, Budé was also dead, Nicolas
Bourbon had abjured Protestantism, and Dolet

himself was lying in the Conciergerie awaiting his sentence of death. A man had been burnt at Chinon, Rabelais's native town, and at the beginning of the year a secretary of the Cardinal du Bellay had been burnt at Paris. If the Cardinal could not protect his secretary, how was he to protect his canon and physician, whose *Gargantua* and *Pantagruel* figured in a list of books that had recently been censured by the Sorbonne?

Rabelais, however, trusted to the King for protection. Some three years before this, probably during his temporary visit to France in the winter and spring of 1541–1542, he had been appointed one of the masters of requests attached to the service of the Court. It was an office without pay and without duties, but one which gave the holder some claim to the royal favour. Whether helped or not by this appointment, Rabelais obtained from the King a privilege for ten years, dated September 19, 1545, in which it was duly set forth that "our well-beloved and trusty Master François Rabelais . . . having caused to be printed several books, especially two volumes of the heroic deeds and sayings of Pantagruel, not less useful than delectable, the printers have in several places corrupted and perverted the said books, to the great displeasure and detriment of the aforesaid petitioner and the prejudice of the readers"; but that "being daily importuned by the learned and studious people in our kingdom to continue the said work, he hath petitioned us for a privilege". It is seldom that such delightful humour is allowed to appear in an official document. The advantage of it was that it enabled Rabelais to lay the blame of any heretical or irreverent passages in his earlier books on the shoulders of the wicked printers.

Armed with this privilege, Rabelais prepared his new book for publication. It appeared in 1546, printed and published by Chrestien Wechel, hitherto known solely as a publisher of learned works. For the first time the author allowed his name to stand on the title-page. In the prologue Rabelais, as usual, invited all honest topers and all honest gouty gentlemen to drink frankly and freely of the wine which he offered them, for "good hope lies at the bottom". But "of the searchers after minute corrections do not speak to me, I beseech you . . . of the hypocrites still less . . . because they are not of good but of evil. . . . Back, dogs! out of my course! Back, hypocrites! Out of the way, Pharisees (*caphards*)!"

This was hardly calculated to appease the

Sorbonne, and it is not surprising that before Easter that body passed the same formal censure on the Third Book that it had passed on its predecessors. In spite of the confident tone of his prologue, in spite of the privilege he had obtained from the King, Rabelais evidently anticipated this treatment of his book.

On the 6th of February we find him at Metz, writing to his patron, Jean du Bellay, the following letter:

"MY LORD:

"If M. de Saint-Ay, on coming here lately, had had the advantage of taking leave of you at his departure, I should not now be in so great necessity and anxiety, as he will be able to explain to you more at large. For he assured me that you were well minded to give me some alms, provided that he could find a trusty man coming from your parts. Indeed, my lord, unless you take pity on me I know not what I am to do, unless in the extremity of despair I take service with some one about here, to the detriment and evident loss to my studies. It is not possible to live more frugally than I do, and you cannot make me so small a gift from the abundance of goods that God hath placed in your hands but that I can manage, by living from hand to mouth, to maintain myself honourably, as I have done up to the present, for the honour of the house from which I came on my departure from France. My lord, I commend myself very humbly to your kind favour, and pray our Lord to grant you a very happy and long life, with perfect health.

"Your very humble servant,

"FRANÇOIS RABELAIS, Physician.

"From Metz, this 6th of February (1546)."

TURIN: METZ: ROME

We have also a Latin letter from Jean Sturm, the distinguished educationalist, to Jean du Bellay, dated Saverne, March 28, and, though also without the year, proved by internal evidence to belong to 1546, which contains the following passage: "The times have driven Rabelais out of France. Alas for the times! He has not yet reached us. I hear he is stopping at Metz, for he sent us salutations from there." It is clear from these two letters that Rabelais had made a hurried flight from France some time in January, 1546, and it is impossible not to connect this flight with the publication of his Third Book. Probably it was published quite early in 1546—or even before the end of 1545, for in that age publishers sometimes anticipated the beginning of a new year—and Rabelais's flight took place either immediately before or immediately after the publication.

At Metz he was not long in obtaining employment, being appointed physician to the public hospital at an annual stipend of one hundred and twenty livres. He held the post from Easter (April 25), 1546, or possibly from the beginning of April, to midsummer, 1547. Traces of his residence at Metz are to be found in the Fourth Book, where he refers to the Graulli, or image of a winged serpent, which it was the custom to carry in procession on St. Mark's Day (April 25) and the Rogation days as a memorial of the dragon put to flight by St. Clement. He also introduces a few words of Metz patois.

At midsummer, 1547, he probably returned to France, and a passage in the *Sciomachie* seems to point to his being at Paris on July 10 of that year, the day on which the celebrated duel between Jarnac and La Châtaigneraie was fought at Saint-Germain. François I. had died on the 31st of March, and had been succeeded by his only surviving son, under the title of Henri II. If Rabelais had thought that the new reign would inaugurate a milder policy towards Protestantism and other forms of heterodoxy, he was speedily undeceived. Though in their foreign policy Henri's rival advisers, the Constable de Montmorency and the Cardinal de Lorraine, were diametrically opposed to each other, they were united in a common aim to repress Protestantism by severe measures, and their views were shared by the King's all-powerful mistress, Diane de Poitiers. Moreover, there was no longer any need to angle for the alliance of the German Protestant princes. Accordingly, on October 8, 1547, a second criminal court of the Parliament of Paris was specially created for the trial of heretics. This was the famous *Chambre*

98

Ardente. Beginning its operations in December, it sat continuously for twenty-five months, during which period it passed at least five hundred sentences.

Rabelais, however, undeterred by past experiences, continued the publication of his book. The Fourth Book opens with the statement that Pantagruel put to sea on June 9, and this may indicate that Rabelais began the new book on that day. The year would be 1546, for there is an allusion in the next chapter (the fifth of the complete edition) to the proposed meeting of the Council of Trent for its sixth session on July 29 of that year.* Possibly also the story of Panurge's adventure with the sheep-merchant (chapters v–viii of the complete edition) and the greater part of the account of the storm (chapters xviii–xx) were written at Metz. Then after his return to Paris he added some more chapters (ix–xi, part of xii, xvi, xvii, xxi–xxiv, part of xxv) and a prologue. In 1548 this fragment, containing eleven chapters, was published as the Fourth Book, Rabelais's name again appearing on the title-page. There is no publisher's

---

* The date of July 29 was fixed at the fifth session on June 16, but on July 18 the meeting was postponed. Chapter v must therefore have been written before Rabelais had heard of the postponement.

name, but Lyons is given as the place of publication, and Pierre de Tours was certainly both publisher and printer. There was little or nothing in the chapters themselves to which the ever vigilant Sorbonne could take exception, but in the prologue there is a characteristic attack on the "canting bigots, booted monks, and hypocrites" who had calumniated his writings. "Seeing all the world in eager appetite to see and read my writings, on account of the preceding books, they have spit in the basin; that is to say, they have by their handling befouled, decried, and calumniated them, with this intention, that no one should read them save their own poltroon selves."

Once more Rabelais thought it advisable to leave France. We learn from a receipt which he signed for the value of a bill of exchange drawn at Paris on a Roman banker that he was at Rome on the 18th of June, again as physician to Cardinal du Bellay. For on the accession of Henri II. Du Bellay had fallen out of favour, and to ensure his absence from the Court had been sent on a special mission to Rome. He expected it to last only a few months, but the months went by, and in spite of repeated letters to the Constable and to the Cardinal de Lorraine, in which he complained in moving terms of his gout and the Roman climate, he was not recalled. The advent of his friend and physician must therefore have been very welcome. His palace was in the Piazza de' Santi Apostoli, where he lived on his usual magnificent scale, with an establishment of over a hundred persons and thirty-seven horses. There were also numerous stray pensioners on his charity, who never begged in vain. No wonder that in his letters home he complained of his limitless expenses, and became more urgent than ever for his recall.

With another French cardinal who was at Rome at this time, Georges d'Armagnac, Bishop of Rodez, Rabelais had long been on friendly terms. Like the Bishop of Montpellier, he had done good service to François I., not only as a diplomatist, but as a collector of Greek manuscripts. In his service at Rome were Guillaume Philandrier, the architect and commentator on Vitruvius, of whom Rabelais speaks in his Fourth Book as his "great friend", and Pierre de Paschal, to whom several of the sonnets in Joachim du Bellay's *Regrets* (*Les Regrets*) are addressed, and who was also a friend of Rabelais.

On March 14, 1549, Cardinal du Bellay gave a splendid entertainment in the Piazza de' Santi Apostoli, to celebrate the birth of a son (who died in infancy) to Henri II. The chief feature of the entertainment was a sham fight between the attackers and the defenders of a great wooden castle which had been erected in the Piazza. This was followed by a sumptuous supper, at which thirty puncheons of wine were drunk, by a performance of Spanish dancers, by several masks, and finally by a ball which lasted till daylight, "when the most reverend lords, the ambassadors, and other prelates retired with great jubilation and content". It is from Rabelais's own pen that we have an account of these festivities, for he described them in a series of letters to the Cardinal de Guise, which were published by Gryphius, in the same year, under the title of *The Sham Fight and Festivities Held at Rome* (*La Sciomachie et Festins faits à Rome*). His biographer Le Roy, indeed, tells us that he was the author of some of the mechanical contrivances which formed part of the entertainment.

The next remarkable event which took place at Rome during Rabelais's visit was the election of a new pope. On November 10, 1549, Paul III. died, and at once the wheels of French and Spanish diplomacy were set in motion. There were only three French cardinals on the

spot, Meudon, Armagnac, and Lenoncourt.
Jean du Bellay had returned to France, but
he was promptly ordered back, and on December 11 he entered the Conclave with Guise,
Châtillon, Tournon, and Vendôme. Before
the arrival of this French contingent the Englishman, Cardinal Pole, had been first favourite.
Indeed, on December 5 his election had been
regarded as practically certain. But his combined supporters, the Imperialist party and
the followers of Cardinal Farnese, a grandson
of the late Pope, could never muster more
than twenty-three votes, while the French
party, after they had been reinforced, polled
nearly as many for their candidate, Cardinal
Caraffa. Both parties were equally determined, the Frenchmen declaring that they
would conquer or rot. In the middle of January
matters were still at a dead-lock; the Conclave
was expected to drag on till March, and the
betting had become very open. At last Guise,
who, though the youngest of the French cardinals, acted as their leader, came to an agreement with Farnese, with the result that on
February 7, 1550, Cardinal del Monte was
duly elected. He took the title of Julius III.
He was the third pope whom Rabelais had
seen, a circumstance which he notes by the
mouth of Panurge in the Fourth Book, adding,

with characteristic irreverence, "and I have profited little from the sight of them".

The long confinement of the Conclave, where there was "a great stench", and where at one time more than four hundred persons were immured, told severely on Cardinal du Bellay's health, and he greatly needed the services of his physician. As soon as he had sufficiently recovered, which was not till the beginning of May, he set out for Naples on some business which had been entrusted to him by Catherine de' Medici. But on the road he changed his mind, and returned to Rome. In June he was still at Rome, evidently expecting his exile to be prolonged, for he ordered a hundred tuns of wine. But before midsummer he received from Montmorency the welcome message that he might return to France as soon as he pleased. In the early days of July he set out, and in spite of a fall from his horse, which necessitated his continuing the journey in a litter, reached Paris by slow stages before the end of the month, accompanied doubtless by his trusty physician.

CHAPTER IV

I⊤ will be recollected that Guillaume du Bellay had charged his estate with an annual payment to Rabelais, which was to cease on his receipt of church preferment of a certain value. It was therefore probably in satisfaction of the latter alternative that he was presented about this time with two livings, that of Meudon, in the diocese of Paris, and that of Saint-Christophe du Jambet, in the diocese of Le Mans, of which Jean du Bellay was also Bishop, having succeeded his brother René in 1546. The document which records his collation to the living of Meudon is extant, and bears the date of January 18, 1550. A century later Antoine Le Roy found there traditions of the care with which he tended his flock. In these traditions, collected as they were by a partial biographer, legend may have been blended with fact, but there is no reason why Rabelais should not have made as good a parish priest as he was a doctor. The proximity of Meudon to Paris, from which it is distant only about four miles, would have enabled him to keep in touch with the intellectual life of the capital, and he doubtless paid frequent visits to that "paradise of salubrity", Jean du Bellay's château at Saint-Maur-des-Fossés. Indeed, in the letter to Odet de Châtillon which he prefixed to the Fourth Book he speaks of meeting the Cardinal there. As regards his other parish of Saint-Christophe du Jambet, he must have discharged the duties through a *vicaire*, or curate.

One of his first concerns after his return to Paris must have been to prepare for the publication of his Fourth Book in a complete form. We cannot say what his reasons were for the fragmentary publication of 1548, with its abrupt ending. Possibly he may have intended it as a *ballon d'essai* to test the disposition of the new government towards his book. Possibly, too, he may have kept back in his portfolio part of what he had already written. But at any rate several references to events which took place in 1548 show that considerable additions were made after this. Moreover, half a dozen chapters were interpolated, three in one place and three in another, in the published portion of the Fourth Book. When he returned to France at the end of July, the book must have been ready for publication; otherwise he would not have applied for a privilege, for privileges were naturally not granted, in those days of strict supervision of the press, until a book was practically complete.

To obtain this privilege it was needful for Rabelais to show even more than his usual circumspection. During his absence at Rome a monk of Fontevrault named Gabriel de Puits-Herbault had introduced into a Latin dialogue entitled *Theotimus* (1549) a passage which represented him as a glutton, a drunkard, and a dangerous heretic. His old patron, Jean du Bellay, was out of favour. He was sorely in need of new protectors. He had already, as we have seen, angled for one in the person of the Cardinal de Guise, or, as he had called himself since his uncle's death, in 1550, the Cardinal de Lorraine, whose influence with the new King rivalled that of the Constable de Montmorency, and was inferior only to that of Diane de Poitiers. But whether Guise, who belonged to the orthodox camp, did not choose to stand sponsor to a new book of *Pantagruel*, or whether the prudent Rabelais thought it advisable to have a second protector, it was to Odet de Châtillon, possibly on the advice of Jean du Bellay, that he applied for assistance in the matter of his privilege. Odet de Châtillon, the eldest of the Coligny brothers, was now a man of thirty-five. At sixteen he had been

made a cardinal; at seventeen, Archbishop of
Toulouse; at twenty-six, Bishop of the rich
see of Beauvais. It was possibly a feeling of
the abuse of church patronage, which was so
well exemplified in his own person, that inclined him in the direction of the new religious
doctrines, and led him, like his two brothers,
to become a Protestant. He had no more of
the churchman in him than Jean du Bellay
or the other high ecclesiastics who were Rabelais's friends, but he was a munificent patron
of literature and learning, and a large proportion of the books published in France during
the reign of Henri II. were dedicated either
to him or to the Cardinal de Lorraine. He
was on friendly terms with Jean du Bellay,
who probably introduced Rabelais to him
when he came to Rome for the Conclave.
In any case, it was he who used his good offices
with Henri II. to procure Rabelais a privilege
for his new book.

Fortunately, the storm of religious persecution had somewhat abated, and the *Chambre
Ardente* was no longer sitting, having been
temporarily suppressed at the beginning of the
year 1550. Rabelais, however, took special
pains to make his book acceptable to the King
by introducing passages of delicate flattery.
He refers to him twice as the *roi megiste* (great-

est king), and once, in a passage interpolated
in the fifth chapter, as King Ohebé, a Hebrew
word which signifies "lover". He also introduces a story of which the point lies in a compliment to the bravery of Claude de Lorraine,
the father of the King's favourites, who had
died in the preceding April. But he went
further than mere personal compliment. As
Brunetière has pointed out, he supported the
King's policy by approbation of his acts and
by satire directed against his opponents. The
patriotic tone of the prologue to the Fourth
Book must have been greatly to the taste of
a monarch as warlike as Henri II. When
we read that the young Niphleseth, Infanta
of the Island of the Chitterlings, was sent
to the great King of Paris, where she was
honourably treated and married in a high
and wealthy position, one is inevitably reminded of how in August, 1548, the young
Mary Stewart was carried off to France to be
educated at the French Court, and formally
betrothed to the Dauphin. Possibly Rabelais
did not really intend any allusion to this
master-stroke of Guise policy, but in the last
chapter of the book there is direct mention of
a minor success gained by the French against
England at this period. When Panurge says
that he thinks "that this very morning the

Isle of Horses near Scotland has been sacked and ransacked by the Lords of Thermes and Dessay [D'Essé], together with all the English who had surprised it", he is referring to the recapture of Inchkeith on the day of Corpus Christi (June 20), 1549. It is true that peace had been made with England on March 24, 1550, but this was a move of Montmorency's against the Guises, and was not altogether to the King's satisfaction. When a special mission was sent from England, in June, 1551, to invest him with the Garter, he naturally made great professions of friendship; but he was not supposed to be in earnest, and the Venetian ambassador, Lorenzo Contarini, says, in the report which he sent to his government in that year, that it was Henri's intention to attack England at some time or other.

Softened, perhaps, by these flattering tributes to himself and his policy, the King acceded to Rabelais's request, and a privilege for ten years was granted him on August 6, 1550, in the presence of Odet de Châtillon. In spite, however, of the privilege, Rabelais delayed the publication of his book. The reasons for this delay are unknown to us, but at any rate after June, 1551, when the severe Edict of Châteaubriand was issued against the Protestants, the publication must have been a dangerous matter. We can get some idea of the stress of the persecution from the fact that nearly three hundred French refugees were received at Geneva in the year 1551, as against one hundred and twenty in the preceding year. They included the well-known printer and scholar, Robert Estienne. Rabelais, however, with his usual tenacity, clung to his idea of making the King, so to speak, an accomplice in his book. The whole episode of Bishop Homenaz and the Decretals so closely reflects, as Brunetière has pointed out, the policy of Henri II., or rather of his advisers (for he was as wax in their hands), that it is difficult to avoid the conclusion that Rabelais was furthering the King's projects. It was not, however, till the close of the year 1550 that this anti-Vatican policy began to develop. We have seen that the new Pope, Julius III., had been elected through a coalition between the French cardinals and the party of Cardinal Farnese. It was the question of Parma and Ottavio Farnese which led to the breach between France and the Pope. In December, 1550, Ottavio, finding that the Pope could not protect him against the hostilities of the Imperial forces or persuade the Emperor to restore to him Piacenza, applied for aid to Henri II., and in the following May a treaty was signed between them. At the same time the Pope threw in his lot with the Emperor, and declared Ottavio deprived of his fief. So the war of Parma, between France and the Holy See, began. On September, 1551, the Council of Trent reopened, and letters from Henri II. were read by Jacques Amyot, the translator of Plutarch, in which the King repudiated the authority of the Council and reproached the Pope with the war. "It seems to me," said Panurge, when he was shown the portrait of an ideal pope, "that this portrait is faulty as regards our late popes, for I have seen them wearing a helmet on their heads; and while the whole Christian empire was at peace and quiet, they alone were furiously and very cruelly carrying on war." The reference is ostensibly to former popes, such as Alexander VI. and Julius II., but the censure must have been intended to apply as well to the actual Pope, Julius III.

On the whole, then, it is extremely tempting to draw the inference that the chapters of the Fourth Book relating to Bishop Homenaz and the Island of the Papimanes were added in 1551, after the privilege had been granted. At the close of the year the complete book, now consisting of fifty-two chapters, was sent to the press. It was furnished with a new prologue, and a letter to the Cardinal de Châtillon by way of preface, in which Rabelais protests most strongly against the calumnious attacks that had been made on his book, and declares stoutly that there is not a word of heresy in it. The printing was finished on January 28, 1552. In spite of the author's precautions, as soon as the book appeared it was pounced upon and censured by the Sorbonne, while the Parliament of Paris prohibited its sale for a fortnight pending the King's pleasure (March 1, 1552). Henri II. was on the eve of invading Lorraine in accordance with his agreement with the Protestant princes of Germany. He occupied Toul on April 13 and Metz on April 18, and accordingly, in a new edition of the Fourth Book, the epithets "great, victorious, and triumphant" were introduced in the prologue before the King's name. But this flattery did not avail to remove the interdict on the book; the revised edition appeared without name of publisher or place of publication, as did also an edition of the four books in 1553.

Just before the printing of the Fourth Book was finished, on January 9, 1552, Rabelais had resigned both his livings. This may have been due to pressure from without, or it may have been in some way or other connected with the publication of the Fourth Book. This

is the last specific act of Rabelais's life that is
known to us, but we hear of him again in November, 1552, when Denys Lambin, the well-
known scholar, writing from Lyons to a friend
at Paris, on the 3d of that month, says that
he has heard a rumour that Rabelais has been
thrown into prison. A few days later he writes
to Henri Estienne that he believes the rumour
to be a mere fable, and on December 5 he
tells the same correspondent that he has heard
nothing about Rabelais. According to an old
tradition, Rabelais's death took place in the
year 1553; at any rate, we know for certain
that he died before May 1, 1554, for an epigram by Jacques Tahureau on *Rabelais Dead*
(*Rabelais trépassé*), which appeared in his collected poems, must have been written before
that date. Guillaume Colletet, writing in the
early part of the seventeenth century, says
that he died at Paris in the Rue des Jardins,
and that he was buried in the cemetery of
Saint-Paul.

The record of Rabelais's life, when it has
been stripped of all legend, is somewhat bare
of incident, while for certain periods it is a
complete blank, which we must fill up as best
we can by inference and conjecture. We do not
know when he was born, or the exact year
in which he died. We know practically nothing

of his life till he was about five-and-twenty. In fact, the whole of our knowledge amounts to little more than this, that he was first a friar, and then a monk; that he took his medical degrees at Montpellier; that he held for a short time the post of physician to the hospital at Lyons; that he wrote certain books; that he made three journeys to Rome; and that he resided for a time at Turin and at Metz. Only a few of his letters have come down to us, and of these the one to Erasmus is in Latin, and more or less formal in character, while those written from Rome to the Bishop of Maillezais are evidently not as they came from his pen, and have lost most of their savour.

In spite, however, of our scanty knowledge, certain facts in his life and character stand plainly out. We must abandon the legend which represents him as a gluttonous and wine-bibbing buffoon, as an unfrocked priest, as a sort of ecclesiastical Falstaff. We have seen what his relations were with Guillaume and Jean du Bellay, two of the foremost men in the kingdom; we have seen how he was respected by men like Geoffroy d'Estissac, the Bishop of Maillezais, and the distinguished jurist, André Tiraqueau, and how humanists like Salmon Macrin and Dolet and Voulté and Jean de Boyssonné spoke in the highest

terms of his learning and of his skill as a
physician. But perhaps it is from the letters
written to him during his sojourn at Turin
by Guillaume Pellicier, the Bishop of Montpellier, that we get the most convincing proof
of the high regard in which he was held, not
only by men of his own rank, but by those
far above him in power and station, princes
of the Church and patrons of humanism.

The light in which he appeared to the more
understanding of his contemporaries may be
judged also from a Latin poem which a learned
physician of Loudun, named Pierre Boulenger,
wrote for his epitaph. Though it did not
appear in print till 1587, it was probably
written soon after Rabelais's death, when the
author was a young man between twenty and
five-and-twenty.

"You will perhaps think the man was a buffoon and a
jester, one who angled for dinners with witty speeches.
No, he was no buffoon, no jester of the market-place,
but one who, with the penetration of a distinguished
mind, laughed at the human race, its foolish wishes and
credulous hopes. He passed his days free from material
care, his sails ever filled with the breeze of prosperity.
Nor would you find any one more learned, when it pleased
him to lay aside laughter for serious topics. . . . If a
great and difficult question had to be solved by industry
and learning, you would have said that he alone saw
into the greatest mysteries, that to him alone were re-
vealed the secrets of nature. . . . He was familiar with

all the learning of Greece and Rome, and like a second
Democritus laughed at the idle fears and hopes of populace
and princes, and at the vain cares and anxious labours
of this transitory life." *

There were, of course, exceptions to this
view. A man with Rabelais's propensity to
laughter and satire is bound to make enemies.
There are some men to whom laughter is the
one unpardonable sin, and who are ever ready
to quote, with Bossuet, "Woe unto you that
laugh, for ye shall mourn and weep". Moreover, in Rabelais's day controversy was carried on with little regard for either decency or
truth. It was little wonder if men so devoid of
humour as Calvin and the elder Scaliger, or
lesser men like Voulté and the monk Puits-
Herbault, attacked Rabelais in Latin epigrams
and other Latin writings in which, fortified by
the classical examples of Cicero and Catullus,
they cast on his character aspersions which
had little or no foundation in fact, and which
no one familiar with the classical commonplaces of the language of abuse will regard for
a moment as worthy of serious attention.

Now that these mists of libel and legend
have been dispersed, we can see that Rabelais
was regarded by the majority of his contem-

---

* *Hippocratis Aphorismorum Paraphrasis Poetica* (cited
in part by Rathery).

poraries as a great physician, a man of varied learning, a charming companion, a loyal and helpful friend, and as the author of a successful and amusing book. That it was the greatest book that had yet been published in the French language they naturally did not suspect. Indeed, it is curious that among the various references to Rabelais by his contemporaries there is hardly one which refers to him as the author of *Pantagruel*. The one notable exception is Joachim du Bellay's allusion to him, in the *Defence and Illustration of the French Tongue* (*Deffence et Illustration de la Langue françoise*), as the man "who has brought Aristophanes back to life, and who imitates so well the satirical wit of Lucian".

When we look for more particular traits in his character, we are baffled by the scantiness of our information. We note, however, that in the conduct of his affairs, and especially with regard to the publication of his book, he combined in a remarkable manner prudence with tenacity of purpose, and courage with caution. In the face of the active and constant opposition of the Sorbonne and the Paris Parliament, and of the dangers which that opposition entailed, it required great courage to publish the successive instalments of his book. But with remarkable adroitness he managed to conciliate the favour of the King, and though neither François I. nor Henri II. had the strength of character and consistency of purpose of a Louis XIV., Rabelais, like Molière, found behind the throne a shelter against extreme measures on the part of his opponents. In less important matters, if our inferences from the dry official record of his academical career at Montpellier are correct, he seems to have shown a similar pertinacity, standing up for his rights and hitting back on occasion. "Friar John," said Panurge, after the conclusion of his quarrel with the sheep-dealer, "hearken to me. Never did man do me a good turn without a recompense, or at least an acknowledgment. I am not ungrateful, never was, and never shall be. Never did man do me an ill turn without repenting it either in this world or in the other. I am not such a fool as that." Here Rabelais is speaking by the mouth of Panurge; for if he was a dangerous enemy, he was a loyal and trustworthy friend, sparing no trouble to serve those who had befriended him. It is noteworthy, too, that as if conscious of the unchristian character of the sentiments expressed by Panurge, he added in the complete edition of the Fourth Book the following reply by Friar John: "Thou damnest thyself like an old devil. It is written, 'Vengeance is mine'. 'Tis in the breviary."

Of the characteristics which make Rabelais so thoroughly representative of his age, the most striking are his devotion to learning, his many-sidedness, and his love of travel. In the piteous letter which he addressed from Metz to his patron, Jean du Bellay, he speaks of "taking service" as a last extremity, because it would be to the detriment of his studies. Like Erasmus, he would have said, "Books first, and then clothes".

Rabelais's learning is remarkable rather for its wide range than for its depth and accuracy in any one subject. The number of Greek and Latin authors from whom he quotes or borrows is very great, even allowing for those with whom he had probably only a second-hand acquaintance; but he had not the knowledge of a professional scholar. He could not have emended a corrupt text, or have surveyed the whole field of antiquity with the comprehensive vision of a Budé. He had studied Roman law up to a certain point with considerable profit, but he was not an expert jurist. He had some Hebrew, but it was hardly more than a smattering. But to these studies of the ordinary humanist he added many more. He was widely read in French and Italian vernacular literature. We shall see in the next chapter that he had a considerable knowledge of architecture, though he was interested in it rather on the technical than on the artistic side. Of the other fine arts his chief interest seems to have been in music, and in the prologue to the Fourth Book he gives us a list of fifty-nine musicians of his day, chiefly Flemish or French, and nearly all belonging to what is known as the Netherlands School. Chief among them are John Okeghem and his pupil Josquin Des Prez, both in their turn heads of the Royal Chapel in Paris, Adrian Willaert, a native of Bruges and choir-master of St. Mark's, Venice, Pierre Certon, choir-master of the Sainte-Chapelle, and Clément Jannequin, a charming composer of popular songs. In spite of his visits to Italy, Rabelais seems to have taken little or no interest in painting or sculpture. The bent of his mind was literary and scientific rather than artistic.

It was in the domain of science that his acquirements were the most remarkable. His knowledge of anatomy and physiology and his skill as a practising physician have already been discussed in a previous chapter. He had also a considerable knowledge of botany and zoology, including comparative anatomy. The positive and scientific bent of his mind is further shown by his acquaintance with the technical terms of various arts and crafts; we have a good instance of this in the prologue to the Third Book, where he pours forth with lavish profusion strings of words relating to fortification and other military matters. On the other hand, according to a competent critic, his famous account of the storm betrays ignorance rather than knowledge of naval matters.

Finally, Rabelais proves himself a thorough representative of his age in his love of travel and his general restlessness. It is true that his journeys to Rome, as well as those to Turin and Metz, seem to have been dictated by prudence, if not by actual necessity. But apart from these he had wandered over a large part of France, and was seldom in one place for long together. Besides the visits recorded in the preceding chapters, there are places which, from the way in which they are mentioned in his book, we feel sure he must have visited at some time, notably Saint-Malo, the port from which the expedition to the Bottle sailed. From Saint-Malo he seems to have visited the Channel Islands of Sark and Herm, for Panurge says that he has seen these islands (IV, lxvi), and Rabelais not unfrequently records his own experiences by the mouth of Panurge.

His love of travel is only another form of

his ardent thirst after knowledge. Wherever he went, he was inspired by what Montaigne calls "an honest curiosity for information about everything". At Rome, as we saw, he threw himself with untiring energy into the study of its ancient remains. At Turin, fired by the martial atmosphere in which he found himself, he took a keen interest in the work of fortification. At La Rochelle and Saint-Malo he made the acquaintance of pilots and sailors, and learned what they had to tell him of the New World. In every town that he visited, he marked with an observant eye its buildings and other noteworthy objects.

During that wonderful period of rejuvenescence of human energy which we call the Renaissance, there were many men who surpassed Rabelais in the variety of their artistic achievements, there were some who were superior to him in scientific knowledge, there were possibly a few who rivalled him in the knowledge of books; but in the combination of both literary and scientific knowledge with artistic achievement it would be difficult to find his equal.

CHAPTER V

GARGANTUA

THERE was until recent years considerable discussion as to whether the character of Gargantua was invented by Rabelais, or whether he already existed in popular tradition. But the occurrence of the name in a document of 1470 conclusively proves his prior existence. M. Sébillot's researches into the folklore on the subject point to the same conclusion; for, while stories relating to Gargantua are comparatively rare in Touraine, Anjou, and Poitou, where Rabelais's younger days were spent, they are most plentiful in Brittany, which apparently he did not visit till a later period of his life. This Breton predominance of the legend agrees, too, with the fact that in *The Great and Inestimable Chronicles* Gargantua is connected with the Arthurian Cycle. Shakespeare, when he makes Celia say to Rosalind, "You must borrow me Gargantua's mouth first", is doubtless thinking, not of Rabelais's book, but of the giant of popular legend.

But there is a further question. Did Rabelais write *The Great and Inestimable Chronicles*, or did he merely revise an existing chap-book? On this point critics are generally agreed in thinking that the work as a whole is unworthy of Rabelais, and that at most he added to it some characteristic touches. But crude though it is, it had, we have seen, a tremendous success, for it appeared at a time when the prose romances of chivalry were the favourite reading of the French public. While the older and more aristocratic Arthurian romances, printed in sumptuous folios, were read chiefly by noble lords and ladies, the middle classes preferred the fifteenth-century prose versions of the *chansons de geste* in their last decadence, or the *romans d'aventure*. Among the more popular were *Valentine and Orson, The Four Sons of Aymon, Melusine* and its continuation, *Geoffrey with the Great Tooth, Ogier the Dane, Fierabras*, and *Robert the Devil*. But even in the days of François I. these romances must also have appeared, as they certainly did later, in versions which appealed to the lowest stratum of readers, and which therefore dealt largely in exaggeration and burlesque—in short, chapbooks. It is such a chap-book, embodying the popular legends relating to the beneficent giant Gargantua, that we may suppose Rabelais to have been employed to edit by the Lyons publisher, Claude Nourry.

FRANÇOIS RABELAIS

It was apparently while he was engaged upon this task that it occurred to him to use the popular story as a starting-point for an original work dealing with the history of Pantagruel, the son of Gargantua. This, as we have seen, appeared probably before the end of the year 1532. Encouraged by its success, Rabelais determined to write a new and worthier account of Pantagruel's father, and the new *Gargantua*, though written after *Pantagruel*, thus became the first book of Rabelais's great narrative. But he did not altogether reject the materials of the popular story. The description of Gargantua's clothes, the marvellous mare which he rode, the story of his carrying off the bells of Notre-Dame at Paris —all have their origin in *The Great Chronicles*.

The prologue to *Gargantua* is comparatively short, but it is well worth attention. In the first place, it is addressed to "the very illustrious drinkers" for whose entertainment Rabelais professes to write his books, thereby laying up for himself much misinterpretation at the hands of ill-disposed persons. Secondly, he impresses upon his readers that his book is not one of entertainment only, not, as Montaigne carelessly termed it, "simply amusing" (*simplement plaisant*). Referring to Alcibiades's comparison of Socrates to certain boxes, called

Sileni, which were painted outside with wanton figures to stir people to laughter, but contained within precious drugs, such as balsam, ambergris, musk, or civet, he says that in the same way the matters treated of in his book are not so frivolous as the title indicates. Just as a dog gnaws and sucks a bone in order to extract from it the marrow, so he bids his readers by careful reading and frequent meditation to suck the substantial marrow from his book. So they will find in it "high sacraments and dread mysteries as well concerning religion as concerning public polity and private life".

The book itself may be said to consist of four main episodes, the birth and childhood of Gargantua (chapters i–xiii), Gargantua's education (chapters xiv–xxiv), the war between Grandgousier and Picrochole (chapters xxv–li), and the abbey of Thelema (chapters lii–lviii). As has been already pointed out, the account of Gargantua's birth is remarkable for its numerous references to the neighbourhood of Rabelais's home. It also contains the famous chapter (v) entitled *The Talk of the Drinkers* (*Le Propos des Buveurs*), which affords a striking example of the author's astonishing verve and command of language. Here is the opening of it:

"Then they fell to chat after the collation in the same spot: and forthwith began flagons to go, gammons to trot, goblets to fly, glasses to rattle.

"Draw, reach, fill, mix.—Give it to me without water, so, my friend.—Whip me off this glass gallantly.—Bring me here some claret, in a glass weeping over.—A truce to thirst.—Ha! false fever, wilt thou not away?—By my faith, gossip, I cannot get in the drinking humour.—You have catched a cold, gammer?—Yea, forsooth, sir.—By the belly of St. Quenet, let's talk of drinking.—I only drink at my hours, like the Pope's mule.—I only drink in my breviary, like a good father guardian.—Which was first, thirst or drinking?"

The ninth chapter, which treats of the colours and livery of Gargantua, is interesting as a satire on the popular craze for heraldry, which showed itself not only in the direct study of the subject, but in less important ways. Thus even printers and publishers had their devices, which in many cases are a beautiful feature on the title-pages of their books. Poets, too, had their mottoes, and called themselves by names borrowed from the language of disguised knights-errant. Just as Amadis of Gaul was *Le Beau Ténébreux*, Rabelais's worthy friend Jean Bouchet was *Le Traverseur des Voies Périlleuses*. A similar fashion, which Rabelais also ridicules in this chapter, was the love of emblems and hieroglyphics, which led to the publication of various popular books on the subject. It was all part of the cult of chivalry, in its outward forms rather than in its true spirit, which marked the reigns of François I. and his successor—of François I., who was knighted by Bayard on the field of Marignano, and of Henri II., who was wounded to death by the splintered lance of his opponent in the lists of the Tournelles.

The second section of the book deals with the education of Gargantua, and is partly a satire on the old methods of education which prevailed in Rabelais's childhood, partly an exposition of his own ideas on the lines of the humanistic method which was coming into favour when he was writing *Gargantua*. Gargantua's first teacher was a famous doctor of theology named Thubal Holofernes, the latter part of whose name Shakespeare has borrowed for his pedant in *Love's Labour's Lost*. He began by teaching his pupil his A-B-C so thoroughly that he could say it by heart backwards. This took five years and three months. He then spent several years with him over the time-honoured grammars and text-books of mediæval education, such as the Latin grammar of Donatus and the *De Modis Significandi* of Jean de Garlande. Then he died, and was succeeded by Master Jobelin Bride, who introduced Gargantua to the celebrated *Doctrinale Puerorum* of Alexander de Villa

Dei, a grammar which, amid much murmuring of conservative pedagogues, was superseded in 1514, to various moral treatises, and to a favourite collection of sermons which bore the suggestive title of *Sleep Peacefully* (*Dormi Secure*).

But though Gargantua was an industrious pupil, his father found that he profited nothing by this instruction, and that he cut a sorry figure by the side of young Eudemon, the page of a neighbouring potentate, who had been studying for only two years. So he packed off Master Jobelin, and sent Gargantua to Paris in the company of Eudemon and the tutor Ponocrates.

Then follows the account of Gargantua's journey to Paris, riding on his enormous mare, and of how he carried off the bells of Notre-Dame, and how the Sorbonne, after much deliberation, sent the oldest member of the theological faculty, Master Janotus de Bragmardo, to point out to him the terrible inconvenience that was caused by the loss of the bells. The discourse which follows is an amusing parody on the harangues of university orators of that day, with their parade of learning and logic and their mixture of French and bad Latin.

In chapters xxiii and xxiv we have an account of the system of education which

Ponocrates, after first demonstrating the vicious effects of the old system, now adopted for Gargantua. It must be remembered that when Rabelais was writing, probably in the year 1533, the new studies had just begun to get a firm foothold in Paris in the face of the opposition of the obscurantist party. In March, 1530, the new Regius professors had entered on their duties. Even in the University itself some of the colleges were distinguished for enlightened views, especially the College of Sainte-Barbe, under the headship of Jacques de Gouvea and of his nephew André, who succeeded him. It was here that Maturin Cordier, who devoted himself to the work of reforming the education of the younger students of the University, lectured for three years. As recently as 1530 he had published a little treatise in which he waged war against the monkish jargon which passed for Latin among the students. Another educational reformer was Jean de Tartas, principal of the College of Lisieux, who in 1533 left Paris to become the first principal of the new College of Guyenne at Bordeaux. Outside the University there was the famous German humanist, Jean Sturm, who came to Paris in 1529, and soon afterwards opened a school in which education was conducted on humanistic lines,

and which attracted a large number of pupils.
With these men, or at least with their work,
Rabelais must have been familiar, if he resided
at Paris from 1528 to 1530. In fact, we know
from the letter of Sturm to Jean du Bellay
referred to in a previous chapter that at some
time or other Rabelais became personally acquainted with Sturm; and this was doubtless
before January, 1537, when Sturm left Paris
to become rector of the new gymnasium at
Strasburg.

This is how Gargantua spent his day. He
got up at four, and while he was being rubbed
(after a bath, let us hope) he had a page of
the *Bible* read to him by a young page. During the process of dressing he repeated his
lessons of the previous day; then a book was
read to him, accompanied doubtless by explanations, for three hours. This was followed
by some form of moderate exercise, such as
tennis, after which he and his companions
returned home to dinner, which was probably
at ten. During the meal a book was read,
and everything on the table was made a subject for instruction, passages from ancient
authors bearing on the subject being learned
by heart. The hour of digestion was devoted
to the study of the four subjects which formed
the *quadrivium* of mediæval education—arith-

metic, geometry, astronomy, and music; but
these were taught in an amusing and interesting fashion, arithmetical problems, for instance,
being solved with the help of dice and cards.
Then came hard study again for three hours,
consisting partly of repetition of the morning
lesson, partly of a continuation of the book
read in the morning, and partly of a writing
lesson.

This was followed by instruction at the hands
of a young gentleman of Touraine, named
Gymnaste, in every form of exercise on horseback. On some days there was swimming
and diving, and instruction in the arts of
rowing and sailing, followed by the climbing
of trees or gymnastic exercises. Then, after
changing their dress, they walked home through
the meadows, botanising on the way. It was
now time for supper, which was made the principal meal of the day. If dinner was at ten,
supper would be at six. Like dinner, it was
accompanied by reading and improving conversation. The evening was spent in music
or games of cards or dice, varied by visits to
learned men or travellers. Then came a lesson
in practical astronomy, and the pupil briefly
recapitulated to his tutor all that he had read,
seen, learned, and done during the course of
the day. Finally they returned thanks to God

for His past mercies, and commended themselves to His divine clemency for the future.

It will be noticed that we are not told what the books were which were read at the long morning and afternoon lessons; but we may infer, partly from Rabelais's known enthusiasm for the new studies, partly from Gargantua's letter to Pantagruel in the Second Book, that they were principally Greek and Latin authors, with the addition, probably, of Hebrew and history.

On wet days, instead of violent outdoor exercise in the afternoon, there was carpentering, painting, sculpture, and visits either to various workshops in the town or to the fencing rooms, where they showed themselves masters of every form of the art. Once a month there was a whole holiday, which was spent in an excursion into the country, to Chantilly or Saint-Cloud. But even on those days, though there were no books or lectures, instruction was not forgotten. They recited passages from Virgil's *Georgics* or Hesiod's *Works and Days*, or they composed Latin epigrams and then translated them into French ballades or rondeaux.

In considering this remarkable scheme of education as a whole, two things must be borne in mind. In the first place, it is in several important respects little more than a general outline, without much attempt to go into detail as regards either method or subjects, and with no attempt to distinguish between the various stages of intellectual development. Secondly, like many of Rabelais's schemes for the improvement of human society, it is an ideal scheme. It presupposes a pupil endowed with physical and intellectual capacity beyond that of an ordinary mortal, with any number of teachers at his command, and with exceptional opportunities for instruction in every branch of knowledge. It is the education, in short, not only of a prince, but of a giant.

What strikes one at first sight in the scheme is the perpetual instruction, which, except for the hours devoted to physical exercise, and even during some of these, goes on from four in the morning to six in the evening. According to modern ideas, a boy who repeated his lessons while he was dressing, who had to learn by heart passages of Pliny and Aristotle during his dinner, who had on his way home after three hours of hard exercise to compare plants with their descriptions in Theophrastus and Dioscorides, would inevitably grow up a monstrous prig. But in Rabelais's day this enthusiasm for learning was not priggish, because it was perfectly natural. Moreover, in Gargantua's education, though every available moment is occupied and the pupil has literally no leisure, the actual time allotted to severe study is not long. The six hours of lessons, three in the morning and three in the afternoon, compare favourably with what was the actual practice in schools and universities. When Henri de Mesmes was a student in the University of Toulouse, from 1545 to 1548, he attended lectures, as he tells us in a well-known passage of his memoirs, from five to ten in the morning without a break, and again in the afternoon from one to five. In addition to this he read Greek or Latin authors after dinner and after supper, and spent an hour before supper in going over his notes on the lectures.

It is a remarkable feature in Rabelais's scheme that five hours of the day are allotted to physical exercise. Moreover, in other respects we see the hand not only of the educationalist but of the physician. The dinner, or morning meal, is "sober and frugal", but the supper is "copious and plentiful". The hour of digestion is spent in gentle instruction, or in music or games. The pupil changes his clothes after exercise, and is rubbed and dried. Never before, or indeed since, in France has the training of the body played so important a part in an educational system.

Another noticeable feature is the care that is taken to develop the faculty of observation. Morning and evening the pupil has to note the face of the sky and the position of the stars; in the afternoon he has to compare the plants in the fields with their descriptions by ancient writers. If the day is wet, there is a visit to the druggist and the apothecary—to see how they adulterate their goods; or there are visits to the workshops of all kinds of artisans, as jewellers, clock-makers, printers, and dyers. Of course, this falls far short of modern ideas on the teaching of science; notably, there is no attempt at instruction in experiments. But in the heyday of the humanistic movement, when all wisdom and all knowledge were supposed to be contained in the works of Greek and Latin authors, and when even students of the natural sciences— physiologists, anatomists, botanists, zoologists —for the most part confined themselves to the work of collecting and classifying the ancient lore on their respective subjects, it was a great step in advance that things as well as books should be regarded as fitting objects of study, and that a pupil's powers of observation should be trained, as well as his memory. Not that the training of his memory is neglected. Three times a day he repeats by heart some passage from the book that has been read to him. Twice a day he goes over with his tutor the work of the previous afternoon. If there is any deficiency, it is in the cultivation of the logical faculty and of the imagination. As regards logic itself, it is no wonder if Rabelais, impelled by a spirit of reaction against the overwhelming importance which was attached to it in the old education, gave no place to it in his scheme; but at least such studies as arithmetic and geometry, which tend to develop the logical faculty, might have had more attention paid to them. On the other hand, we miss any attempt to train or encourage the imaginative faculty. Naturally, the Greek and Latin authors which are read to the pupil include poets in their number, and the pupil has to recite passages of Virgil and Hesiod. But it is the subject-matter and not the form which is regarded as of importance, and neither poetry as such nor any other kind of imaginative literature is recognised as an essential feature in mental training. Moreover, the fact that the pupil is allowed no leisure, that he is never free from the supervision of his tutor, that he is allowed no play in the true sense of the word, would all tend to make him unimagina-

tive and wanting in originality. Had one of
the popular romances of chivalry, even *The
Great and Inestimable Chronicles of Gargantua*,
been substituted for some of the improving
conversation or some of the references to Athenæus and Julius Pollux, it might have been to
the advantage of Gargantua's general mental
development.

In its broad outlines, Rabelais's scheme is
modelled on that which had been gradually
developed under the influences of humanism,
partly by practical teachers like Vittorino da
Feltre and his successors, and partly by writers
of educational treatises from Vergerius down-
wards. In the attention paid to physical
training, and especially in the insistence on
martial exercises as a necessary part of the
education of a prince, Rabelais is carrying out
the practice and precepts of men who had been
tutors to Italian princes; and the central position occupied in his scheme by classical literature, which, however, is implied rather than
insisted upon, is, of course, of the essence of
humanism. Moreover, he is also indebted to
his predecessors for certain details: to Vergerius, whose treatise *On a Liberal Education*
(*De Ingenuis Moribus*) remained a classic
throughout the sixteenth century, to More,
and to Erasmus. But in some important

respects he has improved on his models. His medical experience and the importance which he attached to health—"Without health life is no life," he says in the prologue to the Fourth Book—led him to pay special attention to the care of the body, while to his interest in science is due what is perhaps his most original contribution to the subject—his insistence on the cultivation of the powers of observation. On the whole, the scheme is remarkable for its large-mindedness, its good sense, its freedom from those fads and prejudices to which educationalists of all ages have been prone, rather than for any subtle or deep insight into the human mind. A fighter in the vanguard of humanism, yielding to no one in his veneration for antiquity, he was yet cool-headed enough to remember that the aim of education is not so much to fill the pupil with learning as to train both his mind and his body. His genius was none the less bold, none the less original, because it was always controlled by the dictates of common sense.

The story now returns to Touraine, and to the relation which forms the longest section of the book, that of the war between Grandgousier and his neighbour, King Picrochole. In the days when some high political personage was supposed to lurk behind each of the prin-

cipal characters of Rabelais's book, Picrochole
was said to stand for either Ferdinand the
Catholic or his grandson, Charles V., but there
can be little doubt that he is of humbler origin. According to the fullest and earliest version of a local tradition which was current
at least as far back as the seventeenth century, and which was repeated both to Ménage
and to Bishop Huet, the original of Picrochole
was Gaucher de Sainte-Marthe, physician to
François I. and to the abbess of Fontevrault,
who had made over to him her seignorial
rights over the village of Lerné. He was the
father of Charles de Sainte-Marthe, a contemporary of Rabelais, though somewhat younger,
an indifferent poet, but of some note as a
scholar and a religious reformer; grandfather
of Gaucher or Scévole de Sainte-Marthe, the
author of a well-known Latin poem on the
education of children (*Pædotrophia*), and of
the *Lives of Illustrious Men* (*Vies des Hommes
illustres*); and great-grandfather of the brothers Sainte-Marthe, the authors of the *Gallia
Christiana*.

The war between this choleric monarch and
Grandgousier began, like all great wars, from
small causes. The cake-bakers of Lerné refused to sell their cakes to Grandgousier's
shepherds, who, as it was the season of vint-

age, were guarding the vines and preventing the starlings from eating the grapes. The refusal was accompanied with insulting epithets, and a free fight took place, in which one of the cake-bakers, named Marquet,* was severely wounded; and the shepherds carried off about four or five dozen cakes, paying for them at the usual price.

On their return to Lerné the cake-bakers at once brought their complaint before their king, Picrochole. "He incontinently broke into a furious rage, and without asking any further why or how, had the ban and arrière-ban proclaimed throughout his kingdom." The operations of the war which ensued were carried on in the district round La Devinière, and may be traced on the map with perfect precision. As we saw in the first chapter, the villages of Lerné, La Roche-Clermaud, Seuilly, and Vaugaudry all play an important part in the narrative, while there is frequent mention of the Ford of Vedé. This tiny area to which the operations are confined forms an amusing contrast to the largeness of the armies engaged and to the grave tone of the narrative.

Picrochole at first met with no resistance. His army, plundering on the way, marched

---

* Gaucher de Sainte-Marthe married a Mlle. Marquet.

to Seuilly, which it pillaged with the usual license of armies of that day. A force was then detached to attack the abbey, but here they met with their first check. Among the monks was a certain Brother Jean des Entommeures, whose portrait must be given in Rabelais's own words:

"Young, gallant, frisk, lusty, nimble, bold, adventurous, resolute, tall, lean, wide-mouthed, long-nosed, a rare mumbler of matins, a rare unbridler of masses and scourer of vigils; in a word, a very monk, if ever there was one, since the monking world monked a monkery. For the rest, a clerk to the teeth in the matter of breviary."

The heroism of this young monk saved the abbey. Single-handed, and wielding only the staff of the Cross, he threw himself upon the enemy to such good purpose that they were completely routed, and left many of their number dead on the field.

Meanwhile Picrochole captured the stronghold of La Roche-Clermaud, which was undefended, and Grandgousier, who was of a peaceful disposition, sent an ambassador to him to offer satisfaction. The speech of this ambassador, Ulrich Gallet, is a remarkable specimen of manly eloquence, modelled to some extent on Cicero, but serving to remind us that Rabelais himself had a considerable reputation as a lecturer and speaker. But Picro-

chole turned a deaf ear to Grandgousier's proposals, which included an offer of five cartfuls
of cakes. Then follows a chapter (xxxiii)
of admirable satire, in which some of Picrochole's advisers conjure up before him a magnificent vision of universal conquest. To such
an extent is the king's imagination inflamed
that he begins to look on his conquests as
already accomplished, and speaks of them in
the past tense.

" 'But,' said he, 'all this time what is being done by
that part of our army which discomfited the swillpot
clown Grandgousier?'

" 'They are not idle,' said they; 'we shall soon meet them.
They have taken Brittany, Normandy, Flanders, Hainault,
Brabant, Artois, Holland, and Zealand. They have
crossed the Rhine over the bellies of the Switzers and
Landsknechts, and part of them have subdued Luxemburg,
Lorraine, Champagne, Savoy, as far as Lyons, in which
place they have found your garrisons returning from
the naval conquests of the Mediterranean Sea; and they
have reassembled in Bohemia, after having sacked Suevia,
Wurtemberg, Bavaria, Austria, Moravia, and Styria;
then they have fiercely set upon Lubeck, Norway, Swe-
den, Riga, Dacia, Gothia, Greenland, and the Easter-
lings as far as the Frozen Sea. This done, they have conquered the Isles of Orkney and subjugated Scotland,
England, and Ireland. From there sailing through the
Sandy Sea and by the Sarmatians, they have conquered
and dominated Prussia, Poland, Lithuania, Russia,
Wallachia, Trans-Silvania and Hungary, Bulgaria and
Turkey, and are now at Constantinople.'

" 'Let us go,' said Picrochole, 'and betake ourselves

to them as soon as possible, for I wish also to be Emperor of Trebizond.' "

Meanwhile Grandgousier had informed his son of what had happened, and Gargantua had set out from Paris immediately on receiving his letter. His arrival on the scene speedily changed the fortunes of the war, for his studies at Paris had evidently taught him the secret of military success. After a few preliminary engagements he marched on La Roche-Clermaud, where Picrochole had intrenched himself, took it by storm, and totally defeated the opposing army. Picrochole himself fled in despair, and in his flight a miller whose ass he was going to take beat him and stripped him. "From that time," adds the narrator, "no one knows what has become of him. Nevertheless, I have been told that he is a wretched porter at Lyons, choleric as ever."

In the operations under Gargantua Friar John does good service, and he becomes a conspicuous figure in this part of the narrative. The conversation at the supper to which he is invited by Gargantua recalls that of the drinkers, at the beginning of the book.

"And Friar John made merry. Never was any one so courteous and gracious.

" 'Come, come,' said Gargantua, 'a stool here near me at this end.'

" 'With all my heart,' said the monk, 'since it is your good pleasure.—Page, some water. Pour it, my boy, pour it; it will refresh my liver. Give it me here, that I may gargle.'

" '*Deposita cappa*,'* said Gymnaste, 'let us take off this frock.'

" 'Ho, pardy,' said the monk, 'my good sir, there is a chapter in the statutes of the order which would not allow this point.'

" 'A fig for your chapter,' said Gymnaste. 'This frock burdens both your shoulders; put it off.'

" 'My friend,' said the monk, 'leave it with me; for I swear I drink only the better for it. It makes all my body right merry. If I should lay it aside, the pages will make garters of it, as I was once served at Coulaines. Besides, I shall have no appetite; but if I sit at table in this habit, I will drink, pardy, to thee and to thy horse, and heartily to it. God save the company! I have supped, but for all that I will eat not a whit the less, for I have a paved stomach, as hollow as the boot of St. Benet,† ever open like a lawyer's pouch.' "

Friar John's joviality leads Eudemon to ask why it is that men drive away monks from all good companies, calling them trouble-feasts. The explanation is given by Gargantua:

" 'A monk—I mean one of those lazy monks, doth not labour like the peasant, nor guard the land as doth the man-at-arms, nor heal the sick like the physician, nor preach to and instruct the world like the good Evangeli-cal doctor and the pedagogue; he doth not import goods and things necessary for the commonwealth, like the

---

* An irreverent quotation from the ritual of the Church.
† This was the name of a huge cask at Bologna.

merchant. That is the reason why by all men they are hooted at and abhorred.'

" 'True,' said Grandgousier, 'but they pray to God for us.'

" 'Nothing less,' answered Gargantua. 'True it is that they disturb the whole neighbourhood with the jangling of their bells.'

" 'Yea, verily,' said the monk, 'a mass, a matins, and a vesper well rung are half said.'

" 'They mumble a great store of legends and psalms in no ways understood by them. They count a number of Paternosters, interlarded with long Ave Marias, without thinking of or understanding them. And that I call a mockery of God, and not prayer. But may God be their aid if they pray for us, and not through fear of losing their manchets and rich soups. All true Christians of all estates, in all places, in all times, pray to God, and the Spirit prayeth and intercedeth for them, and God receiveth them into favour. Now such is our good Friar John. Therefore every one wisheth for him in his company. He is no bigot; he is not a tatterdemalion; he is honest, merry, resolute, and a good companion; he works, he labours, he defends the oppressed, he comforts the afflicted, he succours the distressed; he guards the abbey-close.' "

It will be seen from the above citation that Rabelais's chief objection to monks and friars, like Colbert's in the next century, is their idleness. In his eyes they are an idle race, of no use to the commonwealth. He has the same objection to pilgrimages—that they take men away from their work.

" Go your ways, poor men," says Grandgousier to the pilgrims, "go your ways, in the name of God the Creator, and may He be your perpetual guide. And henceforth do not lend yourselves to these idle and unprofitable journeys. Maintain your families, labour every one of you in his vocation, instruct your children, and live as the good apostle St. Paul directeth you."

These pilgrims, it should be mentioned, had met with a strange misadventure. In fear of the soldiers they had hidden in a garden among the cabbages and lettuce, whence they had been gathered by Gargantua along with the lettuce to make a salad. Then the giant had inadvertently put them in his mouth, and it was only owing to the fact that one of the pilgrims had prodded a hollow tooth with his staff that Gargantua became aware of their presence, and so called for his toothpick and dislodged them. This incident is told by Rabelais in his most comic vein, and is a good example of how things grave and gay are blended in his narrative.

Gargantua showed remarkable moderation in the use of his victory. After making a long harangue to the vanquished, in which he cited instances of clemency on the part of conquerors, and especially the case of his own father, he declared his terms. He promised that with a few exceptions they should all be sent to their homes in safety, receiving three months' pay. The exceptions were the cake-bakers and Picrochole's evil counsellors, who were to be delivered up to him for punishment. But the only punishment he inflicted on them was to make them work at the printing-press which he had just set up. Then Grandgousier, after "the most magnificent, the most abundant, and the most delicious feast that had ever been seen since the time of King Ahasuerus", distributed presents of money and silver plate among Gargantua's captains, and crowned his beneficence by giving to each in perpetuity one of his castles with its adjoining lands. It is interesting and important to note that the majority of the places mentioned belonged at one time to Rabelais's family. La Devinière, however, Grandgousier kept for himself; it was his home—and almost certainly Rabelais's.

The realistic basis of this part of Rabelais's narrative has been made even more apparent by recent investigations on the part of M. Lefranc. Following up a statement of M. Clouzot's, he discovered in the departmental archives at Orléans the documents relating to a legal dispute between Gaucher de Sainte-Marthe, on the one hand, and the merchants of the Loire and its tributaries, especially the Vienne, on the other, with regard to certain rights of navigation. The complaint of the merchants was that Sainte-Marthe, who had a property at Chapeau on the Loire as well as one at Lerné, had, by the erection of a mill, piles, dams, and other obstacles, and especially by the undue development of his own fisheries, greatly impeded the navigation. The proprietors on the banks of the Loire above Sainte-Marthe were naturally affected as well as the merchants, and among these proprietors was Antoine Rabelais, the father of François, who had inherited from his mother the estate of Chavigny, in the parish of Varennes, about six miles above Chapeau. The case had come before the local courts as far back as 1522, and by 1529—such were the delays of the law—had been transferred to the Parliament of Paris. Then it slumbered for a season, until the early days of September, 1532, when the merchants returned to the charge with renewed energy. This was just the time when Rabelais paid his visit to his native country and finished the writing of *Pantagruel*. M. Lefranc has further discovered that the château of Bois-de-Vedé, which Gargantua demolished (chapter xxxvi), belonged to Sainte-Marthe, and that one Jean Gallet, king's advocate at Chinon and a near relation of Rabelais, was sent to Paris to represent the merchants, just as his namesake, Ulrich Gallet, was sent as Grandgousier's ambassador to King Picrochole.

GARGANTUA

After Grandgousier had duly rewarded his followers, there remained Friar John to provide for. Gargantua wished to make him abbot of Seuilly, but he refused this, as well as other abbeys that were offered to him. He would have, he said, no charge or government of monks, "but if you think that I have done you acceptable service, give me leave to found an abbey after my own device". Thereupon Gargantua offered him all his country of Thelema along the river Loire, and Friar John proceeded to unfold his scheme for the ordering of the future abbey. It was to be a complete negation of the monastic system. Because all abbeys were strongly walled, it was to be built without walls; because all monasteries were regulated by fixed hours, it was to have no clocks; because men were not admitted to convents of women, there were to be no men in his abbey without women, and no women without men; because they placed in religious houses no women save those who were ugly or ill-made or senseless, and no men save those who were sickly or silly, no women should be admitted to his abbey that were not fair and of a good disposition, and no men that were not handsome and well-conditioned; because monks and nuns after their year of probation had to remain monks and nuns all their lives, the brothers and sisters of Thelema were to be at liberty to depart when they pleased; because members of the religious orders took a three-fold vow of chastity, poverty, and obedience, at Thelema every one might marry, every one might be rich, every one might live as he pleased. There was one feature in the constitution of Friar John's abbey which was not entirely new, and that was the one which seems the most novel: namely, the inclusion of men and women in the same community. The great abbey of Fontevrault in the neighbourhood of Rabelais's home had been founded for both monks and nuns, under the rule of an abbess, and this arrangement was maintained in Rabelais's day.

Then follows the description of the abbey, which is of considerable interest as showing at once the style of architecture prevalent in France at the time when Rabelais wrote and his own ideas on the subject. It should be noted, in the first place, that in the edition of *Gargantua* published in 1535 he speaks of his abbey as "a hundred times more magnificent than Bonnivet", and that in the edition of 1537 he adds "Chambord, or Chantilly". Bonnivet was a château near Châtellerault in Poitou, built by Admiral Bonnivet from 1513 to 1525 (the year in which he was killed at Pavia), and must doubtless have been seen by Rabelais during his residence in Poitou. The royal palace of Chambord was begun in 1526,* but was not in a habitable state till about 1535, and the same may be said of the Constable de Montmorency's château of Chantilly. But Rabelais may well have seen Chambord in its unfinished state before 1533, in which year, as we have seen, *Gargantua* was probably written; and at Chantilly there was an older building of the fifteenth century (destroyed at the Revolution), to which Rabelais's imaginary abbey bears certain resemblances.

Thelema was a hexagonal building with a great round tower at each angle. As Charles Lenormant points out in his little treatise on *Rabelais and the Architecture of the Renaissance* (*Rabelais et l'Architecture de la Renaissance*), it was just at this time that great round towers were beginning to disappear from French architecture. They existed at Bonnivet and at the older château of Chantilly, and especially at Chambord, where the outer towers are the same in number (six) and the same in diameter (sixty feet) as at Thelema. Another feature which recalls Chambord is "the mar-

---

* Most commentators of Rabelais give the date wrongly as 1536.

vellous winding staircase, the entry to which was outside the building in an arch six fathoms broad. It was built with such symmetry and breadth that six men-at-arms with lance in rest could ride abreast right to the top of the whole building." It is in similar terms that the Venetian ambassador Lippomano, writing in 1577, speaks of the great spiral staircase at Chambord. Yet another feature in which Thelema recalls Chambord—and in this it adopts the architectural style of the future rather than of the past—is its extreme regularity. The six sides of the hexagon are all of the same length. Two of these, those facing the east and the northeast, are occupied by the women's apartments, two more, those facing the west and the southwest, by the men's apartments, while the remaining two are devoted to the libraries and the picture-galleries respectively.

The libraries contained books in Greek, Latin, Hebrew, French, Italian, and Spanish, these being regarded in Rabelais's day as the six literary languages of Europe. Arabic had fallen out of favour; English and German were as yet of little account. The picture-galleries were painted with "ancient feats of arms, histories, and descriptions of the earth". These last, no doubt, as Lenormant suggests, were maps, for the maps of the sixteenth century were extremely decorative. To quote Lenormant: "They glitter with gold and purple and blue; whales and dolphins gambol in the ocean, which vessels of Columbus and Vasco da Gama plough; the Arab has planted his tent on the site of the desert; the American savage and the African nomad are drawn each in his place after the most authentic accounts." Two famous specimens of such maps, well known by reproductions, are the map of the world made by Diego Ribeiro in 1529 and the so-called "Map of Henri II.", which really belongs to the year 1546, and is probably the work of the celebrated Dieppe cosmographer, Pierre Desceliers.

Another noticeable feature of the abbey of Thelema is its height. It has no less than five stories, besides the underground cellars. This again is a survival of the old fortress style of architecture. So also is the vaulting of the first or ground-floor story in the form of the handle of a basket. But there are signs of the increasing regard for comfort in the roof of "fine slate with a backing of lead", and in "the gutters which came out of the walls between the casements, painted in diagonal shape in gold and azure down to the ground, where they ended in great conduit-pipes".

In the fifty-fifth chapter we have an account
of the court, the gardens, the park, the tennis-
court, and other appurtenances, and it should be
noticed that some of the descriptions here,
especially that of the fountain surmounted by
figures of the three Graces, are evidently, as
Mr. W. F. Smith has pointed out, borrowed
from the famous *Hypnerotomachia Poliphili*
of the Dominican monk, Francesco Colonna, a
book which was well known to Rabelais, and
which he mentions in the ninth chapter of
Gargantua under the title of the *Dream of
Loves* (*Songe d'Amours*) of Polyphilus.

Then follows an account of how the brethren
and sisters were dressed, and M. Quicherat,
the author of the *History of Costume in France*
(*Histoire du Costume en France*), has declared
that the chapter is a complete and exact account of French costume about the year 1530.
The men wore doublets, trunk-hose, and
stockings of the same colour, with mantles
or long cloaks of cloth of gold or silver, and
caps of black velvet surmounted by a white
plume. The ladies wore tight-fitting bodices
(*vasquines*) of camlet and farthingales of
taffeta, embroidered petticoats of various materials and colours, and gowns according to
the season. In winter these gowns were of
taffeta, while in summer, on some days, they

GARGANTUA

wore instead of gowns "fair flowing robes".
Their stockings were scarlet or purple, and
their shoes were of "crimson, red, or violet
velvet, pinked like lobsters' beards". Their
head-dresses were in winter of the French fashion, in spring of the Spanish, in summer of the
Tuscan fashion.

Next we have an account of their daily life,
some touches of which may have been suggested
by the account of the palace of Alcina in the
seventh canto of Ariosto's *Orlando Furioso*.

"All their life was laid out, not by laws, statutes, or
rules, but according to their will and free pleasure. They
rose from their beds when it seemed good to them; they
drank, ate, worked, slept, when the desire came upon
them. None did awake them, none did constrain them
either to drink or to eat, or to do anything else whatsoever; for so had Gargantua established it.

"In their rule there was but this clause:

DO WHAT THOU WILT; *

because that men who are free, well-born, well-bred,
conversant in honest company, have by nature an instinct and spur which always prompteth them to virtuous actions and withdraweth them from vice; and this
they style honour. These same men, when by vile sub-
jection and constraint they are brought down and en-
slaved, do turn aside the noble affection by which they
are freely inclined unto virtue, in order to shake off this
yoke of slavery; for we do always strive after things
forbidden, and covet that which is denied unto us.

* *Fay ce que vouldras.*

FRANÇOIS RABELAIS

"By means of this liberty they entered into a laudable emulation to do all of them what they saw did please one. If any one of the men or ladies said, 'Let us drink', they all drank. If any said, 'Let us play', they all played. If one said, 'Let us go disport ourselves in the fields', they all went thither.

"So nobly were they taught that there was neither he nor she amongst them but could read, write, sing, play on musical instruments, speak five or six languages, and compose therein in verse as well as in prose.

"Never were seen knights so worthy, so valiant, so dexterous both on foot and on horseback, more vigorous, more nimble, better at handling all kinds of weapons, than were these.

"Never were seen ladies so handsome, so dainty, less froward, better taught with their hands, with their needle, in every womanly action that is honest and gentle, than were these.

"For this reason, when the time was come that any man wished to go forth from the said abbey, either at the request of his parents or for some other cause, he carried with him one of the ladies, her who should have taken him for her faithful servant, and they were married together. And if they had formerly lived in Thelema in devotion and friendship, still more did they so continue in wedlock; insomuch that they loved one another to the end of their days as on the first day of their marriage."

The abbey of Thelema is not, like Plato's Republic or Sir Thomas More's Utopia, a philosopher's reasoned conception of an ideal society. It is rather the passing dream of a poet, of a poet who has been a monk, and who, though he is no longer confined within the monastery walls, still feels the weight of his

broken chains. We must not, therefore, crit-
icise it too closely, or treat it as if it were the
serious embodiment of Rabelais's philosophy
of life. The famous *Fay ce que vouldras* is
the expression neither of an ignoble Epicurean-
ism nor of individualism run mad. It is not
the former, because the brethren and sisters of
Thelema "have by nature an instinct and spur
which always prompteth them to virtuous
actions". It is not the latter, because they
are in such perfect harmony with one another
that the wish of one is the wish of all—that
when one says, "Let us drink", they all drink.

On one subject, however, there is complete
individualism. They have no common place of
worship, but each member has a private chapel
in his or her apartments. "Worship God as
thou wilt" is the only command of the Thele-
mite religion. It is the logical conclusion of
the principle which was at the root of Protestantism, that there should be no intermediary
between God and the human soul.

But if not only in this general conception of
religion but by more special references to
Protestant doctrine Rabelais in this part of
his work shows a considerable sympathy with
the new religious teaching, he differs funda-
mentally from the man who was shortly to
become its leader. Without insisting on a too

liberal interpretation of this delightful dream, we may be sure that the dreamer held optimistic views on the subject of human nature; that, far from accepting in the Calvinistic sense the doctrine of original sin, he was almost ready to believe, like Rousseau and his followers, in the perfectibility of man. Unlike Rousseau, however, he would not have gone to the savages of the new world to find a perfect state of society, but rather to the "well-born and well-educated" citizens of Europe, to such a company as held converse together in Castiglione's *Courtier* or in the *Heptameron* of Margaret of Navarre.

With the account of the manner of life among the Thelemites we might expect *Gargantua* to end. But there is a final chapter which treats of an enigma which was found among the foundations of the abbey, and which was read aloud to the company. "The style is of Merlin the prophet," says Friar John, and in fact, with the exception of the first two and the last ten lines, the whole enigma is to be found in the works of Merlin or Mellin de Saint-Gelais, and was doubtless either written by that poet for Rabelais or used by Rabelais with his permission, for it was not published at the time. In the form in which it appears in Saint-Gelais's works, it is evidently meant, at any rate on the surface, to be a description of a game of tennis, written in the prophetic style of an enigma. And such is Brother John's interpretation, though in Gargantua's opinion it signifies "the progress and maintenance of divine truth".

What is Rabelais's own meaning? The view that Saint-Gelais, while using terms which might be applicable to a game of tennis, is really referring to the persecution of the Protestants, and that Rabelais adopts this signification, is improbable, especially when we remember that in 1533 there had as yet been no organised or severe persecution of the Protestants in France. It is more likely, as M. Fleury suggests, that Rabelais, while taking the enigma from Saint-Gelais as a mere description of a game of tennis, adopted it in the sense attributed to it by Gargantua, and with that intention added to it the lines at the beginning and the end. The question of what he meant by "divine truth" must be reserved for inquiry in a later chapter. Finally, it is in accordance with his habitual practice that he should apparently reject this interpretation for the more material one suggested by Friar John. But for those readers who "suck the substantial marrow" of his book there is "a more abstruse doctrine".

CHAPTER VI

PANTAGRUEL

IF anything were wanting to convince us that *Pantagruel*, which eventually became the Second Book of the whole romance, was written before *Gargantua*, we might find an additional argument in its general inferiority. *Gargantua* is perhaps the most admirable of all the books. If it is less philosophical than the later ones, it shows greater freshness, more action, more genuine fun, less display of learning. In *Pantagruel*, on the other hand, Rabelais has not yet freed himself from the tone of the conventional giant-story; it is written largely in the vein of *The Great and Inestimable Chronicles*. This is especially the case with the first four chapters, which deal with the genealogy, birth, and childhood of Pantagruel.

The name Pantagruel, though not, like Gargantua, famous in popular legend, is not of Rabelais's invention. It is found before his time both as a proper name and as the name of a certain malady which affects the throat. It is in view of this latter meaning that Rabelais interprets it as "the all-thirsty one".

For Pantagruel, like his father Gargantua, is a patron of drinkers. His mother Badebec, who died at his birth, was the daughter of the King of the Amaurotes in Utopia, the first of many instances of Rabelais's acquaintance with Sir Thomas More's famous work. The best of these four chapters is the third, with its description of Gargantua's comical perplexity as to whether he shall weep for the death of his wife or laugh for the birth of his son.

The four following chapters (v to viii) are all in their way notable. The fifth, which contains the account of Pantagruel's experiences in the provincial universities of France, has already been cited almost in entirety. The next contains the encounter at the Paris gate of Orléans with the Limousin scholar, which commentators of the more careless sort have till quite recently persisted in regarding as a satire on the reforms of the Pleiad, forgetful that in the year 1532 Ronsard and Joachim du Bellay were still children. As a matter of fact, the Latinised jargon in which the scholar speaks is a caricature, and no unfair one, of the style of the *grands rhétoriqueurs*, whose reign in French literature had only just come to an end. The opening of the scholar's first speech is identical almost word for word with a passage which Geoffroy Tory, in his *Champ fleury* (1529), gives as a specimen of the style of those whom he calls "skimmers of Latin" (*escumeurs de Latin*). Either Rabelais borrowed the passage from Tory, who died in the year after the publication of *Pantagruel*, or it was a stock joke among university students.

The seventh chapter contains a burlesque catalogue of the library of the abbey of St. Victor at Paris, founded in the twelfth century, and celebrated in Rabelais's day for the antiquated character of its books. According to Scaliger, there was nothing of any worth in the library. Rabelais's catalogue is of his own invention; some of the titles are in Latin, some in French, some are parodies on the titles of real books, some contain a satire on existing persons. The most interesting, perhaps, is the last, *Merlinus Coccaius de Patria Diabolorum*. It demands a word of explanation.

Girolamo Folengo, whose name in religion was Teofilo and in literature Merlin Coccaye, belonged to a noble family of Mantua. The date of his birth is variously given as 1492 and 1496; he was therefore about the same age as Rabelais. After studying at Bologna he entered a Benedictine convent at Brescia, and it was there that he wrote seventeen cantos, or, as he called them, *Macaronica*, of his princi-

pal work, entitled *Macaronea*, and written in
what is known as macaronic verse—that is to
say, Latin interspersed with vernacular words
formed like Latin. In 1515 he fled from his
convent, and two years later published his poem.
There was a second edition in 1520, and a third
edition, with eight additional *Macaronica*, in
1521. He afterwards returned to monastic
life, and died in a convent of his order, near
Padua, in 1544. Thus his monastic career
somewhat resembled Rabelais's, and his principal work is, like Rabelais's, though to a far
greater extent, a burlesque of the romances of
chivalry. In the last two cantos there is a description of the infernal regions, and it is to
this that Rabelais refers in "*de Patria Diabolorum*".

After seven chapters of burlesque and satire
Rabelais suddenly becomes serious, and gives
us a letter from Gargantua to his son, in which
the former no longer appears as a foolish giant,
but as an enlightened monarch. The letter
may be regarded as a first sketch of the two
famous chapters on education, in *Gargantua*.
But it also supplements them, for in one point,
at any rate, namely, the subjects which the
pupil is to study, it goes more into detail.

"It is my intention and desire that thou learn the languages perfectly; first the Greek, as Quintilian will have

it, secondly the Latin, and then the Hebrew, for the sake of the Holy Scriptures, and the Chaldaic and Arabic likewise; and that thou form thy style, as to the Greek, in imitation of Plato, and as to the Latin, of Cicero. Let there be no history which thou hast not ready in thy memory, whereunto shall aid thee the cosmography of those that have written thereon. Of the liberal arts of geometry, arithmetic, and music I gave thee some taste when thou wert yet little, at the age of five or six years. Proceed to learn what remains, and of astronomy learn all the rules. But leave, I pray you, divining astrology and the art of Lullius.* Of civil law I would have thee know by heart the admirable texts, and compare them with philosophy.

"And as to the knowledge of the works of nature, I would have thee devote thyself to its exact study, so that there be no sea, river, or fountain of which thou dost not know the fishes; all the fowls of the air, all the trees, shrubs, and evergreens of the forest, all the herbs of the earth, all the metals hidden in the womb of the abysses, the precious stones throughout the East and the South— let nothing be unknown to thee.

"Then carefully go over again the books of the Greek, Arabian, and Latin physicians, not despising the Talmudists and Cabalists; and by frequent dissections acquire perfect knowledge of the other world, the microcosm, which is man. And at some hours begin to attend to the Holy Scriptures, first in Greek, the New Testament and the Letters of the Apostles, and then the Old Testament, in Hebrew. In brief, let me see thee an abyss of knowledge."

It will be seen that the course of study thus sketched out is not less comprehensive than the scheme which was put into practice in

* Raymond Lully, a writer of the thirteenth century.

Gargantua. And it is worth noting that Gargantua prescribes it to his son as a preparation, not for the life of a student, but for the active life of a great prince. "Hereafter," he says, "when thou becomest a man, thou must needs come forth from this tranquillity and repose of study; thou must learn chivalry and warfare, to defend my house and succour our friends in all their needs against the assaults of evil-doers."

Another interesting feature in the letter is the contrast which Gargantua draws between the condition of learning in his youth and in his old age. He says to his son:

"I had no supply of such teachers as thou hast had. The time was still dark, and savouring of the misery and calamity wrought by the Goths, who had entirely destroyed all good literature. But by Divine goodness its own light and dignity has been in my lifetime restored to letters, and I see such amendment therein that at present I should hardly be admitted into the first class of the little grammar-boys, although in my youthful days I was reputed, not without reason, as the most learned of that age. . . .

"But now all methods of teaching are restored, the study of the languages renewed—Greek, without which it is a disgrace for a man to style himself a scholar, Hebrew, Chaldean, Latin; impressions of books most elegant and correct are in use through printing, which has been invented in my time by divine inspiration, as on the other side artillery has been invented by devilish suggestion.

FRANÇOIS RABELAIS

"All the world is full of knowing folk, of most learned preceptors, of most extensive libraries, so that I am of opinion that neither in the time of Plato nor Cicero nor Papinian was there ever such conveniency for study as is seen at this time. Nor must any hereafter adventure himself in public, or in any company, who shall not have been well polished in the workshop of Minerva. I do see robbers, hangmen, freebooters, grooms, of the present age, more learned than the doctors and preachers of my time.

"What shall I say? Women and young girls have aspired to this praise and celestial manna of good learning. So much is this the case that at my present age I have been constrained to learn the Greek tongue, which I had not contemned, like Cato, but which I had not had leisure to learn in my youth; and I do willingly delight myself in reading the Morals of Plutarch, the fine Dialogues of Plato, the Monuments of Pausanias, and the Antiquities of Athenæus, whilst I wait for the hour when it shall please God my Creator to call me and command me to depart from this earth."

This is a faithful picture of the change which had come over the condition of learning in France during Rabelais's own lifetime. Only two or three years before Rabelais wrote the above words, François I. had established the royal professorships, and had laid the foundation of his collection of Greek manuscripts; the printing of Greek books had made a definite start in Paris; Budé had published his great work, the *Commentarii Linguæ Græcæ;* and at Lyons a new college, that of the Trinity, had been founded, which was to have a consider-

PANTAGRUEL

able influence on the development of humanistic studies. Thus Gargantua's letter is an
important document for the history of humanism in France. So might Budé in his old age
have written to Adrien Turnèbe, the future
Greek professor, when the latter was pur-
suing his studies at Paris.

There is still another feature to be noticed
in Gargantua's letter, and that is its profoundly
religious tone. These are the concluding sentences:

"But because (according to the wise Solomon) wisdom
entereth not into a malicious soul, and science without
conscience is but the ruin of the soul, it behoveth thee
to serve, love, and fear God, and in Him to put all thy
thoughts and all thy hope, and to cleave to Him by
faith formed of charity, so that thou mayest never be
separated from Him by sin.

"Hold in suspicion the deceits of the world. Set not
thy heart on vanity; for this life passeth away, but the
Word of the Lord endureth for ever. Be serviceable to
all thy neighbours and love them as thyself. Revere thy
preceptors. Flee from the company of those whom thou
wouldest not resemble, and receive not in vain the graces
which God hath given thee.

"And when thou shalt perceive that thou hast attained
unto all the knowledge that is acquired in those parts,
return unto me, that I may see thee and give thee my
blessing before I die.

"My son, the peace and grace of our Lord be with thee.
Amen."

Soon after the receipt of this letter, Pantagruel, acting upon a suggestion of his father's,

169

"put up in all the cross-ways of the city con-
clusions [theses] to the number of 9764 in
all manner of knowledge, touching in them
on the most debated points in all sciences".
In this he was following the example of the
famous Pico della Mirandola, who in the winter of 1486–1487 offered to maintain at Rome
nine hundred theses about every subject of
knowledge (*de omni scibili*). Accordingly, in
the famous Rue du Fouarre, or Feurre, the
Street of Straw, which is immortalised in
Dante's poem, Pantagruel "held dispute against
all the regents, students in arts, and orators,
and routed them all. Afterwards, in the Sorbonne, he disputed against all the theologians
for the space of six weeks, from four o'clock
in the morning till six in the evening, except
two hours' interval to take his repast and to
refresh himself." This is hardly an exaggeration of what habitually took place in the Paris
schools, as may be seen from the following account written by the Spaniard Vives, who
studied there from 1509 to 1512:

"A boy is set down to dispute the first day he goes to
school, and bidden to wrangle before he can speak. It
is the same in grammar, in poetry, in history, in dialectics,
in rhetoric—in short, in every branch of study. Nor is it
enough to dispute once or twice a day. They dispute till
dinner, after dinner, till supper, after supper. . . .
They dispute at home, abroad, at the dinner table, in the

bath, at church, in the town, in the country, in public, in private, in all places and at all hours."

A similar account is given by the well-known Pierre Ramus, who, when Rabelais was writing, was a student at the same university:

"If I had to defend a thesis or a category, I thought it was my duty not to yield to an opponent, however right he might be, but by searching for some subtlety to embroil the whole discussion. . . . The categories were like a ball given to us to play with, which, if we lost, we had to recover by shouting, and if we held, we had to resist its being taken from us, however much we were shouted at. I was persuaded that the whole sum of logic consisted in disputing as bravely and as loudly as possible."

Pantagruel acquired such fame by his success as a disputant that he was invited to decide a legal case which had baffled equally the Parliament of Paris and a special assembly composed of the four most learned Parliaments of France, the great Council, and all the principal regents of the universities of France, England, and Italy. For forty-six weeks this assembly had been considering the case without being able "to get their teeth into it". At last, by the advice of one of them, named Du Douhet (Rabelais's friend Briand de Vallée), they sent for Pantagruel and begged him to sift the case thoroughly, and "delivered into his hands the sacks and documents, which nearly made up the load of four great jack-asses". Pantagruel, after inveighing against Accursius, Baldus, Bartolus, and the other mediæval glossators, "those old mastiffs who never understood the least law of the *Pandects*, and were no more than great tithe-calves, ignorant of everything that is necessary for the understanding of the laws", had all the papers burnt, and proceeded to hear the plaintiff and defendant in person. The speeches which follow, with their mixture of obscurity and irrelevance, are a satire on the legal procedure of Rabelais's day. Pantagruel's judgment is equally unintelligible, but "the councillors and other doctors who were present remained entranced in ecstasy for three good hours, all ravished with admiration at his more than human wisdom".

Meanwhile Pantagruel had made the acquaintance of a very remarkable person. One day, as he was taking a walk without the city, he met "a man of a handsome figure and elegant in all the lineaments of his body, but pitiably wounded in divers places, and in such disarray that he seemed to have escaped from the dogs". On being asked his name, he answered in German, and then in twelve other foreign languages, including three which are

perfectly unintelligible. The known languages
are Italian, English (or, rather, Scots), Basque,
Dutch, Spanish, old Danish, Hebrew, Greek,
and Latin. Of these the Basque first appeared
in the edition of 1542, and the English in that
of 1533, the text of the latter becoming more
and more corrupt in later editions. There
are only two lines of Hebrew, and these are
far from correct. Of the three speeches which
are evidently intended to be gibberish, one is
interesting as containing the names of four
properties belonging to Rabelais's family,
Gravot, Chavigny, La Pomardière, and La
Devinière. Panurge, for so the illustrious
stranger is named, says that it is *Lanternois*,
or the language of Lantern-land, just as Pantagruel says of another of Panurge's answers,
in which some of the older commentators
have tried to detect a French provincial
dialect, that it is the language of his country
of Utopia.

At last the stranger condescends to explain
in good French—we need not trouble ourselves
with the inconsistency that Pantagruel and
his tutor Epistemon must have understood
perfectly well several of the languages in which
the stranger had already spoken—that his
name is Panurge, that he comes from Turkey,
where he was taken prisoner after the defeat

of the French at Mitylene, and that he has
"a very urgent necessity to eat".

Later on we have a description of his personal appearance and his character:

"Panurge was of middle stature, neither too tall nor
too short, and had somewhat of an aquiline nose, made
like the handle of a razor; and at that time was five-and-
thirty years of age or thereabouts, smart enough for
gilding, like a leaden dagger, a fine fellow in his person,
except that he was a bit rakish and by nature subject to a
malady which was called at that time

'The lack of money, pain unparallelled'.

However, he had sixty-three ways to find some at his
need, the most honourable and common of which was by
means of larceny stealthily perpetrated; he was mischievous, a sharper, a tippler, a roisterer, a dissolute
footpad, if there was one in Paris,

'And for the rest, the best lad in the world'.

And he was always contriving some trick against the
sergeants and the watch."

In the Third Book we learn that his beard
was turning gray, and Brother John compares
it, with its mixture of gray, white, tan, and
black, to a map of the world.

The description of Panurge's appearance and
character is followed by an account of various tricks which he played on the peaceful
citizens of Paris. The most amusing of these
is the visit which he made in company with

Rabelais (who here introduces himself into his
narrative, as he seldom does except in the
Fifth Book) to various churches, for the purpose of buying indulgences. But whenever
Panurge put in a denier, he took out four or
five dozen, so that at the end he produced, to
his friend's horror, ten or twelve purses full
of money. But "if he had sixty-three ways
of finding money, he also had two hundred
and fourteen ways of spending it".

The next episode is the dispute by signs
between Panurge and a learned Englishman,
named Thaumast, who had been attracted to
Paris by the fame of Pantagruel's learning, and
who now wished to "dispute" with him, not
after the usual method, by declamation, but
by signs only, without speaking. Pantagruel
agreed, but Panurge eventually took his place
and thoroughly discomfited the Englishman,
who at last confessed himself beaten. He was
amazed at so much learning. "What would
the master have done, seeing that the disciple
hath shown such prowess!" Then Pantagruel
took Thaumast with him to dinner, and "believe it that they drank with unbuttoned
stomachs". Some of the commentators suggest that Thaumast stands for Sir Thomas
More, who had just resigned the chancellor-
ship. His reputation in France at this time

exceeded that of any other Englishman, and indeed he retained this preëminence almost throughout the sixteenth century.

Soon after this Pantagruel received news that his father Gargantua had been "translated" to the Land of the Fairies, and that the Dipsodes, or Thirsty People, had taken advantage of this to ravage part of his kingdom of Utopia, and were besieging Amaurot, the capital. On hearing this, Pantagruel, accompanied by Panurge, Epistemon, Eusthenes, and Carpalim, set sail for Utopia, and after a successful voyage engaged in battle with the Dipsodes, who were assisted by three hundred giants. The account of the fighting is given with Rabelais's usual verve and gusto, but in the burlesque and exaggerated form of a giant-story, very different from the more or less serious narrative of the war between Gargantua and Picrochole.

In the midst of all this buffoonery we suddenly come upon the admirable prayer in which Pantagruel, before entering on the battle with the giants, recommends himself to the protection of God. Another noteworthy feature is the account of Epistemon's visit to the other world. Having had his head cut off in the battle, he is skilfully healed by Panurge, but he regrets that he has been brought back to life so quickly, for he was taking a singular

PANTAGRUEL

pleasure in seeing the dead. "They are not treated," he says, "so badly as you would think, but their condition of life is changed in a strange manner. For instance, I saw Alexander the Great mending old breeches, and so earning his miserable living." Then follows a long list of distinguished persons, famous Greeks and Romans, popes, Homeric and Virgilian heroes, and heroes of the romances of chivalry, with the addition of their profession or occupation in the other world. Xerxes was a crier of mustard, Cyrus a cowherd, and Nero a fiddler; Julius II. was a tart-seller, and Alexander VI. a rat-catcher; the four sons of Aymon were dentists; Cleopatra sold onions, and Dido mushrooms. "In this fashion those who had been great lords in this world gained their poor, wretched, scurvy livelihood there below. On the other hand, the philosophers and those who had been poor in this world were, on the other side, great lords in their turn." Thus Diogenes strutted in a purple robe, and beat Alexander the Great when he had not mended his breeches properly. Epictetus, surrounded by a gay company, drank and danced and made good cheer; and when Cyrus begged a penny of him to buy onions for his supper, he threw him a crown, but "the other rascals of kings who are down there, such as Alexander, Darius, and others, robbed him in the night". Then there was Patelin, now treasurer to Rhadamanthus, who took Pope Julius's tarts without paying for them, and Jean Le Maire des Belges, who played at being pope, and made all the kings and popes of this world kiss his feet; and there was François Villon, who asked Xerxes the price of his mustard, and brutally insulted him, and the Franc-archer of Baignolet,* who was an inquisitor of heretics, and would have had Perceforest† burnt alive had it not been for Morgant the giant.

The main idea of this chapter, that the lives of men in the other world are an inversion of their lives in this, is borrowed from Lucian's *Menippus* or *Nekuomanteia*, but the Greek satirist gives only a few instances, and those chiefly in general terms, as that Xerxes and Darius were beggars. The only cases that he mentions more particularly are those of Philip of Macedon, who mended old shoes, and Diogenes, who made fun of Midas, Sardanapalus, and others who, having been wealthy in

---

* The hero of a well-known fifteenth-century poem, often printed with Villon's works, but not written by him.

† The hero of a romance of chivalry which was very popular in Rabelais's day,

this world, were suffering in the other from extreme poverty.

Epistemon's narrative suggests to Panurge a fitting treatment for Anarchus, the defeated King of the Dipsodes. With the full approval of Pantagruel, he is made a crier of green sauce and married to an old hag, and Pantagruel gives the pair a little lodge, and a mortar wherein to pound their sauce.

After these two chapters of high satire we return to the giant-story vein, and presently the book concludes with a promise that the narrative shall be continued, and that we shall learn how Panurge was married, and how Pantagruel found the philosopher's stone, how he crossed the Atlantic, how he married the daughter of Prester John, and how he visited the moon.

CHAPTER VII

THE THIRD BOOK

THE Third Book was published, as we have
seen, at the beginning of 1546, that is to say,
more than eleven years after *Gargantua* and
more than thirteen after *Pantagruel*, the book
to which it forms the immediate sequel. There
was hardly less interval between its composition
and that of the earlier books, for *Gargantua*
was probably written in 1533, while the main
portion of the Third Book must have been
written, at the earliest, after Rabelais's return
from Turin at the beginning of 1543, and probably not before 1544. This being so, it is not
surprising if we find that a considerable change
has taken place in the character and treatment
of the work and even in the style.

The plans which Rabelais announced at
the conclusion of *Pantagruel*, though doubtless with no great seriousness, for the future
conduct of the story, if not altogether lost
sight of, are at any rate abandoned for a time.
Pantagruel's second voyage is postponed. Panurge becomes the principal figure though not
the hero of the story, and his marriage is its

main theme. And with this change of subject
there is a corresponding change of treatment.
The form of a popular giant-story is definitively
abandoned. Henceforth Pantagruel stands
above his fellows only by his superior wisdom
and virtue. The whole tone of the book becomes more philosophical; there is less action
and more discussion; there is less fun and more
learning, more heaping up, sometimes to the
point of tediousness, of citations from classical and other learned authorities. The actual
style, too, shows considerable differences.
Rabelais's syntax has become more Latinised,
and he makes an even bolder use of inversion
than was permissible in the older language.
We have a good instance of this in an altera-
tion which he introduced into the prologue
to the Second Book for the new edition of 1542,
and to which M. Stapfer has called attention.
In the earlier editions the passage, to which
reference has already been made, ran as follows: "*Je m'en suis venu visiter mon pays de
vache, et savoir s'il y avoit encore en vie nul de
mes parens.*" But in the 1542 edition Rabelais
altered the last part of the sentence to "*si en
vie estoit parent mien aulcun*".

Further, his command of vocabulary has
increased, and he exults in his power like a
giant at play. He indulges in a veritable de-

bauch of words, stringing together substantives or adjectives or verbs with a profusion possible only to one whose command of vocabulary is prodigious. We have a first-rate instance of this in the prologue to the Third Book, where he gives us a page of technical terms relating to the art of fortification (a reminiscence of his sojourn at Turin), and then strings together no less than sixty verbs describing Diogenes's treatment of his celebrated tub.

For the theme of this remarkable prologue is a comparison between Rabelais and Diogenes. Writing during the first seven or eight months of 1544, when Frenchmen were expecting a combined attack on Paris by the Imperial and the English forces, he compares himself to Diogenes, who, when all the citizens of Corinth were employed in making preparations for the defence of their city against the expected attack of Philip of Macedon, finding himself the only person to whom no duty was assigned, found vent for his martial ardour by rolling his tub up and down and performing various exercises with it. So Rabelais invites all honest drinkers, but not hypocrites or prying critics, to come and drink from his cask "frankly, freely, and boldly, without payment and without stint".

THE THIRD BOOK

"It has a living spring and a perpetual source. . . . 'Tis a true cornucopia of joyousness and raillery. If sometimes it seems to you to be exhausted even to the dregs, for all that it will not be drawn quite dry. Good hope lies at the bottom, as in Pandora's box; not despair, as in the cask of the Danaids."

The first five chapters are closely connected, at any rate in subject, with the Second Book, and though the style is the same as that of the main portion of the Third Book, they were, as we have seen, probably written at Saint-Maur-des-Fossés between 1538 and 1540, before Rabelais went to Turin. The first chapter describes Pantagruel's treatment of the conquered country of the Dipsodes, and serves as an occasion to controvert the "erroneous opinion of certain tyrannical minds", that is to say, Machiavelli, whose famous *Prince*, dedicated to the father of Catherine de' Medici, had been published not many years previously (1532). In the second chapter we learn how Pantagruel bestowed on Panurge the barony of Salmigondin, which produced an immense revenue, and how "the new baron managed so well and prudently that in less than a fortnight he squandered the revenue for three years . . . taking money in advance, buying dear, selling cheap, and eating his corn in blade". Pantagruel, when informed of this, "was not in any way indignant, angry, or grieved.

FRANÇOIS RABELAIS

Only he took Panurge aside, and gently pointed
out to him that if he chose to live in this way,
and not manage his household otherwise, it
would be impossible, or at least very difficult,
ever to make him rich." This calls forth a
long outburst from Panurge, half serious and
half paradoxical, in which he first defends his
conduct as based on the four cardinal virtues,
and then breaks forth into an eloquent panegyric on debtors and borrowers:

"Debts, a thing rare and honourable. . . . Think you
not that I am glad when every morning round me I see
these creditors so humble, serviceable, and profuse in rev-
erences? . . . These be my fawners, my parasites, my salu-
ters, my givers of good-morrows, my perpetual orators.

"And I verily thought that in debts consisted the hill
of heroic virtue described by Hesiod, on which I kept the
first degree of my licentiate. At this degree of excellence all
human beings seem to aim and aspire; but few climb
thither by reason of the difficulty of the way, seeing to-
day the whole world is in fervent desire and bustling appetite of contracting debts and making new creditors. Notwithstanding, it is not every one who wishes that is a
debtor; it is not every one who wishes that makes creditors. And yet you would deprive me of this sovereign
felicity. You ask me when I shall be out of debt. And
the case is far worse than that. I give myself to St.
Babolin, the good saint, if I have not all my life looked
upon debts as a connection and colligation of the heavens
and the earth, the one single mainstay of the race of man-
kind—I say, that without which all human beings would
soon perish—perhaps that it is the great Soul of the uni-
verse, which, according to the Academics, gives life to
all things."

THE THIRD BOOK

Pantagruel, however, is very far from being convinced by Panurge's eloquence, and after stating his view bids his follower drop the subject and make no more debts.

The next chapter (vi), in which they discuss the question why newly married men are exempt from active service, forms a transition to what becomes the principal theme, not only of the rest of the Third Book, but of the whole work. The next day Panurge appears with a gold ring in his ear, in which is set a black flea, and a long gown, and spectacles fastened to his cap. On Pantagruel's inquiring the meaning of this disguise, he replies that he wishes to marry, in order that for a year at least he may rest from warfare. But he is troubled by various doubts, and especially as regards three points. Will his wife be faithful to him? Will she beat him? Will she rob him? Pantagruel makes mirth of his perplexities, but finally gives him serious advice.

"Are you not assured of what is your own wish? The principal point lies there: all the rest is fortuitous, and dependent on the fateful dispositions of Heaven. We see a goodly number of people so happy in this encounter that in their marriage there seemeth to shine forth some idea and representation of the joys of Paradise. Others in it are so unlucky that the devils who tempt the hermits in the deserts of Thebais and Montserrat are not more miserable. It behoves you therefore to put the business to a venture

185

with eyes bandaged, bowing your head, kissing the earth, and recommending yourself to God for the rest, when once you wish to make trial of it. Other assurance I can give you none."

Ever since Jean de Meun, towards the close of the thirteenth century, had attacked the character of women with cynical effrontery in the second part of *The Romance of the Rose* (*Le Roman de la Rose*), the subject had been a favourite one in French literature. A little later the clerk Mathéolus repeated the attack. His original Latin work is lost, but a translation into French verse, made about 1340, was printed several times at the close of the fifteenth and the beginning of the sixteenth century. It was left to a woman, Christine de Pisan, at the beginning of the fifteenth century, to champion the cause of her sex, but she was supported by Martin Le Franc, who, between 1440 and 1442, wrote a long allegorical poem entitled *The Champion of Women* (*Le Champion des Dames*). Then the controversy slumbered for a time, till Giovanni Nevizzano, an Italian living in France, published at Paris in 1521 an elaborate attack on women, written in Latin and bearing the fanciful title of *Six Books of the Nuptial Forest* (*Sylvæ Nuptialis Libri Sex*). It was reprinted in 1526 at Lyons, and in the same year Cor-

THE THIRD BOOK

nelius Agrippa, who was then practising as a physician in that city, wrote, and probably published, his *Declamation on the Sacrament of Matrimony*. In 1526 also there appeared Erasmus's admirable treatise, *The Institution of Christian Marriage*, while in 1529 Agrippa composed for Mary of Hungary, the Regent of the Netherlands, in whose service he then was, his *Declamation on the Nobility and Superiority of the Female Sex*. In the following year (1530) Galliot Du Pré reprinted *The Champion of Women*—a sure sign of the popularity of the subject. Then came Gratien Du Pont's *Controversies of the Masculine and Feminine Sexes* (*Controverses des Sexes masculin et féminin*) (153⅘), a long poem full of violent invective against women. Rabelais's copy of it still exists.*

But the contribution to this controversy which had the greatest influence on Rabelais was a Latin work by his friend André Tiraqueau entitled *On the Laws of Marriage* (*De Legibus Connubialibus*). It was first published in 1513, and again in 1515, and when the scene opens upon Rabelais's residence at Fontenay-le-Comte, Tiraqueau was engaged in pre-

* See A. Lefranc, in the *Revue des Études rabelaisiennes*, II, 1 ff. and 78 ff.

paring a third and much enlarged edition. This appeared at the end of 1524, the year in which Rabelais left the monastery, the publisher being Galliot Du Pré. Originally a short treatise, it had now grown into a stout volume of nearly six hundred pages, consisting almost entirely of citations, each accompanied by its proper reference. M. Barat, who has written an extremely interesting study of the subject, reasonably conjectures that in this enormous labour of collecting the citations Tiraqueau was helped by his friends, including Rabelais. The latter is mentioned several times in the course of the work, and a Greek epigram from his pen, in which he compares the author to Plato, stands at the head of it.

This new edition of Tiraqueau's book had a great success, but it was not till twenty years later (February, 1546) that he brought out a fourth edition, with a large number of new citations. He was probably incited to this fresh labour by the interest which had been recently aroused by the publication of Antoine Heroet's *The Perfect Mistress* (*La Parfaicte Amye*), in 1542, in which that philosophic but prosaic poet had expounded with great clearness the Neoplatonic doctrine of spiritual love. Moreover, in the same year there had been begun a poetic controversy on the subject of love in general, the various contributions to which were published collectively in 1544 by two separate publishers, one of them being Galliot Du Pré. This controversy seems to have been in its origin quite independent of Heroet's poem, which, however, was printed with the contributions referred to. Since Rabelais had helped Tiraqueau with the third edition of his book many years had elapsed, and the impression which it had made on him must have been long since effaced. But certain passages in the Third Book to which M. Barat has called attention make it probable that Rabelais had seen the fourth edition before it was printed, and had thus renewed his former acquaintance with the work. Tiraqueau was now living at Paris, having been appointed a member of the Paris Parliament in 1541. Rabelais, who had returned from Turin early in 1543, was now a canon of the Benedictine abbey of Saint-Maur-des-Fossés, near Paris, and, as has been suggested in an earlier chapter, he may have resided there during parts of the three years 1543 to 1545. This would have given him opportunity for frequent intercourse with Tiraqueau; and even if M. Plattard is right in supposing that Tiraqueau became estranged from his old friend, we may fairly conjecture that it was owing to Tiraqueau and the new edition which he was preparing of his book that Rabelais's mind was diverted to the subject of the great controversy on the character of women.

Pantagruel himself has no belief in a power to foretell the future, or, at any rate, not sufficient faith in it to accept it as a guide to human conduct, but his well-furnished memory provides him with many classical instances of supposed intimations of impending fate. He is therefore quite willing that Panurge should try, if he pleases, every known method of forecasting the future, and it is under his advice that most of the experiments are conducted. They first have recourse to a method which has found favour in all ages, and which consists in opening some special book at random and regarding as prophetic the passage which first catches the eye. In ancient times the chosen book was Homer or Virgil, usually Virgil, so that the name for the proceeding was "Virgilian lots" (*sortes Virgilianæ*). In the Middle Ages the *Bible* was generally used, but Pantagruel and Panurge, as good humanists, consult the works of Virgil, having first determined by a throw of the dice the number of the line on the page. Pantagruel, however, is careful to point out that the use of dice in general is pernicious, and that it had been abolished throughout his father's kingdom. This is perhaps a reminiscence of More's *Utopia*, where we are told that the Utopians "do not so much as know dice or any such foolish and mischievous games".

Pantagruel next suggests divination by dreams, and accordingly Panurge is ordered to make a frugal supper of good bergamot pears, an apple, some plums, and some cherries. But he is no better satisfied with this experiment than with the former one, so he proceeds to consult in turn various persons who are popularly supposed to have the gift of second sight: a sibyl, a deaf-mute, and an old man at the point of death. Among the instances which Pantagruel cites, with his usual wealth of information, of dying men who have foretold the future, there is one of great interest, namely, that of Guillaume du Bellay, at whose death, as we have seen, Rabelais was present, and who is here said to have "employed the three or four hours before his death in vigorous words with tranquil and serene understanding, predicting to us that which in part we have seen and in part we wait for". The dying man selected on this occasion is an old poet named Raminagrobis, in whom Étienne Pasquier recognised Guillaume Cretin, a leading poet of the *rhétoriqueur* school who died before 1525. The identification is possible, but except that the poem which Raminagrobis writes. down for Panurge is found in Cretin's works, there is nothing to connect the two.

On arriving at the old man's house, they find him in his last moments "with a joyous bearing and open face and a luminous look". Panurge explains the motive of his visit and asks for his advice, whereupon the "good old man" orders ink, pen, and paper to be brought him, and writes down a rondeau, which he puts in their hands, saying to them:

"Depart, my children, in the keeping of the great God of the heavens, and disquiet me no more on this business or any other whatsoever. I have this very day, which is the last of May and of me, with great labour and difficulty driven out of my house a rabble of ill-favoured, unclean, and pestilent beasts, black, piebald, dun, white, ash-coloured, speckled, which would not let me die in peace, but by fraudulent stingings, harpy-like clutchings, waspish importunities, all forged in the shop of I know not what insatiability, would fain call me forth from the sweet thought in which I was reposing, contemplating and beholding, yea, already touching and tasting the blessing and happiness which the good God hath prepared for his faithful and elect in the other life in a state of immortality. Turn aside from their courses and be not like unto them, and leave me in silence, I beseech you."

On hearing this, Panurge, who is extremely orthodox, is utterly confounded and exclaims:

"'By the powers, I believe that he is a heretic. He slanders the good mendicant fathers, the friars and Jacobins, who are the two hemispheres of Christianity. But what have those poor devils the Capuchins and Minims done to him? Are they not woebegone enough already, poor devils? Are not they sufficiently pervaded and permeated with misery and calamity, the poor wights, extracts of ichthyophagy [*i.e.*, a fish diet]? By thy faith, Friar John, is he in a state of salvation? In good sooth, he is on his way, damned like a very serpent, to thirty thousand basketfuls of devils. To slander these good and sturdy pillars of the Church! . . . I am greatly scandalised at it.'

"'I care not a button about it,' quoth Friar John. 'They slander everybody; if everybody slanders them, I do not pretend to any interest in it.'"

On the other hand, Epistemon declares that Panurge has put a wrong interpretation on the old man's words, and that he was really referring to various sorts of insects. Of Rabelais's real meaning there can be no doubt, and Raminagrobis's speech recalls the entry in Louise of Savoy's diary: "In the year 1522 my son and I, by the grace of the Holy Ghost, began to understand the hypocrites, white, black, gray, smoky, and of all colours."

As regards Raminagrobis's poem, Panurge is as little satisfied with it as with his former attempts to read the future. He therefore next turns to a professional astrologer, one Her Trippa, who is represented as living on the Ile Bouchard, an island in the Vienne a little above

Chinon. Trippa, in whom the commentators
have agreed to recognise Cornelius Agrippa,
gives even plainer answers to Panurge's questions than he has hitherto received. His wife
will be unfaithful to him, she will beat him,
and she will rob him. But Panurge is still un-
satisfied, so Pantagruel, whose patience is inex-
haustible, advises that they should invite to
dinner a theologian, a physician, a lawyer, and
a philosopher, and lay before them the subject
of their perplexity. The lawyer has a previous
engagement, but the three others accept the
invitation. After the first course Panurge puts
to them in turn two questions. Shall he marry?
Will his wife be unfaithful to him? The theologian's advice on the second point is full of
good sense and good feeling. "Your wife,"
he says, "will be faithful to you if she comes of
honest parents and is educated in virtue and
honourable conduct, loving and fearing God,
and fearing to offend Him and lose His grace by
transgression of His divine law, by which she is
commanded to cleave to her husband, to cherish
him, to serve him, and to love him with all her
heart next to God." On the other hand, Panurge, on his part, must set her a good example,
and live chastely and virtuously. "You wish
me, then," says Panurge, "to marry the strong
woman described by Solomon? She is dead,

without doubt; I never saw her, that I know of.
Many thanks, though, my father."

Panurge then turns to the physician, who is
named Rondibilis, and who is said, with a good
deal of probability, to stand for Guillaume
Rondelet, who, as we have seen, was the proctor
to whom Rabelais paid his fees when he matriculated at the University of Montpellier. "Rondibilis" means "Roly-poly", and Rondelet is
said to have been a little, pot-bellied man.
He gives Panurge a good deal of sound, practical
advice on the subject of marriage in general,
but as regards the second question he is not
reassuring. "When I say woman, I mean a sex
so fragile, so variable, so changeable, so incon-
stant and imperfect, that Nature, when she
made woman, seems to me, speaking in all
honour and reverence, to have strayed from
that good sense with which she created all
things." There are, he adds, virtuous women
who have lived chastely and blamelessly, and
their praise is very great. But when Panurge
asks him how he may keep his wife in the path
of virtue, he puts him off with an allegorical
story. This leads Ponocrates to tell the story
of Pope John XXII. and the nuns of Fontevrault, which Rabelais probably borrowed from
Du Pont's *Controversies of the Masculine and
Feminine Sexes*, though he may have taken it

from an older work which was very popular in his day, Herolt's *Sermones Discipuli*. In the later editions of the Third Book, "Coignaufond" was substituted for "Fontevrault".

It is in the advice given by the theologian and by Rondibilis that Rabelais's debt to Tiraqueau is most conspicuous. Some of the passages in the chapters relating to Rondibilis are directly borrowed from the fourth edition of his book, while the excellent remarks of the theologian are in close conformity with the general spirit of its teaching. For the book is by no means a one-sided attack on women, but a fair-minded and judicial attempt to deal with the evidence on both sides of the question, so far as this is compatible with the axiom upon which Tiraqueau's whole doctrine rests—that woman is by nature inferior to man, and that it is her part to obey and his to command. A husband, however, says Tiraqueau, may take counsel of his wife, even in matters relating to his own duties. But he must not trust her with secrets, for what she does not reveal when she is awake she reveals in her dreams. Tiraqueau himself, we learn, was exceedingly happy in his marriage, and doubtless acted up to one of his precepts—that if a husband wishes his wife to love him, he must be rigorously faithful to her. That was the advice which the theologian gave to Panurge, and which Panurge so little relished.

Rabelais's own attitude towards women has been often discussed. In spite of the part played by them in the abbey of Thelema, his views when he was writing *Gargantua* are probably more nearly expressed by his contemptuous remark with reference to the death of Grandgousier's wife, that he cared mighty little for her or for any other woman. But during the ten or twelve years which had elapsed since he expressed this sentiment his horizon had been considerably widened. From convent and university he had passed into the life of the world. Especially, he had spent a considerable time in Italy, where the fame of many learned and highly cultivated women must have reached his ears, even if he did not meet them in personal intercourse; for those were the days of Olympia Morata and Vittoria Colonna.

Thus he brought to the reperusal of Tiraqueau's book a more open mind than heretofore, and, like Tiraqueau, he tried to treat the question with judicial fairness. The result is that he seems to have emerged from the discussion which occupies so great a part of the Third Book with a distinctly greater respect for woman. In the Fourth Book she is certainly treated better, and we have a graceful female character in Niphleseth, the Queen of the Chitterlings. But she is, it must be confessed, a shadowy person, for Rabelais to the end of his life probably knew very little of women at first hand. It is this absence of experience which makes his treatment of the subject decidedly lacking in freshness and originality.

One remaining point must not be forgotten. The Third Book is dedicated to a woman—to Margaret of Navarre, whose eager sympathies and quick intellect had so marked an influence upon the whole movement of the French Renaissance; and it is dedicated to her in a form which, although Rabelais himself evidently had little sympathy with the Neoplatonic doctrine of spiritual love, gracefully recognises her interest in the subject. The dedication runs as follows:

"FRANÇOIS RABELAIS TO THE SPIRIT OF THE QUEEN OF NAVARRE

> Abstracted Spirit, rapt in ecstasy,
> Who, haunting now thy home, the firmament,
> Hast left thy servant and thy hostelry,
> Thy body, well attuned, obedient
> To thy commands, in life 'mong strangers shent,
> Without all sense, and as in apathy;
> Wilt thou not deign a little while to fly
> Thy mansion all divine, perpetual,
> And here below a third time to descry
> The jovial feats of the good Pantagruel?" *

* W. F. Smith's translation.

After this digression we may return to Rabelais's narrative, which we left at the close of Panurge's discussion with Rondibilis.

"Without a word he put into his hand four rose nobles. Rondibilis took them very well, and then said to him in dismay, as if he were indignant, 'Oh, sir! nothing was needed. Many thanks, all the same. From bad people I never take anything; from good people I never refuse anything. I am always at your command.' 'For a fee,' said Panurge. 'That is understood,' said Rondibilis."

Rabelais may have borrowed from Merlin Coccaye this satirical reference to the fees of doctors, but it is found elsewhere and has become almost a literary commonplace. Molière has utilised it with great effect in *The Doctor in Spite of Himself* (*Le Médecin malgré lui*).

It is next the turn of Trouillogan, the philosopher. But just after Panurge has put the first question to him, Pantagruel sees near the door of the banqueting-hall his father's little dog, "which he called Kyne, because that was the name of Tobit's dog". (As a matter of fact, the *Apocrypha* is silent on this important point.) So he bids the company rise, for the King, he says, cannot be far off. As he speaks, Gargantua enters, and with his usual courtesy bidding them be seated, orders a chair to be brought him, and inquires the subject of their discussion. The reader will remember that towards the

close of the Second Book we were told that
Gargantua was translated to the Land of the
Fairies, but as none of the company seem to be
in the least surprised at his appearance in their
midst, we may infer that Rabelais has forgotten,
or chosen to forget, this incident. Inconsis-
tencies of this kind trouble him little.

The discussion is then resumed. Trouillogan
in his character of Sceptic gives nothing but
ambiguous answers to Panurge's questions,
till that worthy is driven to desperation.

"P. Will my wife be honest and chaste?
T. I doubt it.
P. Have you ever seen her?
T. Not that I know of.
P. Why then do you doubt of a thing which you do
not know?
T. For a reason.
P. But if you knew her?
T. Even more.
P. Page, my little friend, here is my cap; I make you
a present of it, except the spectacles. Go into the court
and swear for me for a little half-hour. I will do the same
for you when you want it."

It will be remembered that Molière has admirably imitated this in a famous scene of *The
Marriage by Compulsion* (*Le Mariage forcé*).

There remains Mr. Justice Bridlegoose (Bri-
doye), who has been unable to accept Pantagruel's invitation because he has been summoned before the Parliament of Myrelingues to

state his reasons for a certain judgment which he has given. Pantagruel, therefore, who has an affection for Bridlegoose, determines to go with his followers to Myrelingues to hear the case, which seems to portend some disaster. For Bridlegoose has sat as a judge for more than forty years, and during all that time not one of his decisions has been reversed. On arriving at Myrelingues they find him seated on the bench with the judges of the high court. His only excuse is that he has grown old, and that his sight is not so good as it used to be. He cannot, therefore, distinguish the pips of the dice as clearly as he has done in the past; in the case in question he may have taken a four for a five. "But what dice," asks Trinquamelle, the president of the court, "do you mean, my friend?" "The dice of judgment," answers Bridlegoose. Then, with many references to the *Digest*, he explains how he first duly reads and rereads all the pleadings in the case.

" 'But,' asked Trinquamelle, 'how do you clear up the obscurity of the claims put forward by the parties?' 'As your worships do (*comme vous autres messieurs*),' answered Bridlegoose; 'that is to say, when there are many bags full of pleadings, I use my little dice; but I also have large dice, which I use when the case is clearer, that is to say, when there are fewer bags.' 'And then,' asked Trinquamelle, 'how do you pronounce judgment, my friend?' 'Like your worships,' answered Bridlegoose, 'I pronounce judgment for the suitor to whom the fall of the dice is favourable.' 'But, my friend,' asked Trinquamelle, 'since you pronounce judgment according to the throw of the dice, why do you not do it at once without any delay? To what uses do all the pleadings that are contained in the bags serve you?' 'The same as to your worships,' answered Bridlegoose; 'they serve me in three excellent things: first, for the sake of formality; secondly, as honest and salutary exercise; thirdly, as do also your worships, I consider that time ripens everything. With time everything comes to light. Time is the father of truth. That is why, as do also your worships, I adjourn, delay, and defer the decision in order that the case, well ventilated, sifted, and threshed out, may by the process of time come to its maturity, and that the lot ensuing thereupon may be borne more lightly by the parties condemned.' "

At last Bridlegoose concludes by telling an appropriate story of one Perrin Dandin, a labourer in the neighbourhood of Poitiers, who used to decide disputes for all the country round, and another of a Gascon in the camp of Stockholm.

Pantagruel has only one suggestion left to make to Panurge: as he is not satisfied with the advice of wise men, let him try that of a fool. Accordingly they send for Triboulet, the famous fool of François I., the hero of Victor Hugo's play, *The King Enjoys Himself* (*Le Roi s'amuse*). As usual, Pantagruel interprets his answer as unfavourable, while

Panurge interprets it as favourable. For Panurge's object throughout the inquiry has been not merely to be assured as to his destiny, but to compel destiny to be favourable to him. He wants to lead a life of sin and self-indulgence, and then escape the penalty. Nothing less will content him. Now, he had given Triboulet a bottle of wine, and Triboulet, having drained it, had given it back to him. What does that signify? "It means," says Pantagruel, "that your wife will be a drunkard." "No," says Panurge, "for it was empty. It means that I am to consult the oracle of the Bottle." Pantagruel with his usual good nature at once gives his consent, subject to his royal father's permission. Gargantua is pleased with the project, and adds that he wishes Pantagruel was similarly inclined to matrimony. This remark leads to a very strong expression of opinion from both father and son that no children should be allowed to marry without the consent of their parents. "I pray God," says Pantagruel, with unusual energy of language, "that I may rather be seen dead at your feet to your displeasure than married and alive without your pleasure."

Accordingly Pantagruel begins to prepare for the voyage, and amongst the preparations collects a large supply of the plant Pantagruelion, of which Rabelais gives the following striking description:

"From the root proceeds a single stem, which is round, cane-like, green without, whitish within, concave like the stalk of smyrnium, beans, and gentian, woody, upright, friable, denticulated a little in form of pillars slightly fluted, full of fibres, in which consists the whole value of the herb. The height of this is generally from five to six feet; sometimes it exceeds the height of a lance. . . . From its stem proceed large and strong branches. It has its leaves three times as long as they are broad, always green, rough like bugloss, hardish, and dentated all round like a sickle and like betony; ending in points like a Macedonian pike or a lancet used by surgeons. The shape of its leaves differs but little from those of the ash-tree or the agrimony. Its leaves are spread all round the stalk in rings at equal distances, to the number, in every rank, of five or of seven."

Any one who is familiar with the appearance of hemp will recognise the spirit and accuracy of this description. Rabelais further remarks that the plant is of two sexes, or, as botanists say, diœcious, but in accordance with the erroneous opinion of his day he calls the fertile plant the male and the barren one the female.

The next chapter contains a learned and interesting dissertation on the origin of the names of plants, and this is followed by an eloquent panegyric on the many virtues of Pantagruelion.

CHAPTER VIII

THE FOURTH BOOK

In his fascinating book, *The Voyages of Pan-tagruel* (*Les Navigations de Pantagruel*), M. Abel Lefranc has opened up a new field of Rabelaisian study, by pointing out how closely Rabelais was in touch with the geographical discoveries of his day, and how a ground-work of fact underlies the fantastic embroidery with which he has adorned his famous account of the voyage to the oracle of the Bottle. Indeed, with his warm enthusiasm for the progress of human knowledge, he could not have failed to watch with ever growing interest the gradual unrolling of the map of the world which took place during his lifetime. In 1492, only a year or two before the probable date of Rabelais's birth, Columbus, sailing for the East by the West, had landed on one of the Bahama Islands and practically discovered the American continent. In 1497 Vasco da Gama, completing the work which Bartolomeo Diaz had begun, had reached India by the Cape of Good Hope. In 1513 Vasco Nuñez de Balboa, climbing "a peak in Darien", had seen the Pacific Ocean stretched at his feet. In 1521 Ferdinand de Magellan had sailed through the straits which bear his name.

The results of these voyages and of others only less epoch-making were recorded in various works, of which perhaps the most popular was the well-known *Decades* of Peter Martyr of Anghiera, an Italian who had risen to high distinction in the service of Ferdinand and Isabella. It was printed at Alcalá in 1530, and reprinted at Paris in 1536. But long before this a collection of voyages had been published in Italian under the title of *Newly Discovered Countries* (*Paesi Novamente Ritrovati*) (1507), and afterwards translated into Latin (1508) and French. In 1532 a German antiquary named Johann Huttich reprinted these, with others, under the title of *The New World* (*Novus Orbis*), with a preface by Simon Grynæus and an introduction by the well-known Hebrew scholar and mathematician, Sebastian Münster. The work was published at Basel, and a Paris edition, with a map of the world by Oronce Finé, the Regius professor of mathematics, appeared in October of the same year. But it must have been the original Basel edition that Rabelais used for his brief account of the voyage of Pantagruel to Utopia, which appears in the Second Book, and runs as follows:

THE FOURTH BOOK

"In a few days, passing by Porto Santo and Madeira, they put ashore on the Canary Islands. Setting out from there, they passed by Capo Bianco, by Senegal, by Capo Verde, by Gambia, by Sagres, by Melli, by the Cape of Good Hope, and disembarked in the kingdom of Melinda."

Every name in the above passage is taken from Sebastian Münster's introduction, but for the rest of the voyage we have names which on the face of them—Meden, Uti, Uden, Gelasim, the Islands of the Fairies, and the kingdom of Achoria—denote, like Utopia, their existence only in the world of fancy. M. Lefranc, however, has ingeniously suggested that Meden and Uden (Greek words meaning "nothing") represent Medina and Aden, a suggestion which is borne out by the mention of these places in Münster's introduction. He further suggests that Gelasim stands for Ceylon; it is, in fact, an imperfect anagram of Seyla, the form which the name takes on Finé's map.

At the end of the Second Book, it will be remembered, Rabelais announced that in the continuation of the story we should hear how Pantagruel "sailed over the Atlantic Ocean, and defeated the Cannibals, and conquered the Islands of Pearls; and how he married the daughter of the King of India, called Prester John". Here again Rabelais is following *The New World*. The "Cannibal Islands" was the corrupt form under which the Carribal or Caribbean Islands were known in Rabelais's day, and by the "Islands of Pearls" are meant the islands off Venezuela from which Pedro Alonzo Niño "returned laden with pearls" With regard to the kingdom of Prester John, it will be noticed that Rabelais places it in Central Asia, and not, with the majority of his contemporaries, in Abyssinia.

Between the composition of the Second Book and that of the Third events had happened which must have aroused in Rabelais a still greater interest in maritime discovery. Hitherto, France, like England, had played a subordinate part in the work of geographical discovery. Not that her people lacked the spirit of adventure. From the early years of the sixteenth century Norman, Breton, and Basque sailors had sent out expeditions from the ports of Dieppe, Saint-Malo, and Bayonne, and French fishermen had fished for cod on the shores of Newfoundland and Labrador. From 1520 to 1540 the enterprising Dieppe ship-owner Ango had despatched his pilots by different routes to the Spice Islands. In 1529 the sailor-poet Jean Parmentier and his brother Raoul had sailed from Dieppe to Sumatra, where they died of fever in the following year. These were all private expeditions, but in 1523–

THE FOURTH BOOK

1524 Giovanni da Verazzano, a Florentine in the service of François I., had been sent by the King ostensibly to find a passage by the West to Cathay, and having explored the whole coast from North Carolina to Newfoundland, he had given it the name of New France. It was the claim of the French King to a share in the spoils of the New World.

It was not, however, till 1534 that a Frenchman made an important addition to geographical knowledge. In the spring of that year a Breton pilot, Jacques Cartier, sailed through the Strait of Belle Isle and reached the entrance to the Gulf of St. Lawrence. Starting again in May of the following year, he touched the coast of Labrador, navigated the St. Lawrence as far as Montreal, visited Prince Edward Island, and sailing between Cape Breton Island and Newfoundland proved the insular character of the latter. He made his third voyage in 1541, as captain-general and master-pilot to Jean François de la Roque, Seigneur de Roberval, upon whom François I. had conferred the title of Viceroy of Canada. Roberval not being ready, he sailed without him, and met him only on his return in the late autumn of 1542. Then in the following year he was sent to fetch Roberval back, returning probably in 1544. His own records have been lost, but a narra-

tive of the second voyage, by an anonymous
writer, was published in 1545.* No account of
the first voyage appeared in print till 1598,
while the third voyage and the whole expedition of Roberval are known to us only from
some fragmentary accounts published in English by Hakluyt.† These voyages, however
imperfectly recorded in print, had a considerable influence upon the maps of the period, and
between 1540 and 1550 various maps were produced by Dieppe cosmographers in which the
discoveries of Cartier were utilised. In these
maps, however, Newfoundland is represented,
not as a single island, but as an archipelago of
numerous small islands.

It was under the influence of Cartier's discoveries that Rabelais began his Fourth Book,
writing, as we have seen, the first chapter and
the episode of Panurge and the sheep (chapters
v to viii) almost certainly at Metz in the summer of 1546. The book opens with the embarka-
tion at the port of Thalasse (Tallard, a portion of
the port of Saint-Malo) of Pantagruel and his
companions. The ships were twelve in number,
Pantagruel's own ship being named the Thala-

---

* The only known copy of this narrative is in the
British Museum.

† For Cartier's voyages, see J. P. Baxter, *A Memoir of
Jacques Cartier*, New York, 1906.

mege, and having for its ensign "a large and capacious bottle, half of silver, smooth and polished; the other half was of gold, enamelled with crimson; whereby it was easy to determine that white and claret were the colours of the noble travellers, and that they were going to consult the oracle of the Bottle". The company being all assembled on the admiral's ship, "Pantagruel made them a brief and pious exhortation, supported by authorities taken from Holy Writ, on the subject of navigation". This was followed by a prayer, and the prayer by the 114th Psalm, sung in Marot's translation, of which Rabelais gives the first line. Thus the religious ceremony with which Pantagruel inaugurated the voyage was a purely Protestant one. Then they all drank to one another, and this was the reason why no one suffered from seasickness. After this follows a remarkable passage, which must be given in full:

"After often renewing their tipplings every one retired to his own ship, and in good time they set sail to the Greek [northeast] wind as it got up, to which point the chief pilot had shaped their course, and set the needles of all their compasses.

"For his advice, and also that of Xenomanes, was—seeing that the oracle of the Holy Bottle was near Cathay in Upper India—not to take the ordinary route of the Portuguese, who, sailing through the torrid zone and the

Cape of Bonasperanza at the south point of Africa, beyond the equinoctial line, and losing the sight and guidance
of the arctic pole, make an enormously long voyage; but
to follow, as near as possible, the parallel of the aforesaid
India and to tack to the westward of that pole, so that
winding under the north they might be in the same latitude as the port of Olonne without coming nearer it, for
fear of coming into and being shut up in the Frozen Sea.
And following this regular turn by the same parallel they
might have the eastward on their right, which at their
departure was on the left.

"Now this turned out to their incredible advantage;
for without shipwreck, without danger or loss of men, in
great calm they made the voyage to Upper India in less
than four months, which the Portuguese could scarcely do
in three years, with dangers innumerable. And I am of
this opinion, that some such route was perhaps followed
by the Indians who sailed to Germany and were honourably treated by the King of the Suevi at the time when
Q. Metellus Celer was proconsul in Gaul, as hath been
described to us by Cor. Nepos, and Pliny after him."

The first thing to notice in the above passage
is that the oracle of the Bottle is "near Cathay
in Upper India". It was Cathay, the supposed
home of the Earthly Paradise, that was the
goal of nearly every explorer. To reach Cathay
by a near way was the primary object which
moved Columbus, fired by the glowing accounts
of Marco Polo, to his great undertaking, and
for a considerable time he was firmly convinced
that the land which he had found actually was
Cathay. Even after the Portuguese explorers
had established the identity of Cathay with

China, the more visionary spirits still clung to their dreams of an Earthly Paradise. They merely placed Cathay further north, in Upper India, as they called it, or the modern Manchuria. Thus Cathay still remained the main object of geographical discovery, and the aim of every Atlantic voyage was to find "a short and straight way open into the West, even unto Cathay".

But opinions differed as to where this "short and straight way" was to be found. Ever since John Cabot, a Venetian in the service of England, had reached Newfoundland and Labrador in 1497, the English, though vaguely and without as yet putting their belief to a practical test, had believed in a Northwest Passage—that is to say, a passage to the northwest of Labrador; and their belief was shared by the Portuguese. On the other hand, the Spanish opinion was that a passage existed somewhere between Florida and Newfoundland, while the French navigators sought for it along the St. Lawrence or the Saguenay, which they believed to be a sea. It was naturally the last of these opinions that was followed by Rabelais, at any rate when he wrote the above passage, for Quebec and the French port of Olonne lie in about the same latitude, which is also that of part of Manchuria.

FRANÇOIS RABELAIS

We are told that Pantagruel in choosing this route was acting on the advice of his chief pilot, named Jamet Brayer, and of Xenomanes, "the great traveller", who was the guide of the expedition. Are these imaginary persons, or are they, as is Rabelais's almost constant practice, real persons under transparent disguises? Nearly forty years ago M. Margry, in his *French Voyages from the Fourteenth to the Sixteenth Century* (*Les Navigations françaises du XIV*e *au XVI*e *Siècle*), conjectured that Jamet Brayer stands for Jacques Cartier, the discoverer of Canada, and Xenomanes for Jean Alfonse of Saintonge, the most experienced French pilot of his day. But this conjecture was inadequately supported by argument, and it was left to M. Lefranc to work it out in detail. In favour of the identification of Jamet Brayer—the name does not appear in Rabelais's text till the complete edition of the Fourth Book (1552)—with Jacques Cartier, we have the facts that Jamet is a diminutive of Jacques, and almost certainly the name of Cartier's father, that Cartier was a native of Saint-Malo, the port from which the expedition starts, and that he had already on three occasions sailed by this route. Further, we have the explicit statement of the oldest historian of Saint-Malo, Jacques Doremet, who was born within twenty years of Rabelais's death, that Rabelais learnt from Cartier at Saint-Malo the nautical terms which he introduced into his book. Though this statement is unconfirmed, it is rendered in some degree probable by the fact already noticed that Rabelais speaks of the two Channel Islands, Sark and Herm, as if he had personally visited them, and that he could only have reached them from the port of Saint-Malo, Cartier's home. The introduction of the name Jamet Brayer into the text after the publication of the partial text in 1548 would seem to indicate that if Cartier is meant, Rabelais made his acquaintance after his return from Rome in July, 1550.

A greater interest attaches to the identification of Xenomanes, for he plays a more prominent part than does Jamet Brayer. From the first Panurge had chosen him to be the guide of the expedition, and throughout the voyage he is represented as giving his advice with regard to the route on every occasion of doubt or difficulty, and as being on terms of perfect equality with the other companions of Pantagruel. Jean Fonteneau, called Jean Alfonse of Saintonge, was, as has been said above, the most experienced French pilot of his day. According to his own statement, made in 1544, his voy-

FRANÇOIS RABELAIS

ages had begun as far back as 1496, and during that period he had navigated every sea and touched at nearly every land then known. He sailed on his last voyage in July, 1544, and in the course of it, probably in the latter half of 1545, was put to death by the Spaniards. Just before sailing he had completed a work entitled *Cosmography* (*La Cosmographie*), the manuscript of which was secured by Mellin de Saint-Gelais for the royal library, of which he was custodian. It was not till the year 1904 that it appeared in print, ably edited and annotated by M. Georges Musset, but Saint-Gelais may well have mentioned its existence to his friend Rabelais, with the result that Rabelais inserted in the 1552 edition of his own book the following passage in the text of the first chapter: "Xenomanes had left with Gargantua and marked out in his great and universal Hydrography the route which they were to take in their visit to the oracle of the Holy Bottle, Bacbuc."

The words "left with Gargantua" fairly represent the fact that the *Cosmography* was composed for François I. This passage then furnishes a strong argument for identifying Xenomanes with Jean Alfonse. Another may be found in the statement that Xenomanes held a small estate in mesne fee of Panurge's

216

barony of Salmigondin,* and the commentators
are agreed that Salmigondin stands for Saintonge, the country of salt-marshes, of which
Jean Alfonse was a native, his home being at
La Rochelle. It was from La Rochelle that
Pantagruel sailed for Bordeaux when he set out
on his tour through the universities, and La
Rochelle is mentioned several times in the
course of the work in a way which shows that
it was familiar to Rabelais. Thus it is quite
possible that Rabelais made the acquaintance
of Jean Alfonse in the days when he resided at
Fontenay-le-Comte, which is only about thirty
miles from La Rochelle. Finally, Jean Alfonse
had acted as pilot to Roberval in the expedition of 1541–1543, with which Jacques Cartier
was also associated. Nor is there any other
French navigator of that day who can be compared with Jean Alfonse, either for general
experience in navigation or, with the exception
of Cartier, for particular knowledge of the route
taken by Pantagruel. We may then with toler-
able confidence accept the identification, and
regard the Fourth Book as being, amongst
other things, a noble monument to one of the
most adventurous Frenchmen of his age, who
died fighting against his country's foes.

---

* III, xlix.

FRANÇOIS RABELAIS

It has been said that according to French opinion the passage which led to Cathay was to be found along the St. Lawrence. This was, in fact, the view of Jean Alfonse, who, we are told, "thought the Saguenay was a sea and led to the Pacific, or the Sea of Cathay". Rabelais no doubt originally intended to conduct Pantagruel and his companions by this route, but certain indications in his narrative seem to show that when he resumed his work on his return from Metz, he changed his intention. For instance, before the travellers reach the island of Ganabin the wind blows for three days from west-southwest, and towards the end of the book we learn that they have reached "the confines of the Glacial Sea", circumstances which clearly point to a voyage along the coast of Labrador (which in Rabelais's day was supposed to trend to the northeast) and to the Northwest Passage. We may conjecture that Rabelais was led to make this change from reading the account of Cartier's second voyage, for Cartier, on being assured that the St. Lawrence ended in fresh water, turned back in order to explore the coast of Labrador, in the hope of finding the passage to China. In any case, it is another instance of how Rabelais's scientific imagination enabled him to foreshadow the results of modern discovery, for it was only in 1850, soon after Franklin had virtually added the last link to the long chain so gallantly forged by the Cabots, Frobisher, Davis, Hudson, Baffin, and Parry, that McClure sailed through the passage, to find it practically useless.

But if Rabelais was in a large measure inspired to write his Fourth Book by the great geographical discoveries of the age, he was indebted for its general framework, that of a voyage among imaginary islands, to a literary source, Lucian's *True History*. But while his prototype's work is exclusively a satire on travellers' tales, Rabelais's does not confine itself to a single theme or a single mode of treatment. He ranges from topic to topic, from grave to gay, from narrative to satire, from myth to matter of fact, just as his fancy leads him.

There was another literary source, however, itself directly inspired by Lucian's *True History*, to which Rabelais was indebted for certain incidents of the voyage narrated in the Fourth Book. This was a species of chap-book similar in character to *The Great Chronicles*, and entitled *The Disciple of Pantagruel* (*Le Disciple de Pantagruel*), with the subtitle of *The Voyage and Navigation Made by Panurge, Disciple of Pantagruel, to Unknown and Strange Islands*, *etc. (Le Voyage et Navigation que fist Panurge, Disciple de Pantagruel, aux Isles incongnues et estranges, etc.).* So far as we know—our information is possibly incomplete—it first appeared in 1538, as a companion to pirated editions of *Gargantua* and *Pantagruel* which were issued at the close of the preceding year from the Parisian press of Denys Janot. Its correspondence to the sequel which Rabelais had promised to *Pantagruel* and the fact that some of its episodes were borrowed by Rabelais for the acknowledged continuation of his story suggest that he himself was the author. On the other hand, its wholly popular character, its lack of any of the higher qualities which distinguish the master's recognised work, and certain marked differences in the style have led the great majority of critics to reject the theory of Rabelais's authorship. Paul Lacroix, however, believed in it, and M. Lefranc has recently pointed out that the question must still be regarded as an open one. In favour of this view it may be said, first, that it is difficult to explain the borrowings except on the theory of at least some connection between Rabelais and the author; secondly, that the difference in style may be accounted for by the character of the book, and that it is at any rate written in well-balanced and harmonious periods of which few of Rabelais's contemporaries had the secret; thirdly, that some of its allusions and references, especially to places, certainly point to Rabelais. Whatever the true explanation, the fact remains that Rabelais borrowed from *The Disciple of Pantagruel* certain episodes for his Fourth Book: namely, the death of the giant Bringuenarilles, the account of the Wild Chitterlings, and that of the source of the winds which he used for the Island of Ruach, and, above all, the idea of Lantern-land, which is introduced almost at the outset of the book.

With these preliminary remarks on the origin and purport of the Fourth Book, we may now accompany the "noble travellers" on their voyage. The first land at which they touched was the Island of Medamothi (Nowhere). Rabelais describes it as "fair and pleasant to the eye on account of the great number of lighthouses and high marble towers with which the whole circuit was adorned", adding that "it was as large as Canada", an interesting reference to the land which Cartier had recently discovered and Roberval had formally claimed in the name of the King of France. On disembarking, the travellers found that it was the third day of the great annual fair, which was frequented by all the richest and most famous merchants of Asia and Africa. Accordingly

FRANÇOIS RABELAIS

Pantagruel bought some wonderful pieces of
tapestry and some rare animals, which included
three fine young unicorns and a *tarande*, or
reindeer.* The description of this latter animal
is borrowed from Pliny, but Rabelais develops
in his usual picturesque fashion the bare statement of his authority that it changes its colour
according to its environment. We thus learn
that Pantagruel wore a scarlet cloak. It
reminds us that, according to Las Casas, the
natives recognised Columbus as the admiral
by his scarlet dress.

The next incident is the unexpected appearance in the harbour of Gargantua's swift-sailing
vessel, the Swallow, which had taken only three
days and three nights to reach the island. On
board was a *gozal*, or carrier-pigeon, which
Pantagruel, having tied to its feet a ribbon of
white silk, set at liberty, and in less than two
hours it brought back to Gargantua the news of
his son's safety. The use of pigeons for the
transmission of news was practised by the
Greeks and Romans, Mohammedans and Christians, but, as M. Lefranc points out, this vision
of a pigeon-post across the Atlantic was realised only quite recently, and that on the very
spot which M. Lefranc believes to be repre-

---

* The scientific name is *Tarandus rangifer*.

222

sented by Medamothi, namely, Newfoundland. This interpretation, however, is at vari-
ance with the fact already noticed, that in
Rabelais's day Newfoundland was regarded as
a group of numerous small islands.

On the next day the travellers sighted a
merchant vessel sailing towards them, and found
to their great joy that the merchants were
Frenchmen from Saintonge who were returning from Lantern-land. Then follows the celebrated episode of Panurge and the sheep, borrowed from Merlin Coccaye, but invested by
Rabelais with a dramatic life of which there is
no trace in the original. The story of how a
sheep-dealer named Dindenault provoked Panurge, of how they quarrelled and were recon-
ciled, of how Panurge, after much boasting on
the part of the sheep-dealer, bought a sheep and
threw it bleating into the sea, of how all the
other sheep leapt in after it, and of how Dindenault, trying to hold one back, was carried
along with it and drowned, is too well known to
repeat here. But the opening of the seventh
chapter may be cited as a specimen of the banter
of the vainglorious Dindenault.

" 'My friend, my neighbour, they be meat for none but
kings and princes. Their flesh is so delicate, so savoury,
and so dainty that it is like balm. I bring them from a
country in which the hogs (God be with us) eat nothing

FRANÇOIS RABELAIS

but myrobalans and the sows are fed only with orange-flowers.'

" 'But,' said Panurge, 'sell me one of them, and I will pay you like a king, on the word of a pawn.'

" 'My friend,' answered the dealer, 'my neighbour, these be sheep bred from the very race of the ram that carried Helle over the sea called Hellespont.' "

In the preceding chapter, it may be noted, there is an irreverent parody of Calvin's *Catechism*.

After this adventure they came to the Island of Alliances, the inhabitants of which "have their noses in the shape of an ace of clubs, and for this reason the ancient name of the island was Ennasin". Then follows an account of the manners of the islanders, who are all related to one another, but the humour of this chapter is not very intelligible to the modern reader. The English reader, however, may like to be reminded that Tristram Shandy compares his great-grandfather's nose to the noses of these islanders. The travellers next touched at the Island of Cheli (Lips), the king of which, Panigon by name, had come down to the harbour to receive Pantagruel and conduct him to his castle. At the gate of the castle the queen appeared to receive them, with her daughters and her ladies, and "Panigon desired her and all her suite to kiss Pantagruel and his men; such was the courteous custom of the country".

224

THE FOURTH BOOK

Some commentators, bent upon allegory, have explained this chapter to be a satire on lip-service and meaningless courtesy, but it is probably nothing more than a reminiscence of Erasmus, who noted with great satisfaction that it was the custom in England for ladies to kiss their guests when they received them or parted from them. In the manuscript, though not in the printed text, of the Fifth Book we read that "Panigon in his last days retired to a hermitage in the Island of Odes, and lived in great sanctity and the true Catholic faith, without desires, without affection, without vice".

On the following day they came to the Island of Procuration, inhabited by Catchpoles. "They invited us neither to eat nor drink; they only told us that they were at our service if we paid them." Then one of the interpreters explained to Pantagruel that the Catchpoles gained their living by being beaten. This led to a long story told by Panurge of the Seigneur de Basché and the Catchpoles, and then Brother John made experiment of the way in which the Catchpoles earned their living. Accordingly he chose out of the whole troop a Catchpole with a red muzzle, and belaboured him so much that he seemed to be beaten to death. Then he gave him twenty crowns, and behold, "the rascal was on his legs, as pleased as two kings".

The same day they passed the islands of
Tohu and Bohu, two Hebrew words which mean
" solitude " and " void ". Here they " found
nothing to fry ". For Bringuenarilles (Nose-
slitter), the great giant, in default of windmills,
which were his ordinary diet, had swallowed
up all the pots and pans in the country.
These, however, had disagreed with him, and
in spite of divers remedies he had died that
morning in a strange fashion. For he had been
" choked through eating a lump of fresh butter
at the mouth of a hot oven by the order of his
physicians ". This incident, to which reference
is again made in a later chapter, is one of those
which Rabelais borrowed from *The Disciple
of Pantagruel.*

The next day they met a ship laden with
monks, who were going to the Council of Chesil
" to discuss the articles of the faith against
the new heretics ", and on seeing them the
orthodox Panurge " fell into an excess of joy ".
Chesil of course stands for Trent, the sixth
session of which was fixed, at the close of the
fifth session, for July 29, 1546. It was, however, postponed, and did not actually open till
January, 1547. Chesil being also the Hebrew
name for a star which was supposed to portend
storm, this encounter with the monks was appropriately followed by a tremendous storm.

THE FOURTH BOOK

Here again Rabelais is following to some extent
Merlin Coccaye, but he has also used as models
the classical storms of the *Odyssey* and the
Æneid, and has borrowed a hint or two from
one of Erasmus's *Colloquies*, entitled *Shipwreck*. M. Jal has severely criticised his nautical
knowledge, but there is no gainsaying the marvellous wealth of language and dramatic expression with which the whole scene is depicted.
In the foreground is Panurge, blubbering with
fear and more loquacious than ever.

"Pantagruel by the pilot's advice held the mast tight
and firm; Friar John had stripped himself to his doublet
to help the seamen; so had Epistemon, Ponocrates, and
others. Panurge remained squatting on the deck, weeping
and lamenting. Friar John perceived him, as he was going
on the quarter-deck, and said to him: 'Pardy! Panurge
the calf, Panurge the weeper, Panurge the wailer, thou
wouldst do much better to help us here than to blubber
away there like a cow, squatting like a baboon.'

" 'Be, be, be, bous, bous, bous!' answered Panurge;
'Friar John, my friend, my good father, I drown, I
drown, my friend, I am drowning. I am clean done for, my
ghostly father, my friend, I am clean gone. . . . Would to
God I were at this moment in the ship of those good and
blessed Concilipetous Fathers whom we met this morning,
who were so godly, so fat, so merry, and so gracious!
Holos, holos, holos! Zalas! this wave of all the devils—
(*mea culpa, Deus*) I mean this wave of God—will break up
our ship. Zalas! Friar John, my father, my friend, confession! See me here on my knees. *Confiteor;* your holy
blessing!'

" 'Come, thou devilish hangdog,' said Friar John,

'come hither and help us; by thirty legions of devils, come!
Art coming?'

" 'Let us not swear at all at this time,' said Panurge,
'my father, my friend; to-morrow as much as you will.' "

The storm over, the travellers landed at the
port of an island called the Isle of the Macræons
(Long-livers). Here they were hospitably received, and an old Macrobius (" for so they
styled their chief sheriff ") showed them all
that was worth seeing, including a deserted
forest in which were several ruined temples,
obelisks, pyramids, and other monuments.
And he explained to them that this was the
habitation of the demons and heroes, who
lived there to a great age, apparently invisible
to the rest of the inhabitants; and that at
the death of each of them there were great
lamentations throughout the forest, and on
earth plagues and disasters, and at sea storms
and hurricanes. He believed that the storm
from which the travellers had suffered and a
comet which had appeared for three nights
portended that one of the heroes had just departed. This gives rise to an interesting conversation, in the course of which the speakers
call to mind the portents which preceded "the
departure of that most illustrious, noble, and
heroic soul of the learned and valiant Knight
of Langey". Then Pantagruel tells, out of

THE FOURTH BOOK

Plutarch's *On the Cessation of Oracles*, the well-known story of the voice calling aloud to the pilot of a vessel and bidding him publish that the great god Pan was dead. And as this is said to have happened when Tiberius was emperor, Pantagruel, following Eusebius, interprets it as referring to the death of the "great Saviour of the faithful . . . for with good right He can be called Pan in the Greek tongue, seeing that He is our All".

The whole idea of the Isle of the Macræons, as well as the story of the death of Pan, is to be found in Plutarch's treatise, and in one passage Rabelais reproduces Plutarch's actual language, though with his usual picturesque amplification. But M. Lefranc has pointed out that he was also inspired by a current popular legend. On most of the maps of the New World from the middle of the fifteenth century to the close of the sixteenth an Island of Demons is to be found opposite the coast of Labrador, while on one dated 1556 it figures as the northernmost island of the group of which Newfoundland was thought to be composed. Of this imaginary island André Thevet, in a passage of his *Universal Cosmography* (*Cosmographie universelle*) (1571) cited by M. Lefranc, gives an account which is strangely similar to that of Plutarch. Though this account appeared long after Rabelais's death, and though Thevet's own travels had not begun at the time of his acquaintance with Rabelais, the latter may easily have heard of the legend from some other source.

The travellers next visited the Island of Tapinois (Sly-land), over which reigned Quaresme-prenant (Lent). Reference has already been made to the detailed description of his anatomy which Rabelais gives, and which shows his remarkably accurate knowledge of anatomy. Of far greater interest to the general reader is the apologue of Physis (Nature) and Antiphysis, borrowed from Celio Calcagnini of Ferrara, which tells how Physis became the mother of Beauty and Harmony, while Antiphysis bore Amodunt and Discordance, who were strangely misshapen. "Since then," adds Rabelais, "she brought forth the apes, bigots, and hypocrites, the maniac Pistols, the demoniac Calvins, impostors of Geneva, the frantic Putherbes, renders, canters, false zealots, cannibals, and other monsters, deformed and made awry in Nature's despite."

In this addition to the apologue Rabelais is paying off two old scores, one against Gabriel de Puits-Herbault, the monk of Fontevrault, who, it will be recollected, had attacked him in 1549, and the other against Calvin, who in his

THE FOURTH BOOK

book *On Scandals*, published at Geneva in 1550, had spoken of him as one who "after welcoming the preaching of the Gospel had been smitten with blindness". The apologue itself may be regarded as a dramatisation of the old precept so much in favour with the Renaissance, "Live according to Nature". But probably neither Rabelais nor Montaigne nor any of the Italian humanists who used the phrase could have given a very clear explanation of what they meant by it. At any rate, they used it in a sense widely different from that which the Academics and the Stoics attached to it. While the Greek philosophers implied by it a rational life in conformity with the general course of the world, the majority of the Renaissance thinkers regarded it as a maxim of liberty rather than of obedience, as an insistence on the rights of natural man against the tyranny of the Church, whether Catholic or Protestant. To Rabelais the fasting of Rome and the strict discipline of Geneva seemed equally violations of the law of Nature, equally the offspring of Antiphysis. "God did not create Lent," he says, in the letter to Antoine Hullot.

The next episode is an encounter with a monstrous whale, which Pantagruel harpooned with great skill. It was then towed ashore to a neighbouring island and cut up for the sake of its blubber. The island was called the Wild Island and was inhabited by Chitterlings, between whom and Lent there had long been a deadly war. The account of how the Chitterlings attacked the travellers, and how Pantagruel summoned his men of arms under the command of Colonel Maul-chitterling and Colonel Cut-pudding the younger, and how by the advice of Friar John it was left to the cooks of the expedition to fight against the enemy, is a purely comic episode, and those who endeavour to find in it any deep philosophical meaning will search in vain.

The travellers next come to the Island of Ruach (Wind), where the inhabitants drink and eat nothing but wind, and from there to the Island of the Popefigs, or those who make mock of the Pope. Here Pantagruel is told the excellent story of the little devil and the labourer, which has been turned into verse by La Fontaine in one of his *Tales*.

We now come to one of the most amusing and humorous episodes in the whole book, that of Bishop Homenaz and the Decretals. The opening scene must be given in Rabelais's own words:

"Having left the desolated Island of Popefigs, we sailed during one day in calm and every pleasure, when the blessed Island of the Papimanes presented itself to our sight. No sooner were our anchors dropped in the harbour, before we had made fast our cables, than there came towards us in a skiff four persons in different garbs: the one as a monk, befrocked, bemired, and booted; the other as a falconer, with a lure and a hawking-glove; the other as an attorney-at-law, with a great sack in his hand full of informations, summonses, pettifoggings, and citations; the other like an Orléans vine-dresser, with fine canvas gaiters, a pannier, and a pruning-knife at his girdle.

"When they were made fast to our ship, they cried out incontinently with a loud voice all together, asking, 'Have you seen him, gentle travellers, have you seen him?'

" 'Whom?' asked Pantagruel.

" 'Him,' they replied.

" 'Who is he?' asked Friar John. 'Ox death, I will maul him with blows,' thinking that they were inquiring after some robber, murderer, or church-breaker.

" 'What is this, strangers?' said they. 'Know you not The One?'

" 'Sir,' said Epistemon, 'we understand not such terms; but explain to us, if you please, whom you mean, and we will tell you the truth therein without dissimulation.'

" 'It is,' said they, 'he that is. Have you ever seen him?'

" 'He that is,' answered Pantagruel, 'by the doctrine of our theology, is God, and in such phrase He declared Himself to Moses. Certainly, we have never seen Him, and He is not visible to eyes corporeal.'

" 'We are not speaking at all,' said they, 'of that high God who rules in the heavens; we are speaking of the God upon earth. Have you ever seen him?'

" 'Upon my honour,' said Carpalim, 'they mean the Pope!'

" 'Yes, yes,' answered Panurge, 'yea, verily, gentlemen;

I have seen three of them, and from the sight of them I have profited little.'

" 'How?' said they. 'Our sacred Decretals declare that there is never but one living.'

" 'I mean one successively after the other,' answered Panurge; 'otherwise I have only seen one at a time.'

" 'O thrice and four times happy folk!' said they, 'be right welcome, and more than doubly welcome!'

"Then they kneeled down before us and wished to kiss our feet, which we would not allow them to do, pointing out to them that they could not do more to the Pope, if by good fortune he should come thither in his own person."

On going ashore Pantagruel and his company were met by all the people of the country, who, hearing that they had "seen *him*", knelt before them and cried, "O happy folk!" for more than a quarter of an hour. So loud were their exclamations that their Bishop, by name Homenaz, bustled up in all haste on a mule with green trappings. He at once took the travellers to the church, on the door of which they saw suspended a huge gilt book covered all over with rare and precious stones. This, explained Homenaz, was the book of the sacred Decretals, "written by the hand of a cherubic angel—you people from over the sea will not believe it"—"Not very easily," answered Panurge—"and miraculously sent down to us here from heaven". After a "low and dry mass" Homenaz showed them a rude painted image of a pope, which he held in particular

veneration. He then took them to dinner. The
conversation at this meal turned chiefly on the
Decretals, the merits of which were proclaimed
by the good Bishop in a long chant. Then the
company in turn related instances of miracles
wrought by the Decretals, mostly of the most
fantastic description. But nothing was too
fantastic for the Bishop's credulity. "Miracle!
miracle!" he cried, at the end of each story.
Then follows a significant chapter entitled
*How by the Virtue of the Decretals Gold is Subtly
Drawn out of France to Rome* (*Comment par
la Vertu des Décrétales est l'Or subtilement tiré
de France en Rome*). It was one of the chief
complaints which the Gallican Church had
against the Roman Curia, and M. Heulhard
aptly cites a letter from Henri II. to the Pope,
in which the King speaks of "the large sums
of money which, contrary to the decrees of
the Church and the liberties of the Church of
France, are drawn by regulation of the Roman
Chancery and other impositions, resulting in
the excessive taxation and oppression of our
subjects, and the diminution of their property
and substance and of the strength and wealth
of our kingdom". This was written in September, 1551, when Henri II., having espoused
the claim of Ottavio Farnese to the duchy of
Parma, was at war with the Pope; and, as we

FRANÇOIS RABELAIS

have seen, there is every probability that Rabelais wrote the account of Bishop Homenaz
about the same time. But if the first idea of
the episode was suggested by a desire to make
himself agreeable to the King, he executed it
with even more than his usual spirit and gusto.
The dinner, with Bishop Homenaz at the head
of the table "quite merry and heartened", calling from time to time to one of the pretty girls
who waited at the table, "A drink here!"
chanting the praise of the Decretals, crying
"Miracle! miracle!" laughing, weeping, and
beating his breast; the guests vying with one
another in the extravagance of their stories;
the giggling girls; Friar John whinnying at
the end of his nose, or pretending to wipe his
eyes with his napkin—this wonderful dinner
is one of the most vivid scenes on Rabelais's
varied canvas. The whole episode of the Decretals is a matchless combination of humour,
satire, and pure jovial fun.

Finally Homenaz gave the travellers a great
number of fine large pears, which, he said, grew
only in that place.

" 'How do you call them?' asked Pantagruel.
" 'Not otherwise than pears,' answered Homenaz;
'we are simple folk, as God would have us, and we call
figs figs, plums plums, and pears pears.'
" 'Verily,' said Pantagruel, 'when I shall come to my
home, I will graft some of them in my garden in Touraine

on the bank of the Loire, and they shall be called *Bon-Chrétien* pears; for never did I see better Christians than these good Papimanes.' "

The account of the frozen words which follows is not productive of much mirth, but it is interesting as showing that the travellers had now reached the confines of the Glacial Sea. Their next landing-place was a rocky and mountainous island of unpromising aspect. But when they had climbed up the mountain of which it was formed, they found the top "so pleasant, fertile, salubrious, and delicious that they thought it was the true garden and Earthly Paradise, about whose situation good theologians dispute and strive so much". Pantagruel, however, told them that it was the dwelling of Virtue described by Hesiod. "The governor thereof was Messer Gaster (Stomach), the first master of arts in the world." The account of Messer Gaster occupies six chapters. In the first of these his service to the world is set forth in a remarkable passage of great eloquence, and in the last two we have a highly ingenious explanation of how all inventions proceed from his endeavours to get and preserve corn.

On the following day, as they were nearing the Island of Chaneph (Hypocrisy), there was a dead calm, and all the company remained "pensive, out of tune, and out of sorts, without saying a word to one another". Each, however, found some occupation: Pantagruel took a nap with a Greek novel in his hand, Panurge made bubbles and bladders, and Friar John, as usual, betook himself to the kitchen. It was Friar John, too, as usual, who restored their cheerfulness by asking the question how a man should raise good weather in a calm. Then each in turn propounded some absurd problem, and, as it was now past nine o'clock, they went to dinner, and found this, as Pantagruel had hinted, a sufficient answer to all their questions. It was a practical example of the power of Messer Gaster. Before dinner was over the wind got up, and presently they perceived a mountainous country, which Xenomanes said was the Isle of Ganabin (Robbers), and was inhabited by thieves and rogues.

The next and concluding chapter contains the interesting reference to the surprise of the English garrison of Inchkeith, otherwise known as the Isle of Horses, by a French force under the command of Thermes and D'Essé (June, 1549). An amusing but not reproducible story in the same chapter shows the same display of patriotic spirit at the expense of England. As France was openly at war with her neighbour from the summer of 1549 to the spring of 1550, we may regard this as another instance of Rabelais's desire to identify himself with the foreign policy of Henri II. It is therefore quite probable that, as M. Lefranc suggests, the Isle of Ganabin is another hit at England. It does not, however, follow that these two chapters were written before the peace of March, 1550, for the Venetian ambassador in his report of 1551 declared that Henri II. meditated a fresh attack on England, and when the French King was invested with the Garter in June of that year, it was said that he was not in earnest in his protestations of friendship. A little mirth at the expense of England would have been quite acceptable at Court when Rabelais's Fourth Book was published.

Shortly before this publication Rabelais wrote a new prologue in place of the one which he had prefixed to the edition of 1548. Here we find an admirable little summary of contemporary history, which shows once more how closely at this time Rabelais watched the shifting scenes of the international drama. The war of Parma and Mirandola, the siege of Magdeburg by Moritz of Saxony, the capture of Tripoli from the Knights of St. John by Dragut Rays and of Mehedia or the Port of Africa by Charles V., the defeat of the Shah of

Persia by Solyman the Magnificent, and the
temporary check given by the Russians to the
Tartars of Kazan are all duly chronicled with
the precision of a writer of universal history.

The prologue opens with a prayer that his
readers may long be kept in health, and an
exhortation to them, in case they have lost it,
to do their best to recover it. "For health is
our life; without health life is not worth living.
. . . I have this hope in God, that He will
hear our prayers, considering the sure faith in
which we offer them, and that He will grant
this our wish, seeing that it is moderate." Then,
after two examples of moderation in wishes,
taken from Holy Scripture, he relates Æsop's
fable of *The Wood-cutter and Mercury*, but in a
manner which is the exact antithesis of Æsop's
dry and concise narrative. Nowhere else has he
developed a story with such profusion of picturesque detail and dramatic invention or such
dazzling *bravoure* of language. The wood-
cutter is represented as a native of Gravot, one
of the small properties which Rabelais's family
held near Chinon, and the story goes on thus:

" It happened that he lost his hatchet. Who was now
perplexed and confounded?—the poor man! for on his
hatchet depended his goods and his life; by his hatchet he
lived in honour and reputation among all rich wood-
merchants; without his hatchet he must starve to death;
if Death had met him without his hatchet six days after,

he would have mowed him with his scythe and weeded him out of this world. In this quandary he began to cry, to pray, to implore, to invoke Jupiter by most eloquent prayers (for you know that necessity was the inventress of eloquence), lifting his face to the skies, his knees on the earth, his head bare, his arms high in the air, the fingers of his hands spread forth, saying at each refrain of his litanies, at the top of his voice, indefatigably: 'My hatchet, Jupiter, my hatchet, my hatchet! Nothing more, Jupiter, only my hatchet, or money to buy another! Alas, my poor hatchet!' "

CHAPTER IX

THE FIFTH BOOK

WE now come to the Fifth Book, and to the much disputed question of its authenticity. The facts of its publication are as follows. In the year 1562, eight or nine years after Rabelais's death, there appeared, without name of printer or publisher or place of publication, a thin octavo volume of thirty-two leaves, entitled *The Ringing Island, by M. François Rabelais* (*L'Isle sonnante, par M. Françoys Rabelays*). It consisted of sixteen chapters, being the first fifteen chapters of the Fifth Book as it is now generally printed, and a chapter entitled *The Island of the Apedefts* (*L'Isle des Apedeftes*). In 1564 appeared the complete Fifth Book, containing forty-seven chapters, that on the Apedefts being omitted. On the last page is a stanza of four lines, beginning "Rabelais is dead; here is another book", and signed *Nature quite*, which is said to be an anagram on the name of Jean Turquet. There is no publisher's name and no place of publication, but the type is identical with that used for a reprint which appeared in the following year with the name of Jean Martin of Lyons. The complete book is also represented by a manuscript in the Bibliothèque Nationale at Paris. It is written in the same hand throughout, which is certainly not Rabelais's. It omits the chapter on the Apedefts and also the account of the game of chess (xxiii, xxiv), but has, after what is now chapter xxxii, an entirely new chapter, entitled *How the Lady Lanterns Were Served at Supper* (*Comment furent les Dames Lanternes servies à souper*), and a different and much longer ending for the last chapter. The numbering of the chapters is irregular, and the prologue is represented by a short fragment, less than a third of the length of the prologue in the printed text.

Thus the Fifth Book was published under circumstances which were calculated to arouse suspicion. In fact, two of Rabelais's contemporaries emphatically denied that it was written by him. One was Antoine Du Verdier, the bibliographer, who was eighteen when *The Ringing Island* was published, and who said, in his *Prosopography* (*Prosopographie*) (1604), that it was the work of a student of Valence. The other was Louis Guyon, a learned physician, who died at an advanced age in 1630, and who in his *Divers Readings* (*Di-*

verses Leçons) (1604) made the following explicit statement:

> "As for the last book that is put with his [Rabelais's]
> works, entitled *The Ringing Island*, which seems only to
> blame and ridicule the functionaries of the Catholic Church,
> I protest that he did not write it, for it was written a
> long time after his death. I was at Paris when it was
> written, and I know well who the author was. He was not
> a physician."

It is not clear whether Guyon is referring to
the complete book or only to the first instalment. It is only the latter which could truth-
fully be said to "ridicule the functionaries of
the Catholic Church".

Attempts have been made to invalidate both
these testimonies, but the special objections
raised to them are of little force. On the other
hand, there is nothing to show that either Du
Verdier or Guyon was in a position to speak
with authority on the subject. Against their
testimony must be set the fact that from the
time of the appearance of the Fifth Book till
within the last half-century it has been generally
though not unanimously accepted as Rabelais's
own work.

Clearly, the external evidence does not help
us. Nor are we much better off when we come
to examine the work itself. It is true that
certain anachronisms, repetitions from earlier

books, and other suspicious circumstances may be detected. But this only shows, what any one acquainted with the methods of sixteenth-century editors would expect, that the text has been tampered with. It does not follow that it is not in the main the work of Rabelais. Another line of argument is founded on general characteristics. It is said with truth that the frequent introduction of the first person is not like Rabelais, that the incidents are less dramatised than is the case in the other books, that the tone is more bitter than that of Rabelais's acknowledged work. But all this is far from conclusive. Still less conclusive is the argument from style and general merit. When critics say that the book is unworthy of Rabelais, they really mean that parts of the book are unworthy of him at his best. But Rabelais in his acknowledged work is often tedious and even dull. On the other hand, those who confidently recognise the hand of the master convince nobody but themselves. Opinions as to style, unless fortified by solid argument, are apt to be purely subjective, and on this particular question most competent judges have differed diametrically.

There is, however, one line of inquiry from which more solid results may be obtained, and that is a comparison between the three different

texts.   Hitherto one factor in this inquiry
has been practically wanting, for only a single
copy of *The Ringing Island* is known to exist,
and till recently that copy has not been
available for collation.   But thanks to the
kindness of its present owner and to the
enterprise of the Société des Études Rabelaisiennes, *The Ringing Island*, admirably edited
by MM. Lefranc and Boulenger, and furnished with an excellent critical introduction
by the latter, may now be studied at leisure.   It presents two noteworthy features.
In the first place, it abounds in printer's errors
both of punctuation and of spelling, the errors
being often of such a nature as to make mere
nonsense.   Secondly, certain incoherences, and
especially the reproduction in one place of two
abbreviations which the writer could never
have intended to appear in print, point to the
conclusion that the manuscript from which
the text was printed was the author's rough
draft, or an uncorrected copy of it.   It is at
any rate certain that the author, whoever he
was, did not see the work through the press.
   Now, supposing that the author was not
Rabelais but some imitator, either writing entirely from his own invention or, what is a
more reasonable supposition, working up Rabelais's fragments with additions and alterations

of his own, we have to account for the remarkable fact that this "editor", having been at pains to execute a skilful forgery, left his handiwork entirely to the tender mercies of an ignorant printer. For the state of the text is such that it precludes the idea of any "editing" having been done after the manuscript reached the printer's hands. Whether the "editor" tampered much or little with Rabelais's work, we have still to explain why he took no part in correcting the proofs. The most natural explanation is that he was dead.

We may now pass on to a consideration of the two remaining forms of the text, the printed text of 1564 and the manuscript preserved in the Bibliothèque Nationale at Paris. The manuscript is the work of a conscientious and fairly careful scribe, but one of little learning and limited intelligence. His occasional errors may be classified as (1) the omission of whole lines, (2) the incorrect transcription of proper names, (3) the leaving of a blank space when he cannot read a word. He had apparently the same manuscript before him as the printer of *The Ringing Island*, but in some places intelligent corrections, not merely due to a better reading of the manuscript, have been introduced. This implies that the manuscript had been revised without being recopied after the publication of *The Ringing Island*. Thus the manuscript in the Bibliothèque Nationale represents, for the first fifteen chapters, a second state of the text.

The third state is represented by the edition of 1564. Here we have abundant traces of a vigorous and not too scrupulous editor. He introduces passages which are neither in *The Ringing Island* nor in the manuscript. Indeed, one of these has been used as an argument that the whole book is not by Rabelais. Where the manuscript leaves a blank and *The Ringing Island* takes a wild shot, he inserts some word or phrase of his own invention. Where his predecessors have disfigured a proper name, he sometimes corrects it happily, but in a great many cases he goes further astray than the conscientious transcript of the manuscript, in the mistakes of which it is easy to detect the true reading. Thus, to take only one typical instance, he prints "the orange trees of Suraine [Suresne]", where it is clear from the *San Rame* of the manuscript that the true reading is *San Reme*. Instances quite as convincing are scattered throughout the book. Whoever the editor was, he was clearly not the author of the main portion of the book. Who, then, was the author?

He was evidently a man of very considerable

learning, notably of far greater learning than his editor; he borrows freely from Plutarch's *Moral Works*, from Servius's *Commentary on Virgil*, from Erasmus and Budé, from the *Hypnerotomachia* of Francesco Colonna, and from *The Disciple of Pantagruel;* he takes a marked interest in travels and voyages, citing in one passage the names of various writers on geography and maritime discovery; he speaks of Touraine with the affection and familiarity of a native; lastly, his style shows certain peculiarities of syntax which at the date when the work was printed were decided archaisms, while in the concluding chapters it is distinguished by a magnificent harmony, the secret of which, so far as we know, was known to only one French writer of the sixteenth century. Above all, he was prevented from seeing his work through the press either by death or by some other equally disabling cause. Who was this unknown author? The simplest supposition is that it was Rabelais himself.

But if Rabelais was the author, to what extent have his editors tampered with his work? We have seen that the condition of the text of *The Ringing Island* practically precludes the supposition that it has been edited at all. It is not till we come to the manuscript

in the Bibliothèque Nationale and to the
printed text of 1564 that we can detect an
editor's presence. The first editor, so far as we
can check him by comparison with the text of
The Ringing Island, seems to have corrected
with a sparing hand, and in this part of the
book he naturally abstained from making any
additions or interpolations. But for the rest of
the book we have no means of judging; for all
we can tell, he may have added and interpolated freely. As for the editor of the 1564
edition, who is probably but not necessarily a
different person from the first editor, we know
that he introduced at least two passages of his
own invention which are neither in *The Ringing Island* nor in the manuscript in the Bibliothèque Nationale, that he added largely to
the prologue, and that he omitted a very considerable passage at the close of the final
chapter.

On the whole, then, such evidence as we
possess would seem to point to the following as
forming at least a working hypothesis: The
chapters included in *The Ringing Island* are
entirely the work of Rabelais; the rest is substantially by him, but probably with a certain
amount of addition and interpolation, possibly
extending to whole chapters. But the amount
of this corruption can only be ascertained, if

at all, by a careful and delicate examination of each chapter.

It does not, however, follow that the Fifth Book is to be regarded as an authentic continuation of Rabelais's narrative. He may have written it, but it is a quite different matter to suppose that he intended it to be printed as it is, or, indeed, to be printed at all. A great many of the chapters strike one as having been written for the Fourth Book and then rejected, either for artistic or for prudential reasons. Some read like first sketches or raw material not yet worked up into an artistic whole. It is only when we come to the final chapters, perhaps the last thirteen, that we feel ourselves, except at intervals, in the true presence of the master, and even here there are passages which seem to want his final touch.

The Ringing Island has no prologue, but in the manuscript of the complete book there is a fragment which in the printed text is considerably expanded. The fragment may have been begun by Rabelais and thrown aside in dissatisfaction. It certainly did not promise well. The continuation is clearly not by him, except so far as it contains passages borrowed from his acknowledged work. Its only interest is the measure it gives of the imitator's capacity for thought and style.

FRANÇOIS RABELAIS

The sixteen chapters of *The Ringing Island* comprise two principal episodes, the one which gives its name to the whole volume (chapters i–viii) and that of the Furred Cats (chapters xi–xv), and three minor episodes, each of which occupies only a chapter. M. Lefranc suggests that the first episode was inspired by Jacques Cartier's account of the Island of Birds in the narrative of his first voyage. If he is right, Rabelais must have known of it by hearsay, possibly from Cartier's own lips, for the narrative did not appear in print till 1598. At any rate, we must not lose sight of another possible source: namely, the voyage of St. Brandan in search of the Earthly Paradise, one of the best known of mediæval legends, which must have been familiar to Rabelais from the pages of *The Golden Legend*. St. Brandan's Isle figured on all the maps of the first half of the sixteenth century, being shifted about, in accordance with the advance of geographical discovery, to various positions between Africa and the New World. In this legend of St. Brandan an Island of Birds plays a conspicuous part. We also read of an abbey of twenty-four monks, which may have suggested the Quavering Friars, of a great storm, and of St. Paul the Hermit, who had resided on his island for seventy-one years.

It is possibly from this source that Rabelais
borrowed the idea of the hermit who makes
Pantagruel and his friends fast for four days
before they land on the Ringing Island. This
island is inhabited by birds which dwell in
cages and much resemble men, and are called
"Clerjays, Monkjays, Priestjays, Abbejays,
Bishjays, Cardinjays, and Popejay, who is the
only one of his species. . . . True it is that
about 2760 moons ago there were in nature two
Popejays produced, but that was the greatest
calamity that was ever seen in this isle." The
reference here, probably, is not to the great
Schism, which began in 1378, but to the election of an antipope in 1328, 2760 moons from
which bring one to the year 1551. As a satire
on the Papacy and the hierarchy of the Catholic
Church this episode is greatly inferior to that
of Bishop Homenaz and the Decretals. It
shows little humour, but considerable bitter-
ness. When Pantagruel asks where the Clerjays
are bred, Ædituus, his guide and host, tells him
that they mostly come from two countries
called Breadless-day and Too-many-of-them,
and that they are commonly hunch-backed,
or one-eyed, or otherwise deformed. Again,
when Friar John says to Ædituus, "In this
island you have nothing but cages and birds.
They neither toil nor cultivate the land; their

whole occupation is to frolic, warble, and sing.
From what country cometh to you this horn of
abundance and store of so many good things
and dainty bits?"—Ædituus answers, "From
all the other world except some countries of
the northern regions. But of what country
are you?" "From Touraine," answers Panurge. "Verily," says Ædituus, "you were
never hatched of a bad bird, since you are
from the blessed Touraine. From Touraine
come to us yearly so much and such good
things that it was said to us one day that the
Duke of Touraine hath not, in all his revenue,
wherefrom to eat his fill of bacon, through the
excessive bounty which his predecessors have
bestowed on these sacrosanct birds."

The good cheer which led Friar John to put
his question lasted for three days, and Pantagruel and even Panurge got rather tired of it,
a feeling which Panurge expressed by relating
the apologue of the charger and the ass, which
is told in Rabelais's best manner. On the third
day they were allowed a ˙glimpse of Popejay,
and were led stealthily to the cage in which he
was squatting, accompanied by two little
Cardinjays and six great fat Bishjays. "Accursed be the beast!" cried Panurge. "He looks
like a hoopoe." "Speak low," said Ædituus,
"for he hath ears. If once he hears you thus

blaspheming, you are lost, good people. Do you see there, in his cage, a basin? From that will proceed thunder and lightning, devils and storms, by which in a moment you will be engulphed a hundred feet below the earth."

Then they returned to their drinking, and Panurge wanted to throw a stone at an old Bishjay who was snoring in an arbour, but Ædituus cried out:

" My good man, smite, strike, slay, and murder all the kings and princes in the world, by treachery, by poison, or any other way, as much as you like; unnestle the angels from heaven—for all this you shall get pardon from Popejay. But touch not these sacred birds, as you love your life, your profit, and your welfare, as well as that of your relations and friends, living and dead; even those who are yet to be born after them would feel the curse of it. Consider well that basin."

It is little wonder if Rabelais determined, on reflection, not to print this bitter and rather heavy-handed satire. To attack the Roman Curia and even the Pope was quite permissible to a good Frenchman, especially in the year 1551, when the relations between France and the Papacy had been strained to the breaking point. But it was another thing to attack the whole hierarchy of the Catholic Church. Not that Rabelais had not considerable justice on his side. In the opinion of many competent observers, snoring bishops, or, in other words, bishops who neglected their dioceses, were the most fruitful source of the evils from which the Church in France was suffering. If we compare Rabelais's picture with that drawn by the Cardinal de Lorraine, a highly orthodox church- man, in a conversation which he held with the papal nuncio in October, 1548, we shall see that they do not differ very much. According to the Cardinal, " Bishops were ignorant and uncharitable; a large number of the priests were worthless; canons refused to pay their bishops, and monks their abbots; and benefices were held by absentees at the Papal Court, who, out of the yearly income of thirty or forty crowns, took twenty-five and left the rest to some poor curé ".* At the sixth session of the Council of Trent decrees had been published relating to the residence of bishops (January 13, 1547).

The episode of the Ringing Island is followed in the printed texts by two short episodes, that of Island of Tools and that of the Island of Cassade, or Sharping. Though in the 1564 text a line has been inserted at the beginning of the tenth chapter, in order to connect the second of these two short episodes with the first, in the earlier text they have no apparent

---

* A. W. Whitehead, *Gaspard de Coligny* (1904), p. 286.

connection either with each other or with what precedes. It is therefore very likely that they are detached chapters which Rabelais threw aside without having worked them up into an artistic form. Certainly, as they stand they are of little interest, but both bear traces of being Rabelais's work, and the Island of Tools is developed from a chapter of *The Disciple of Pantagruel*, which is an additional argument in favour of its being by Rabelais.

The next episode is the important one of the Furred Cats, the satire of which is even more bitter and scathing than that of the Ringing Island. The terrible portrait of Grippeminaud, the Archduke of the Furred Cats, by whose order the travellers (except Pantagruel, who would not go ashore) were made prisoners, with "his hands full of gore, his claws like a harpy's, his muzzle like a raven's bill, his tusks like those of a four-year-old boar, his eyes flaming like the jaws of hell", is one of Rabelais's creations which has impressed itself most strongly on the popular imagination. La Fontaine, for instance, in a well-known fable, *The Cat, the Weasel, and the Rabbit* (*Le Chat, la Belette, et le petit Lapin*),* has borrowed the name for "his Furred Majesty",

---

* *Fables*, VII, 16.

whose other name of Raminagrobis is equally reminiscent of Rabelais. It is curious that the tedious repetition of the words *"or ca"* (ha, now!), which is made a prominent feature of Grippeminaud's conversation, also occurs in a story by Bonaventure Des Periers which did not appear in print till 1558, four or five years after Rabelais's death.

In the text of 1564 we read that the travellers were imprisoned because one of them "wished to sell to a sergeant some of the hats from the Island of Cassade". But these words have obviously been introduced in order to connect the episode with the preceding chapter. Both the text of 1562 and the manuscript give as the reason for their imprisonment that one of them (Friar John) "had beaten the Catchpole". The episode of the Furred Cats, then, must have been written after that of the Catchpoles, in the Fourth Book—that is to say, after 1546. It is then a possible conjecture that it is directed, not against the general administration of criminal justice, but against the *Chambre Ardente*, the newly instituted criminal court of the Paris Parliament, for the trial of heretics, which had begun to sit in December, 1547. It was generally presided over by the First President, Pierre Lizet, whose red face, crimson nose, and bad Latin have been immortalised by Beza in his Latin satire, the *Epistle of Passavant* (1553); and it has been conjectured that Rabelais may have been thinking of him when he portrayed Grippeminaud—not, indeed, his outward appearance, for this is purely imaginary and fantastic, but the inner man. There is nothing, however, to suggest Lizet, whose one virtue, that of being indifferent to money, was certainly not shared by Grippeminaud. If Rabelais had any individual in his mind, it is more likely to have been Matthieu Ory, the Grand Inquisitor for France, who showed extraordinary activity in the repression of heretics, travelling all over the country and presiding at nearly every trial for heresy.

The visit to the Apedefts (Unlearned), "with long fingers and hooked hands", which in *The Ringing Island* follows the adventure of the Furred Cats, is an elaborate—too elaborate—satire, under the simile of a wine-press, on the Chamber of Accounts, which had its habitation in a fine building of the time of Louis XII. near the Sainte-Chapelle. Access to it was by a covered staircase of fifty steps, as Rabelais is careful to note. This chapter is the last of *The Ringing Island*, and is omitted in the manuscript and in the edition of 1564, together with the concluding passage of the preceding chapter.

The heading of the next chapter, the first new one of the complete book, is a good example of the disorganisation which Rabelais's text has suffered. It runs, *How We Passed Forth (outre), and how Panurge Was Nearly Killed*, but there is nothing in the chapter about Panurge being nearly killed, and probably the printed text is a mere fragment which Rabelais had begun as a sequel to chapter xiii and then thrown aside. For *How We Passed Forth* is evidently a pun suggested by Grippeminaud's parting words to the travellers, "Go, my children, and pass forth".

With the seventeenth chapter we make a fresh start, and this and the following seven chapters form a complete episode, that of the visit to the kingdom of Quintessence or Entelechy (Perfection). It derived its names from those of its queen, who was called Entelechy by her godfather, Aristotle, "that first of men and paragon of all philosophy". But though she was thus "eighteen hundred years old, at least", she was "fair, delicate, and gorgeously apparelled"; and she received Pantagruel and his friends with great courtesy, greeting them in such high-flown language that they remained silent, even Panurge, for the whole of their visit, so that the queen believed them to be of the sect of Pythagoras. Then she invited them to dinner, and though she herself never ate anything but categories, abstractions, and other philosophical terms, she treated her guests to such "good meats, sweet dishes, and good cheer" that the narrator professes himself quite unequal to describing them. After dinner they visited the palace, and witnessed a number of cures being performed by the queen and her officers. The queen cured the incurables only, and her officers cured the rest. Consumptives, for instance, were cured "merely by making monks of them for three months". Other officers were engaged in other impossible tasks, such as ploughing the sand, washing Ethiopians white, or gathering grapes from thorns and figs from thistles. Four men were bitterly disputing and ready to tear one another's hair, and it appeared that for four days they had been disputing on three "high and more than physical propositions". The first was about an ass's shadow, the second about the smoke of a lantern, the third about a goat's hair, to know whether it was wool. At this point the queen came up, and after making another speech, consisting of a few commonplace remarks expressed in high-flown language, she enrolled the travellers in the State and Office of her Abstractors, a title, it will be recollected, which Rabelais had already assumed on the title-page of some of the editions of his earlier books. Then came supper, and after supper a ball "after the manner of a tournament", the account of which is simply a description of a game of chess, taken from Colonna's *Hypnerotomachia*.

It cannot be said that this satire on scholastic philosophy affords much entertainment. We miss the lively conversation which as a rule diversifies Rabelais's narrative, though its absence is probably intentional, for we are told that Queen Entelechy so dazzled the senses of the travellers that they were struck dumb. But a careful examination of the text and especially a comparison of the manuscript with the printed editions make it impossible to doubt that Rabelais is substantially the author of the whole episode. There are, however, some clear traces of interpolation, especially in chapter xxi, and much of the work gives one the impression of its being a rough draft which Rabelais, if he had lived, would have revised before publication, and possibly have recast in a more artistic form. Doubt has been thrown especially on the account of the game of chess. This account is omitted in the manuscript in the Bibliothèque Nationale, but as the whole episode concludes with a passage which refers to it in plain terms, it evidently existed when the manuscript was written. That it is borrowed from the *Hypnero-tomachia* certainly points to Rabelais's authorship. On the other hand, it is argued that Rabelais does not usually follow his source so closely as is done here. But though some passages are literally translated from the Italian original, the whole account is considerably amplified. Moreover, whatever one may think of the substance, it is evidently careful and finished work. Here as nowhere else in the Fifth Book, except in the concluding chapters, we find that mastery of clause-architecture and that noble harmony which are so characteristic of Rabelais's style in serious narrative.

The idea of the Island of Odes (Greek for "roads"), where roads move like living beings and travellers find themselves, without any trouble or fatigue, at their destination, has been realised, it is pointed out, in the rolling platform (*trottoir roulant*) of the Paris Exhibition of 1889. But it is doubtful whether Rabelais (to whom this chapter must certainly be ascribed) ever contemplated any practical application of his idea. It is rather to be regarded as a poetical conception which lent itself to picturesque treatment—as, for instance, to the comparison of the road over the Mont Cenis to "St. Jerome in the picture, if his bear had been a lion; for the Road had his long beard quite white and uncombed, and had on him a number of huge rosaries of wild pine-trees badly trimmed; he was, as it were, on his knees, and not standing or lying flat, and he was beating his breast with huge rough stones".

One would gladly regard as spurious the next episode, that of the Island of Sandals, inhabited by the Quavering Friars, for Rabelais has by this time pretty well exhausted the subject of monks, and such fun as he gets out of his new attack on them is in parts laboured and in parts extremely coarse. But there are several indications of his handiwork in the first of the three chapters devoted to this episode, and though one may be permitted to hope that a good deal of spurious matter has been introduced into the next, its conclusion is almost certainly by Rabelais, while the third, with its renewal of the attack on Lent from a medical point of view, is probably also his work in the main. It may be noted that the idea of the monosyllabic answers which the friar makes to Panurge in the middle chapter is not an original one. It appears in a versified dialogue printed in 1532 in an edition of Villon's poems, and was probably a current joke in Rabelais's day. Des Periers makes use of it in one of his stories.

The Island of Frieze, which is next visited,

is a much more interesting place than that of the Quavering Friars. In it is the Land of Satin, where the beasts and birds are of tapestry. The description of this country fills two chapters, and though with its entire lack of action and almost entire lack of conversation it reads like a rough draft, it is undoubtedly by Rabelais. Moreover, if the execution is monotonous and lifeless, the general idea, which is that of a satire on travellers' tales, is decidedly happy, and there is much that is interesting in the details. It begins with a long enumeration of the wonderful animals, all made of tapestry, that were to be seen on the island, elephants, a rhinoceros, unicorns, a chameleon, phœnixes, and many other rare and imaginary creatures, the real and the fictitious being mixed up together after Rabelais's wont.

Then they saw "the Mediterranean Sea parted asunder and uncovered to its lowest abysses", and "in a corner Aristotle holding a lantern, prying, considering, and putting down everything in writing". Behind him were a large company of writers on fishes, whose names are enumerated, and among them a contemporary of Rabelais, the celebrated traveller and naturalist, Pierre Gilles. He is sometimes called the Father of French Zoology, being one of the first writers on natural history who was not content merely to reproduce the learning of the ancients, but who really observed for himself. In his work on fishes, however, he borrowed a great deal from Ælian, that "first-class liar" (*tiercelet de menterie*), as Rabelais calls him.

A great drawback to this Land of Satin was the absence of food. As the travellers were searching in vain to see if they could find any, they heard "a strident and confused noise, as though it were women washing linen, or the mill-clappers of Bazacle at Toulouse".

"Without waiting longer we betook ourselves to the place where it was, and saw a little, hunch-backed, misshapen, and monstrous old man. He was called Hearsay. He had his mouth slit open right to his ears, and within his throat seven tongues, and each tongue slit into seven parts. However this might be, he spoke with all seven together, on different subjects, in different languages; also he had all over his head and the rest of his body as many ears as Argus formerly had eyes; besides which he was blind, and palsied in his legs. Around him I saw an innumerable number of men and women listening attentively, and amongst the group I recognised some who cut a fine figure; and among them one held a *mappa mundi*, and was explaining it to them compendiously in little aphorisms; and so they became learned clerks in no time, and spoke elegantly and with good memory of a multitude of prodigious things, for the knowledge of a hundredth part of which a man's lifetime would not suffice, the pyramids of the Nile, Babylon, the Troglodytes, the Himantopodes, the Blemmyæ, the Pygmies, the Cannibals, the Hyperborean Mountains, the Ægipans, and all the devils, and all by Hearsay."

THE FIFTH BOOK

Then follow the names of various ancient and modern travellers and writers on geography, who were "hidden behind a piece of tapestry, stealthily writing fine stuff, and all by Hearsay". The list of the moderns is particularly interesting and instructive. First come the writers who were not themselves travellers: Albert the Great, Pope Pius II. (Æneas Sylvius), Raffaelle Maffei of Volterra, Paolo Giovio, and Peter Martyr of Anghiera. Then come the travellers who had recorded their own experiences: Marco Polo, Hetoum, Prince of Gorigos in Cilicia, commonly known as Hayton the Armenian, who travelled in Tartary at the beginning of the fourteenth century, Pedro Alvarez de Cabral, the Portuguese navigator who discovered Brazil in the same year (1500) as the Spaniard Pinzon, Jacques Cartier, and Ludovico de Varthema, whose *Itinerary*, an account of his travels in the East, first published in Latin in 1508 and afterwards translated into various modern languages, was exceedingly popular in Rabelais's day. It is a lively record of adventure in lands then little known, for he had penetrated as far as Sumatra and Java, but some parts of it are certainly liable to the reproach of having been written "by Hearsay".

The irony of these two chapters comes in appropriately at the point when the voyage to the oracle of the Bottle is nearing its conclusion. Hitherto, except in the eyes of those who find in the voyage a well-planned moral allegory, none of the episodes can be regarded as essential to the main design of the whole work. Rabelais has conducted his travellers from island to island without any guiding plan, just as his fancy prompted him. This absence of logical connection between the different episodes made it at once easier for the editors of the Fifth Book to piece together the various fragments that they found amongst Rabelais's papers, and more difficult, or rather impossible, for modern critics to discover Rabelais's own intentions.

But the travellers have now reached a stage in the voyage which was deliberately planned from the first. Panurge had declared that his intention was to sail by Lantern-land, and there take some learned Lantern to serve as their guide to the Bottle.* In Lantern-land, the general idea of which, as well as some details, is derived from Lucian's *True History*, Pantagruel and his friends are now arrived. On entering the port they recognise the lanterns (or lighthouses) of La Rochelle, "which gave a good clear light", Pharos (the island off Alex-

---

* III, xlvii.

THE FIFTH BOOK

andria), Nauplia, and the Acropolis at Athens.
"Near the port was a little village inhabited
by the Lychnobii, who are a people living by
lanterns, a good, studious, honest folk."
Thus Lantern-land, of which we have already
heard a good deal in the course of Rabelais's
narrative, signifies the land where men search
after truth. The travellers are presented to
the queen, and Panurge briefly sets forth in
Lantern language, with which, it will be
recollected, he has already shown himself well
acquainted, the causes of their journey. Thereupon the queen commands them to be present
at her supper, that they may the more easily
make choice of a Lantern for a guide.

The account of how the lady Lanterns were
served at supper forms a chapter which is
found only in the manuscript in the Bibliothèque Nationale. It must be confessed that
the names of the imaginary dishes that were
set before the travellers show little wit or fun in
their composition, but there is a certain interest
in the long list of songs and dances which follows,
and which is taken, with some alterations,
from *The Disciple of Pantagruel*. When the
time comes for the travellers to choose their
guide, they select the Lantern of Pierre Amy,
"whom," adds the narrator, "I had formerly
known, and she also recognised me, and she

appeared to us more divine, more sprightly, more learned, more wise, more eloquent, more kindly, more gracious, and more suited to conduct us than any other that was in the company". This tribute to Rabelais's old friend can hardly be by any other hand than that of Rabelais himself. Just as the light of Pierre Amy's knowledge guided him in the monastery of Fontenay-le-Comte when he first set forth to explore the fields of knowledge, so it now guides him at the end of his voyage in the search after absolute truth.

With their noble Lantern lighting and leading them, they arrived at the desired island, in which was the oracle of the Bottle. The approach to the temple was through a large vineyard, where by order of their Lantern they ate three grapes each, put vine-leaves in their shoes, and took a green branch in their left hand. Then passing under a vault which reminded Pantagruel of the painted cellar at Chinon, they descended a marble staircase underground. At this point Panurge began to be horribly afraid, and begged that they might go back, but encouraged by Brother John, and bidden to keep silence by their Lantern, he laid aside his fears. At the bottom of the steps they found a portal, on the front of which was written a Greek sentence signifying, "In wine is truth". The description of the temple, with its two brass gates, its mosaic pavement, its wonderful hanging lamp, and its still more wonderful fountain, is borrowed largely from the *Hypnerotomachia*, whole passages being literally translated, while that of the mosaics which lined the walls and which represented the victory of Dionysus over the Indians is taken from Lucian's *Dionysus*. While the travellers were contemplating this marvellous temple, the venerable priestess Bacbuc appeared, and invited them to drink from the fountain. Then she asked them what they thought of the water. They answered that it seemed to them good, fresh spring-water, whereat she ordered her ladies in waiting to bring hams, tongues, caviar, and other incentives to thirst, "and when their stomachs were thoroughly scoured" bade them drink again. This they did, and to Panurge it seemed to be wine of Beaune, and to Friar John wine of Graves, and to Pantagruel wine of Mirevaux.

" 'Drink,' said Bacbuc, 'once, twice, and three times again, changing your fancy each time, and you will find the taste, savour, and liquor such as you shall have fancied it; and hereafter never say that anything is impossible with God.' I answered: 'Never was that said by us; we maintain that He is all-powerful.' "

FRANÇOIS RABELAIS

Then Bacbuc asked which of them it was that wished to consult the oracle of the Holy Bottle; and on Panurge's answering that it was he, he was wrapt up in a green gaberdine and otherwise solemnly prepared for initiation into the mysteries. Thus accoutred, he was led into a circular chapel, in the middle of which was a fountain of fine alabaster full of clear water, and half immersed in the water was the Sacred Bottle. Then Bacbuc made Panurge kneel and kiss the brink of the fountain, and bade him rise and dance round it; that done, she ordered him to sit on the ground between two stools, and made him sing a vintage song. Then she threw something into the fountain, and the water at once began to boil. Panurge listened with one ear in silence, when from the Sacred Bottle there issued a noise like that of bees or of a heavy shower, and then was heard this word—Trinch.

"Then Bacbuc rose, and took Panurge under the arm gently, and said: 'My friend, render thanks to Heaven; reason requires it of you. You have promptly had the answer of the Holy Bottle—I say, the most joyous, divine, and certain word that I have yet heard from it the whole time that I have ministered here to her most sacred oracle. Rise, let us go to the chapter, in whose gloss that fine word is interpreted.'

" 'Let us go,' said Panurge, 'in Heaven's name; I am as wise as I was last year. Enlighten us: where is this book? Turn it over; where is this chapter? Let us see this merry gloss.' "

Returning to the temple, the priestess drew forth a huge silver book in the form of a breviary, and bidding Panurge open his mouth made him swallow every drop, for it was really a venerable, true, and natural flask full of Falernian wine. "See here," said Panurge, "a notable chapter and most authentic gloss. Is this all that is meant by the answer of the Bottle?" "Nothing more," answered Bacbuc, "for Trinch is an oracular word, in use and understood by all nations, and signifying Drink." After a few more words of explanation they all proceeded to drink, and were forthwith seized with poetic frenzy, and burst forth into rhyme. Then Bacbuc, having made them write their names in a register, dismissed them with parting words of wisdom. "So we passed through a country full of all delights, more pleasant and temperate than Tempe in Thessaly . . . scented, smiling, and pleasant as is the country of Touraine; and at last we found our ships in the harbour."

With this commendation of his native country Rabelais's Fifth Book, as it has come down to us, ends. Was this meant to be the conclusion of the whole narrative? Or, if more time had been granted to him, would he have continued the story, telling us of how the travellers returned to their native country, and of Panurge's marriage, and possibly also of Pantagruel's? It is impossible to say. At any rate, the conclusion as we have it is a singularly noble one, and anything that came after it would have been something of an anticlimax.

CHAPTER X

WE have seen that Rabelais began *Panta-gruel*, the book which eventually became the second of the whole work, as a continuation of a chap-book or popular giant-story which he had edited for a Lyons publisher. In accordance with this intention, the first four chapters, except for the touches of real humour contained in the third, are written in the giant-story vein. But in the fifth chapter, which relates Pantagruel's visits to the provincial universities of France, and which is clearly founded on Rabelais's own experiences, we are introduced to an element of realism which is never afterwards long absent. Then follow two chapters of satire, one on the Latinised language of the *rhétoriqueur* school and the other on the time-honoured books of the old learning. After this comes the famous letter, wholly serious, from Gargantua to Pantagruel, on the subject of education, and then we have more satire, first on the university and then on the law-courts. Meanwhile Panurge has appeared on the scene, and the doings of that worthy, told for the most part in a thoroughly popular manner, occupy several chapters. The book concludes with the expedition against the Amaurotes, in which, except for one chapter of high satire (the account of Epistemon's experiences in the other world), there is a complete return to the tone of a simple giant-story.

In the book next written, *Gargantua*, the giant-story element is greatly diminished. It predominates, indeed, in the first seventeen chapters, but for the rest of the book it appears only in the amusing episode of the pilgrims, and in one or two other places. On the other hand, the realistic element is greatly increased, the whole book being full of reminiscences of the neighbourhood where Rabelais was born and spent his childhood. The satire of this book is chiefly directed against the old methods of education and university training, against monastic life and pilgrimages, and especially against unjust warfare and plans of universal conquest. The constructive part is represented by the admirable account of Gargantua's education, by Gargantua's treatment of his defeated enemies, and by the abbey of Thelema, though this latter must be regarded rather as a poet's dream than as the serious speculation of a philosopher.

It is possible that this satire on existing

conditions, accompanied by proposals, in part
Utopian, for their reform, may have been suggested to Rabelais by More's *Utopia*, of which,
as we have seen, there is a direct reminiscence
at the very outset of the Second Book. But
while satire of existing institutions is introduced by More only in a casual and intermit-
tent fashion, in Rabelais's earlier books, at
any rate, it decidedly preponderates over the
constructive part. But it is a mistake to
regard Rabelais as nothing more than a satirist, and to say, as some of his critics have
said, that he pulls down and never builds
up, that he ridicules everything and suggests
nothing. The constructive element is by no
means absent from his book, but it differs from
More's in being far less Utopian. His proposed
reforms, whether in education or in the administration of justice or in the conduct of foreign
relations, are always practical—capable of
being realised, not only in Utopia, but in the
France of his day.

While the first two books consist of various
episodes loosely strung together, the quest of
Panurge, which from this point becomes the
central theme of the narrative, confers a certain unity on the later books. The method,
however, by which the latter part of this quest
is conducted, that of a voyage from one

imaginary island to another, admits of numberless digressions which have no apparent bearing on the main subject. Further, with the Third Book a change takes place in the objects of Rabelais's satire. It is henceforth directed less against the institutions of his age, his attitude towards which has become decidedly more conservative, than against its ideas. He now occupies himself with deep philosophical problems, such as fate and free will, the future destiny of man, the relations between the world of phenomena and the unseen world. The only important exceptions are the episodes of Judge Bridlegoose in the Fourth Book and the Furred Cats in the Fifth, both satires on the administration of justice, and the attacks on the Papacy represented by the account of Bishop Homenaz and the Decretals and by that of the Ringing Island; and of these it is very doubtful whether the last was definitely intended for publication.

Thus, though the contents of the various books correspond to their titles, in so far as the First Book deals with the adventures of Gargantua and the remaining ones with those of Pantagruel, their construction is exceedingly loose. If the framework is that of a romance of chivalry, the treatment is that of a mediæval *fatrasie*. While a sufficient interest is sustained in the narrative, its many digressions and halting-places enable Rabelais to give free rein to his overflowing learning, his exuberant gaiety and fun, his interest in every form of human activity, his speculations as to the future of man, and through all, and perhaps above all, his joy in the sound of words and the weaving of harmonious periods.

But first, as to his learning. Rabelais was a humanist, in an age when the best humanists were encyclopædists. When Thaumast declared that Panurge had opened for him "the true well and abyss of universal learning (*encyclopédie*)", he was borrowing from the Greeks not only a word, but an idea which played an important part in their theory of education. From the Greeks the idea passed to the Renaissance. Thus we find Budé, for instance, frequently insisting, in his writings, on the importance of encyclopædic or universal learning, without which, he says, there can be no true philosophy. So thoroughly were his precepts carried out by his pupil, Jacques Toussain, one of the first royal professors of Greek, that he was nicknamed "the living library".

It would be a mistake to suppose that Rabelais's knowledge of ancient literature was equal to that of a Budé or a Toussain. Nor was he an expert in any single department of classical study. He was neither a trained philologist, nor a trained jurist, nor a trained archæologist. But he was an omnivorous reader of Greek and Latin literature. The two Greek authors to whom he owed most were Lucian and Plutarch. From Lucian he borrowed the general idea of Pantagruel's voyage, and especially that of the Island of Ruach; the account of Epistemon's experiences in the other world; the idea of prayers ascending to Jupiter through a trap-door, and the story of the countryman and his axe, in which the idea occurs; and the description of the battle between Dionysus and the Indians. His debt to Plutarch is even greater, for besides the more important borrowings, such as the advice given to King Picrochole by his counsellors, the account of the Island of the Macræons, and the story of the death of Pan, he is frequently indebted both to the *Lives* and to the *Moral Works* for ideas, or for anecdotes or other illustrations. Plutarch's genial temper and contented mind no doubt appealed as strongly to Rabelais as they did to Montaigne.

Next to Lucian and Plutarch, his favourite Greek authors seem to have been Homer, whom he calls, oddly enough, "the paragon of all philologists", and the "divine Plato", with whose dialogues he was evidently very familiar. It will be recollected that in his letter to Antoine Hullot he refers to a Plato which had been lent him, but he afterwards possessed a copy of his own, which is still in existence. Among other survivals of his library are two copies of Plutarch and a Galen in five volumes. Other Greek writers for whom he had a special affinity were travellers like Herodotus and Pausanias and biographers like Diogenes Laertius and Philostratus, also Athenæus, whose vast and varied collection of miscellaneous information must have been greatly to his taste. He makes some references to Aristotle, but not many, considering the extent and importance of his work. Euripides, who seems to have been his favourite tragedian, and Aristophanes, whom he calls in one place the Quintessential, both supply some material. Notable absentees are Æschylus and Sophocles, and though Demosthenes is mentioned two or three times, there are few, if any, references to his works.

Naturally, it is the writers who give the most information that are best represented in Rabelais's book. Thus, among Latin authors his greatest debt is to the elder Pliny, and he draws largely on Servius, Aulus Gellius, and Macrobius, on Suetonius and Valerius Maximus. Cicero does not figure largely in proportion to the amount of his writings. Rabelais's favourite Latin poet would seem to have been Virgil, but he has borrowed more from Ovid. He refers occasionally to Plautus, Catullus, Martial, and Juvenal.

Besides these classical writers to whom he is directly indebted, there are several others, less known and for the most part dealing with technical subjects, whom he cites as authorities. It does not follow that he cites them always at first hand, and probably he does not. The practice of quoting or referring to authors at second hand, as if one had read them oneself, was habitual and quite permissible in Rabelais's day, and there were several books, by Italian humanists, miscellaneous collections of anecdotes and multifarious information in the manner of Athenæus or Aulus Gellius, which lent themselves admirably to such a practice. Chief among these was a work by Ludovico Ricchieri, better known as Cœlius Rhodiginus, a native of Rovigo (Rhodigium), who resided for some years in France in the reign of Charles VIII., and after a wandering and chequered career in his own country was appointed by François I. to a Greek chair at Milan in 1515. In the following year he published at Venice his principal work, *Readings from the Ancients, in Sixteen Books (Anti-*

quarum Lectionum Libri XVI), which, embrac-
ing as it does every field of human knowledge,
served Rabelais as a convenient storehouse of
information.   Then there was the collection of
Memorable Sayings and Deeds (*De Dictis et
Factis Memorabilibus*), Milan, 1509, modelled
on Valerius Maximus, by Battista Fregoso
(Fulgosus), once, like nine other members of
his family, Doge of Genoa, but who, having
been deposed and banished, spent his latter
days at Lyons in peaceful devotion to literature and learning. His principal work had a
great success, and was frequently reprinted,
notably at Paris in 1518. Rabelais refers to
him once by name. Celio Calcagnini, from
whom Rabelais borrowed the apologue of
Physis and Antiphysis, has been mentioned in
a former chapter. His works, which were
published in a collected form at Basel in 1544,
three years after his death, include several
dissertations on subjects bearing on classical
antiquity.

But Rabelais, to use his own metaphor, had
a lantern to guide him in his exploration of ancient literature that was more illuminating
than any Italian humanist. We have seen in
what terms of gratitude and devotion he wrote
to Erasmus, calling him "father", and saying
that he had ever nurtured him with the purest

milk of his divine learning. There is nothing surprising in this when we remember the enormous influence which Erasmus exercised on the thought of Northern Europe, and the wide circulation of his writings. Nowhere was he held in higher regard than in France. He had been a student of the University of Paris, had frequently visited that city from 1496 to 1500, and had resided there continuously from 1503 to 1507. It was at Paris that the first edition of his *Adages* (1500) was published, and, on a rumour that the Sorbonne intended to put his *Colloquies* (1518) on the Index, a Paris publisher hurried through the press an edition of twenty-four thousand copies. Rabelais's chief specific debt was to the *Adages*, that "manual of the wit and wisdom of the ancient world for the use of the modern", which, containing in its first edition only eight hundred proverbs, numbered four thousand in the complete Aldine edition of 1520. It was from this source, and not directly from Plato, that Rabelais derived that comparison made by Alcibiades of Socrates to the little boxes called Sileni which opens the prologue to *Gargantua*. His debts to *The Praise of Folly*, which was also first printed at Paris, though in an unauthorized edition (1509), and to the *Colloquies* are naturally different in character, for both these works deal, not with the ancient world, but with contemporary society. *The Praise of Folly*, the irony of which is directed chiefly against the monks and the doctors of theology, must have found in Rabelais a most sympathetic reader. It has evidently inspired some of the passages in *Gargantua* relating to monks and pilgrimages, as well as some of Rondibilis's remarks, in the Third Book, on the character of women. Rabelais has also drawn on the *Colloquies*, especially on the one entitled *On the Eating of Fish*, which contains the well-known account of Erasmus's experiences at the Collège de Montaigu. Possibly, too, he has borrowed something from the *Education of the Christian Prince* (1516), dedicated to Charles V. Finally, whether or no his love of Lucian and Plutarch was inspired by Erasmus, with whom also they were favourite authors, the choice at any rate shows that the two men were kindred spirits.

The influence of Erasmus's friend, Sir Thomas More, on Rabelais has already been pointed out. That of Guillaume Budé, Erasmus's rival for the supremacy in Greek learning, was more general in character, but it was only to be expected that the leading humanist of France, who had encouraged Rabelais with sympathy when he was struggling under difficulties to climb the steep ascent of Greek learning, should have left an impress on his book, and as a matter of fact there are to be found in it not only traces of general assimilation, especially in Gargantua's famous letter to Pantagruel, but also some specific debts.

If Rabelais was inferior to Erasmus and Budé in first-hand knowledge of antiquity, he had greatly the advantage of them in familiarity with the vernacular literature of Italy and France. His debts to the two monks, Colonna and Folengo, who in this connection may be regarded as a vernacular writer, have already been sufficiently pointed out. But he was hardly less indebted to the great romantic epics of which Folengo's poem was a burlesque. Naturally, the satire of Pulci and the irony of Ariosto attracted him more than the serious spirit of Boiardo. With Pulci, indeed, he has many features in common, the same mixture of piety and irreverence, the same combination of theological and philosophical speculation with ribald jesting and jovial buffoonery. Pulci's Margutte was the prototype alike of Folengo's Cingar and Rabelais's Panurge, and Rabelais's elder giants, Grandgousier and Gargantua, certainly owe something to the good-natured Morgante of Pulci's epic. With the *Orlando Furioso* Rabelais had an equally good acquaintance, traces of which are scattered up and down his book. Astolfo's journey to the moon may have given him ideas for the voyage of Pantagruel, and the account of the gardens of Alcina certainly furnished him with some details for the abbey of Thelema. He knew also the other two masterpieces of the zenith of the Italian Renaissance, Machiavelli's *Prince* and Castiglione's *Courtier*. To *The Prince* he makes in one place a distinct reference, combating Machiavelli's advice that a conquered country should be ruined, as "the erroneous opinion of certain tyrannical minds". In the Third Book he reproduces a passage of *The Courtier*, and doubtless his social Utopia of Thelema was in part inspired by that noble and attractive picture of the best side of the Italian Renaissance. The writers of the next period, of the Italian Renaissance in its decadence, are represented by Berni, who inspired the discussion between Pantagruel and Panurge as to the advantage of being in debt, and by Aretino, who furnished the story of the camp at Stockholm. Finally, to go back to the fourteenth century, though Boccaccio is cited only once by name, this is by no means a measure of his influence. As we shall see, it was possibly the publication of Antoine Le Maçon's translation of *The Decameron* which gave the impulse to Rabelais's story-telling vein, and we may be sure that the latter was well acquainted, not only with this supreme specimen of the story-teller's art, but with the works of the other Italian novelists.

Nor did Rabelais, like so many of the French humanists, turn his back on his native literature. Ardent opponent though he was of some aspects of mediævalism, he remained faithful, like Marot, to much of the mediæval tradition in literature, and, like Marot, he especially affected those of the older writers who savoured most richly of the native soil. It happened that in the year 1532, in which Rabelais published the first instalment of his great work and Marot the first collected edition of his poems, Galliot Du Pré, a publisher who was quick to catch the shifting breezes of the popular taste, brought out uniform editions of Gringore, Coquillart, Villon, and the immortal farce of *Patelin*. It is therefore interesting to find that Rabelais quotes a line which is common to Gringore and Coquillart, and that he has a special affection for "Master François Villon" and "the noble Patelin", both of whom, as we have seen, figure in Epistemon's account of the other world, in company with the Franc-archer of Baignolet, whose monologue was first added to Villon's works in

Galliot Du Pré's edition. Master François is
also the hero of two stories, into one of which he
is thrust in defiance of chronology; and his
famous refrain,

"But where are the snows of yester-year?"

is quoted, with mention of him as "the Parisian
poet". *Patelin* also is represented by numerous quotations. Rabelais's attachment to
the older literature is also shown, as might be
expected, by his familiarity with the romances of
chivalry, the heroes of which find constant
mention in his book. Towards his contemporaries, Marot and Saint-Gelais, he exercised the
privilege of friendship, borrowing from Saint-
Gelais the enigma which was found on digging
the foundations of the abbey of Thelema, and
from Marot sundry lines and phrases.

Such were Rabelais's principal literary
sources, and he used them freely and without
stint, now translating, now paraphrasing, sometimes with acknowledgment, sometimes without, borrowing an idea here and a phrase there,
just as it suited him. There was nothing remarkable or blameworthy in this; it was the common
practise of the sixteenth century. Ronsard
and the other members of the Pleiad pillaged
Italian poets and writers of Latin verse at their
pleasure; Desportes, when confronted with his

numerous plagiarisms, said that if he had been consulted he could have furnished his critic with many more examples. The English sonneteers, as has been recently shown by Mr. Sidney Lee, treated Ronsard and Desportes in exactly the same fashion. Montaigne's unacknowledged pilferings, "a wing here and a leg there" (as he quaintly puts it), are so numerous that the late Guillaume Guizot, who began an elaborate investigation into his sources, abandoned the task. Historians were even less scrupulous. La Popelinière incorporated nearly the whole of La Place's *Commentaries* in his own history without even mentioning his name, and Machiavelli plagiarised his predecessor, Giovanni Cavalcanti, with equal freedom.

But while recognising the magnitude of Rabelais's borrowings, we must be on our guard against exaggerating them. Some of the resemblances which have been discovered by enthusiastic investigators of sources are too subtle to be recognised by the ordinary reader, and it does not necessarily follow that when two contemporary writers express the same fairly commonplace idea, one is plagiarising from the other. After all is said, whatever Rabelais takes he makes his own, and that, perhaps, is the true test of originality. While one writer who has never consciously borrowed a line recalls at every turn the features of some model, another, who, to use Molière's expressive phrase, "takes his property wherever he finds it", preserves his own individuality throughout.

We have a good instance of Rabelais's treatment of his sources in the character of Panurge. The first idea of the character came to him, in all probability, from Pulci's Margutte, and it was certainly stimulated by Margutte's descendant, Cingar, who stands in much the same relation to Baldus, the hero of the *Macaronea*, as Panurge does to Pantagruel. For the account of his exploits at Paris he may have made use of such popular works as the *Adventures of Til Ulespiegel*, a French translation of which was published in 1532, or the *Repues franches*, or apocryphal anecdotes about François Villon. But when we have enumerated these sources, we have not really accounted for Panurge—for the qualities by which he lives. In all essentials he is the creature of Rabelais's imagination working upon his experience. It is true that Panurge resembles his prototypes in being malicious, vindictive, thievish, and licentious, but he differs from them in being also a scholar. If the character of Margutte was inspired, as some said, by some hungry Greek whom Pulci had encountered at Florence, so Rabelais, during his university experiences, especially at

Paris, may have met the prototype of Panurge. Even his adventures in Turkey are not beyond the range of possibility, and may almost be parallelled in the lives of some of the wandering scholars of that day—in that of Pierre Gilles, for instance, who was compelled by want of money to serve in the Sultan's army, or in that of Pierre Du Chastel, who was stripped by robbers at Memphis, and, after making his way through Arabia, Palestine, and Asia Minor to Constantinople, returnèd to France to become reader to François I. (in which capacity he read *Pantagruel* to his royal master) and Bishop successively of Tulle, Mâcon, and Orléans.

It is the hard loveless life incident to Panurge's student days which is the reason and to some extent the excuse for his ignoble character. Malicious, vindictive, cruel, dishonest, licentious, cowardly, he is, with all his faults, a scholar and a wit. And he has one virtue: he loves Pantagruel. And this also must be recorded in his favour, that Pantagruel, the wise and blameless prince, loves him. "The love that you bear me," says Panurge to his master, "is beyond estimation; it transcends all weight, all number, all measure; it is infinite, eternal." This love was born of pity, the pity which Pantagruel felt for a man who had been reduced to the lowest straits of poverty by "the adventures which befall the curious". Pantagruel must also have loved him for his inimitable wit and his unquenchable vivacity of speech. In every situation he is never at a loss for an answer; even fear does not leave him speechless. His cowardice, it may be noticed, is only dimly foreshadowed in the Second Book; nor is it till the Third Book that we are introduced to another characteristic, his orthodoxy. In fact, between the production of the Second Book and that of the later books the character of Panurge undergoes a marked development. In the earlier books it is chiefly the more ignoble sides of his character which are brought into prominence. In the later books Panurge, if not more virtuous, is less ignoble. Like Sancho Panza in the service of Don Quixote, his character, if not radically improved, has at any rate been refined by contact with the noble and virtuous Pantagruel. But, over and above this, the conception of his character seems to have grown and developed in Rabelais's mind, to have become more philosophical and of wider import.

Panurge, it has been said, is a man without moral sense, but this is somewhat too simple a definition. Rather is he a man of great intelligence, but little character; of infinite wit, but

slender wisdom; full of resource, but a born
coward; an incomparable talker, but a poor
worker. He has learned many things, but he
has not learned how to live. He has often
been compared to Falstaff, and the resemblances between the pair are as obvious as the
differences. Panurge, like Falstaff, might have
said of himself that he is not only witty in
himself, but the cause that wit is in other
men; and it might have been said of him,
as it was said of Falstaff, that his means
are slender, and his waste is great. He has
the same vices, with the additional one of
malice; he has the same irrepressible optimism and the same affection for his prince.
But Panurge's affection is ennobled by respect,
and Pantagruel's feeling for Panurge is far
deeper than Prince Hal's mere liking for Falstaff. We may be sure that when Pantagruel
succeeds to his father's throne, he will not
cast off his follower or declare that he knows
him not.

Friar John, unlike Panurge, has no literary
prototype, and even if it be true that a monk of
Seuilly named Buinard, who afterwards became prior of Sermaise, served as Rabelais's
model, the creation is none the less original.
The dominant characteristics of this simple
and healthy soul are courage, helpfulness, and

an invincible cheerfulness. "I fear no man who wears a beard," he says, and it is less than the literal truth. "He works, he defends the oppressed, he comforts the afflicted, he helps the sufferers," says Gargantua; and the monk adds, simply, that he is "never idle". On one occasion when all the voyagers, even Pantagruel himself, are out of spirits, Brother John preserves his cheerfulness. His learning is confined to the Vulgate and the offices of the Church; he puts aside all philosophical inquiry with his favourite phrase, "It is not in the breviary"; he is fond of good cheer, but not really a glutton; he is passably irreverent and uses large, mouth-filling oaths, but at heart he is a dutiful son of the Church.

Grandgousier, Gargantua, and Pantagruel do not greatly differ from one another. They all represent Rabelais's ideal of a wise and virtuous monarch. They are all pious, clement, tolerant, good-natured; they are all masters of the learning of their day. Their bearing towards others is habitually marked by a grave courtesy. With Pantagruel, as the hero of four out of the five books, we are naturally the most familiar, but though his character is more fully developed than those of his father and grandfather, it is essentially the same. We note in him, however, as befits the representative of a later generation, a keener interest in scientific and speculative inquiry. Though he is sceptical as to the results, he gives every assistance in his power to Panurge's endeavours to lift the veil of futurity. "I have for a long time known that you are a lover of travel and desirous of seeing and learning everything," says Panurge, when he proposes the expedition to the oracle of the Bottle. Pantagruel, in short, has only one weakness: he is too lenient to Panurge.

As befits the characters of what may without undue straining of language be called a prose epic, they are drawn with epic breadth and simplicity. We must not expect to find in them the gradual development and subtle analysis of Shakespearian drama or the nineteenth-century novel. Moreover, Rabelais's interest was not so much in individual men as in man in general—in the possibilities and future destiny of the human race. His characters, therefore, with the exception perhaps of Panurge, are not strongly individualised. Brother John is a broad type of humanity; Pantagruel is the ideal monarch; both alike are the expression in human form of abstract ideas rather than studies from real life. But all three are portrayed with admirable consistency, and when we consider what few models of epic

characterisation Rabelais had before him—
none outside of Homer and Virgil and the
romantic epics of Italy—we must admit that
the achievement is a remarkable one. Where
in the whole of French literature before
Rabelais shall we find any characters to compare with Panurge or Friar John, or even
Pantagruel?

Pantagruel's lesser followers, Ponocrates, Eudemon, Gymnaste, Epistemon (Pantagruel's
tutor), Carpalim, Eusthenes, and Rhizotome,
are little more than names. The only one among
them that can be said to be at all individualised is Epistemon, the amiable pedant who
tries to find in the learning of the ancients a
solution for every difficulty. Outside Pantagruel's immediate circle the two most remarkable and entertaining characters are Judge
Bridlegoose and Bishop Homenaz. They both
possess the two characteristics of humorous
characters. They are completely unconscious
of their own failings, and they inspire affection
and not contempt.

Rabelais's humour is also conspicuous in
some of his stories, as for instance in that of
John XXII. and the nuns of Fontevrault, in
the judgment of Seigny John, and in the apologue of the horse and the ass. The first of
these, happily, is not too long to give in full.

FRANÇOIS RABELAIS

"I have heard it related that Pope John XXII., passing
one day by the abbey of Fontevrault, was besought by
the abbess and other discreet mothers to grant them an
indult by means of which they could confess one to the
other; alleging that religious women have certain little
secret imperfections which it were an intolerable shame for
them to reveal to men confessors, and that they would
more freely and familiarly tell them to one another under
the seal of confession. 'There is nothing,' answered the
Pope, 'which I would not willingly grant you; but in this
I see one inconvenience. It is that confession ought to be
kept secret, and you women would hardly conceal it.'
'Nay,' said they, 'we can keep it very well, and better
than men do.' The same day the Holy Father left in
their keeping a box, in which he had caused to be put a
little linnet, gently praying them to shut it up in some
safe and secret place, promising on the faith of a pope to
grant them what was borne by their petition if they kept
it secret, but, notwithstanding this, enjoining them by a
rigorous prohibition that they should not open it in any
way whatsoever, under pain of ecclesiastical censure and
eternal excommunication. The prohibition was no sooner
made than they were stewing in their minds with impa-
tience to see what was within, and they longed for the
Pope to be outside their gates so that they might devote
their uninterrupted leisure to it. The Holy Father, having
bestowed his benediction upon them, retired to his palace.
He was not yet three steps out of the abbey when the good
ladies, all in a crowd, ran together to open the forbidden
box and to see what was within. The next day the Pope
paid them a visit, with the intention, as they imagined, to
despatch the indult for them; but before beginning that
subject he commanded the box to be brought to him. It
was brought, but the little bird was no longer there. He
then pointed out to them that it was a matter much beyond them to conceal confessions, seeing that they had
not kept secret for so short a time the box that was so
strongly recommended to their discretion."

RABELAIS'S ART

The apologue of the horse and the ass and the story of the labourer and the little devil, both admirably told and with great humour, are considerably longer than this. But as a rule Rabelais's stories are briefly told, and even the longer ones are without digressions or other unnecessary developments. There is, however, one notable exception. The fable of the countryman and his axe, which fills only a page of Æsop, occupies nearly the whole of the long prologue to the Fourth Book, and is rendered with a profusion of detail and an exuberant gusto which even Rabelais has never surpassed.

The use of stories as a regular feature of his narrative was a late development. In the first two books there is only one story, or at any rate only one of any length. It is not till the Third Book that they become numerous. What was the reason for their introduction? Was it because Rabelais felt that the more serious tone of this book required some relief? Or was he moved by some impulse from without? It is impossible to say, but it is worth noting that in the very year (1545) in which he was engaged upon the Third Book there appeared Antoine Le Maçon's successful translation of Boccaccio's *Decameron*. Moreover, a year before this Bonaventure Des Periers had died, leaving behind him a collection of stories, of which possibly

Rabelais may have heard, though they were not printed till many years later. The mention of Des Periers suggests a comparison between the two craftsmen. Both excel in the lively and dramatic conduct of their stories, so that the whole scene lives before one. Both are brief and concise—Rabelais as a rule, Des Periers invariably. Des Periers's art, without being obtrusive, makes its presence clearly felt; Rabelais's greater art cannot be detected, for it is as simple as nature. Des Periers always tries to be amusing, and generally succeeds; Rabelais's note is more varied, for his stories are often told by way of illustration, and not purely for the story's sake. Finally, Des Periers writes in a style which is always deliberately popular; Rabelais changes his style with the subject, but, whatever the subject, his style never lacks distinction.

Great though Rabelais is as a wit and a humourist, it is perhaps in the province of pure fun that his greatest triumphs have been achieved. The account of how Gargantua ate six pilgrims in his salad, the description of the same giant's perplexity as to whether he shall weep over the death of his wife or laugh over the birth of his son, the scene between Panurge and the sheep-merchant, and the same worthy's behaviour in the storm, all move one to laughter not so much by their wit or their humour as by their simple fun. And not only in these continuous episodes but in a thousand unexpected and irrelevant touches we find proof of Rabelais's exuberant gaiety of heart, which bubbles over with mirth and nonsense from sheer inability to contain itself.

Yet this delightful element in Rabelais's genius, this "cataract of laughter", to borrow a phrase of Mr. Meredith's, has proved more of a stumbling-block to Rabelais's readers than perhaps anything else in his book. For nearly three centuries it led the majority of them to regard him as a mere buffoon, and when at last a truer estimate of his work and character began to prevail, it helped to create the equally mistaken view that his laughter is only a mask, and that behind the mask he is all gravity and philosophy. Both these views have their source in the same delusion, that laughter is incompatible with true seriousness. But Rabelais's outlook on the world is none the less serious because he can laugh heartily; nor, on the other hand, because he appreciates to the full the graver issues of life is his laughter less an integral part of his whole being.

"Better is it to write of laughter than of tears,
For laughter is the special gift of man."

301

FRANÇOIS RABELAIS

So he wrote in the verses which he prefixed to the First Book, and the words aptly express his creed. For of all the great masters of laughter hardly one is so entirely free from melancholy. Molière's gaiety can be just as exuberant, but there is an undercurrent of deep melancholy in many of his later comedies; Cervantes's book is shot through and through with melancholy; in Heine it overflows in bitter tears, or hides itself under cruel mockery. Aristophanes alone can compare with Rabelais in the unflagging joyousness of his laughter; if the Frenchman has no portion of the poetic gift which distinguishes his Athenian predecessor, he shares with him his exuberant overflow of good humour, and the power of expressing it in cascadinous outpourings of harmonious language. Thus when Joachim du Bellay spoke of Rabelais as the reincarnation of Aristophanes, he made an apter comparison than he probably realised.

Like Aristophanes, too, Rabelais often indulges in fun which the modern reader, unless he be a thorough-going Rabelaisian, finds exceedingly coarse. It is said in his defence that he is merely following the fashion of his day, that the sixteenth century was not as squeamish as ours in these matters, and that comedy was almost expected to be indecent. All this

is perfectly true, but it is not very compli-
mentary to Rabelais. A man of his intellectual and artistic stature should rise above
the ordinary standard of his contemporaries.
It will be paying him a truer compliment
if we look into the matter a little more closely,
and consider what the nature of his offence really
is. In the first place, then, there is nothing
licentious or immoral in his book; he does
not portray vice in pleasant colours, or excite
the imagination with prurient suggestions.
There are no hints or innuendoes, no transparent veils; his laughter, if coarse, is at any
rate open; he is "naked, and not ashamed".
So far as he merely uses words and expressions
which a more reticent age has banished from
polite society and literature, the defence of
"other times, other manners" is a perfectly
good one. But over and above this there are
some whole chapters—not many, half a dozen
at the most—in which Rabelais, to use La
Bruyère's word, is "inexcusable". Yet, without excusing him, one may offer explanations
for his grossness. It is no doubt due in part to
his medical knowledge, which, with the naïve
pedantry of his age, he delights in displaying
in and out of season. It is also due to his
monastic training, to the absence of all feminine
influences in his life. The refinement of thought

and language in society and literature is naturally woman's work, and it was accomplished
in France, during the first half of the seventeenth
century, mainly by the agency of Madame de
Rambouillet and her famous salon. Even in
Rabelais's day a beginning had been made.
In one of those interesting discussions which
follow the stories of the *Heptameron* it is pretty
well agreed by the speakers that there are
certain words and phrases which no modest
woman ought to use, and Parlamente, who
represents Margaret herself, adds that she
ought not even to listen to them. Though
the stories themselves show that the standard
of modesty was not a very high one, judged
by modern ideas, it was something that the
subject should be discussed at all. But whatever refining influence woman had in those
days, Rabelais missed it. Woman played a
very small part in his life, and in spite of
the sisters of Thelema, and Queen Entelechy,
and the Queen of the Chitterlings, she plays
an insignificant part in his book.

There is a third cause for Rabelais's grossness,
which must not be forgotten, and that is his
conservatism in the matter of literary tradition.
His fun is coarse because coarseness was a traditional element of comic literature. Indeed,
in this respect Rabelais was not more conserva-

tive than other writers. The comic drama of both the Italian and the French Renaissance is not a whit cleaner than *Pantagruel*, and it is immoral into the bargain. It was not till the days of Corneille that French comedy became really decent. Thus Rabelais's offence is, in a large measure, of literary origin, and does not imply a corresponding coarseness either of mind or of conversation. In fact, the whole question is a literary rather than a moral one. It is against Art that Rabelais has sinned. Conforming too faithfully to the literary fashions of his day, courting an immediate popularity by methods unworthy of his genius, he forgot that Art is eternal. And Art has avenged herself. No writer of anything like his greatness is read so little.

Another characteristic of mediæval humour is its cruelty, and here again we find Rabelais continuing the mediæval tradition. The story of Panurge and the sheep ends with the drowning, not only of the sheep-dealer, but of the wholly inoffensive shepherds. Panurge's tricks, which are related with considerable gusto and apparent appreciation, for the most part involve some cruel act. He knocks all the watchmen down "like so many pigs"; he whips the pages without mercy; and his treatment of women shows a coarse malice which is simply fiendish. In the story of Villon and Friar Tappecouc we read how the friar very properly refused to allow Villon a cope and stole for the purpose of a passion-play; and how Villon, to revenge himself, lay in wait for him with a company of those who were to act as devils in the play; and how they jumped out on him, as he rode by, and frightened his young mare with squibs and crackers; and how he was thrown and dragged, and how the mare kicked him till she burst his head right open, and his arms and legs were broken into pieces. This story, from which some of the horrid details are omitted, is appropriately introduced into the longer story of the Seigneur de Basché and the Catchpoles, in which one of the Catchpoles is belaboured with merciless cruelty. Both here, however, and in the account of Brother John's treatment of his foes when he is defending the abbey of Seuilly, Rabelais's main object, no doubt, is to display his anatomical and pathological knowledge. But one reads with a feeling of special repulsion how the little monklings, by Friar John's orders, "cut the throats of those whom he had already crushed". Yet, in spite of all this, Rabelais was for his age a humane man. He objected as strongly as Montaigne to the cruel flogging of children which was

practised by many pedagogues; and when the
schoolmaster in the Island of the Papimanes
whipped his scholars in order that they might
remember the arrival on their shores of the
wonderful travellers who had seen the Pope,
Pantagruel expressed his displeasure in a
"stentorian voice".

These are the blemishes of Rabelais's art,
but in spite of them he is a great artist, and it
will help us to understand his art if we try to
discover how his imagination worked, and what
kind of sensations called forth its fullest powers.
Now, if we consider the episodes in his book
which are most characteristic of his genius,
such as those of Panurge and the sheep-dealer,
Panurge and Thaumast, the storm, Brother
John's defence of the abbey of Seuilly and his
entertainment at dinner by Gargantua, the
"talk of the drinkers", and Bishop Homenaz
and the Decretals, we see that they all portray animated movement. Even the three
last-mentioned episodes, in which the characters do not move from their seats, are not
really exceptions, for in these no small part
of the picture is formed by the bustle of the
attendants, the animated gestures and tones of
the talkers, the clink of the bottles, the gur-
gling sound of the wine. Further, we note that
the success of these marvellous scenes is due

partly to the inimitable conversation. It is
not only that the remarks themselves are
strikingly natural, but we seem actually to
overhear the speakers and to catch their very
tones.

It seems as if Rabelais's imagination were
roused rather by objects in motion than by
objects at rest, and by sounds rather than by
sights. It is not that he went about with his
eyes shut, or that the material world did not
exist for him; far from it. He must have been
a close and accurate observer, or he would
not have gained his remarkable knowledge of
anatomy and his considerable knowledge of
botany, architecture, and other subjects which
require observation. But he observed as a
man of science, and not as a man of imagination. When he describes an object, he
does it by accumulation of details, not as a
poet does, by seizing hold of some vital feature
and making the object live before us in some
"lonely" epithet. His descriptions, it is true,
are generally picturesque, but they are most
picturesque when he is portraying change or
movement. Is it fanciful to suggest that in
his admirable description of the herb Pantagruelion he is stimulated by the idea of growth
inherent in a plant? And even here the similes
are furnished by an intellectual rather than by

a true imaginative process. We are told that "it exceeds the height of a lance"; that the stem is "serrated like slightly fluted columns"; that its leaves "end in points like a Macedonian pike, or a lancet used by surgeons". According to the valuable distinction made by Coleridge and accepted by Wordsworth, and far too lightly dismissed by some latter-day critics, all these descriptive images are products of the "sportive fancy", and not of the creative imagination.

An instructive example of Rabelais's lack of imaginative sensibility to visual impressions is furnished by his treatment of the Eternal City. Though he visited Rome three times, spending there in all from two and a half to three years, and though on his first visit he diligently inspected her ancient monuments with the view of describing them in a guide-book, the only references to them in his book are a bare mention of the Column of Trajan, the Arch of Septimius Severus, and the obelisks. Neither by their intrinsic beauty nor as memorials of fallen grandeur do they seem to have touched his imagination, as they did that of his compatriot and fellow-humanist, Joachim du Bellay. He is equally unmoved by the noble buildings with which the architects of the Renaissance had adorned, and under Paul III.

were still adorning, the Eternal City. He merely notes that St. Peter's was without a roof. Rome seems to have made an abiding impression upon him as a city of many bells, and it is as the Ringing Island that she figures in his book. His sensibility to sound is also shown by his interest in music, which he displays after his wont by the long list of musicians in the prologue to the Fourth Book and by the unfailing harmony of his prose.

There is another quality of Rabelais's imagination which must not be left out of sight. Like Homer and Scott, he excels in the portrayal of lively and vigorous action. A good instance of this is the narrative of the war between Grandgousier and Picrochole. Rabelais's imagination, then, is affected more by sounds than by sights, more by action and animated scenes than by isolated objects. It is lively rather than deep; it plays round its subject rather than penetrates it; it illustrates rather than interprets; it is kindled more readily by crowds and intercourse with men than by solitude and inward contemplation. Above all, it is fanned, like a flame, by expression. With some artists the imaginative process, which is the germ of all art-production, seems to be a complete act wholly distinct from the subsequent work of expression, and artists of this class often find the medium of their particular art inadequate to render the imaginative truth of their spiritual vision. With others the two processes, imagination and expression, appear to be inextricably commingled; their birth is almost simultaneous; and the imagination gathers heat and swiftness from the expression, like chariot-wheels from their own velocity. This is preëminently the case with Rabelais. He is a master of expression. He is as plenteous, as various, as resourceful as Rubens.

The most obvious characteristic of Rabelais's style, the one which cannot fail to strike the most careless reader, is the richness of his vocabulary. This richness is all the more wonderful because Rabelais, at any rate when he was writing his first two books, had no dictionaries to help him. It was not till 1537–1539 that Robert Estienne published his Latin-French and French-Latin dictionaries. Thus in acquiring his prodigious vocabulary Rabelais must have been chiefly helped by his wide reading, by his intimate knowledge of different parts of France, by his insatiable curiosity for every kind of knowledge, especially technical knowledge, and by his accurate ear. His vocabulary is drawn from every conceivable source: archaisms, patois, Italian, Spanish,

Latin, Greek. With careless prodigality he coins hundreds of new words, a few of which have become a permanent possession of the language, while the rest hardly survived their birth. It was the habitual practice with writers of the sixteenth century to use two words to express the same idea, but Rabelais, even in the earlier books, frequently indulges in three, while in the later ones he is even more prodigal. In the prologue to the Third Book, written in 1544, we have, as we have seen, first, a long list of technical terms for various operations and objects of war, and then a string of verbs to describe Diogenes's treatment of his tub. Nor is he content with printing his litanies of nouns or adjectives or verbs in the usual way; he draws them up in columns of two or three, like a general marshalling his troops. He loves puns and alliterations and other repetitions of sound; words have a positive fascination for him, till sometimes, becoming intoxicated, as it were, by their music, he uses them without any precise meaning.

Less obvious than his mastery of words, but even more remarkable, is his mastery of the phrase. Secure in this mastery, he performs feats of construction which none but the greatest writers can attempt with impunity. He not only makes free use of ellipsis in the case of grammatical forms, but he even omits essential words. He does not shrink from parenthesis, that stumbling-block of all writers of the sixteenth century. He strings clause to clause, like the links of a long but firmly welded chain. And his success is astonishing. Sometimes, indeed, the sentence is unduly cumbrous, sometimes slightly obscure, but there is hardly ever any real doubt as to his meaning, and as a rule he is remarkably clear. In one thing he never fails: his phrase, whether long or short, always falls upon the ear with a perfect cadence.

It must be remembered that in Rabelais's day French prose was in a highly fluid and unsettled condition. The attempts made during the fifteenth century by Alain Chartier and his successors to give weight and dignity to the simple, picturesque style of Joinville and Froissart by imitating Latin models had as yet been crowned with only moderate success. Indeed, the pedantry of the *grands rhétoriqueurs*, whose prose, in its endeavour to become more like Latin, had almost ceased to be French, had tended to disgust sensible men who loved their native language with a reform which, after all, was in the right direction. The vocabulary was no less fluctuating than the syntax. When Panurge says of the court-language of Lantern-land that he will "make a pretty dictionary of it, which will not last much longer than a pair of new shoes", he might have been speaking, with almost equal truth, of the French of that day. This variety and disorder, this absence of rule and standard, which to weaker men was a stumbling-block, is to Rabelais a source of strength. Just as in his vocabulary he now coins neologisms with the help of Greek and Latin, now rescues old words from forgotten corners, so in his syntax he uses archaisms and Latinisms whenever it suits him.

It is to this mastery of expression that he owes another remarkable quality of his style— its variety. He is like a skilled musician who can play on several instruments, but who impresses upon all alike the stamp of a vigorous personality. In the first place, his narrative style is a model of straightforward brevity. This is especially noticeable in the account of the war between Grandgousier and Picrochole. What can be more succinct or more business-like than the following recital of Gargantua's attack on La Roche-Clermaud?

"This advice was found good. Therefore he drew out all his army into the open field, putting his reserves on the side of the rising ground. The monk took with him six companies of foot and two hundred men-at-arms, and with great diligence crossed the fen and occupied the ground above the well right up to the highway from Loudun. Meantime the assault went on. Picrochole's men did not know whether it was best to sally forth and receive them, or rather to keep within the town without stirring. But he set out madly with a troop of men-at-arms of his guard, and there was received and treated with great cannon-shot which hailed on the hill-sides; whereupon the Gargantuists retired to the valley in order better to give way to the artillery. Those of the town defended themselves the best they could, but their shots passed over and beyond without striking any one. Some of his company that had escaped the artillery set fiercely upon our men, but got little by it, for they were all received betwixt the files and dashed to the ground. Seeing this, they would have retreated, but in the meanwhile the monk had seized upon the pass; whereupon they took to flight without order or discipline. Some would have given them chase, but the monk held them back, through fear lest, as they followed the fugitives, they might lose their ranks and at this pass those from the town should set upon them. Then after waiting some space, and none appearing to encounter him, he sent Duke Phrontistes to advise Gargantua to advance so as to gain the hill on the left, to cut off the retreat of Picrochole by the gate on that side. This Gargantua did with all diligence, and sent thither four legions of the company of Sebastus; but they could not reach the height so soon, but they must needs meet face to face Picrochole and those who were dispersed with him. Then they charged them stoutly; notwithstanding, they were much damaged by those who were on the walls, by their archery and artillery. Seeing this, Gargantua went with a strong party to their relief; and his artillery began to play upon the walls in this quarter so strongly that the whole force of the town was withdrawn thither."

There is not an unnecessary word; the whole affair is related with a military precision worthy of Wellington, and with a crisp brevity of style which rivals that of Cæsar or Thucydides.

As a specimen of a different style, we may take a short passage from the speech of Ulrich Gallet, the envoy sent by Grandgousier to remonstrate with Picrochole:

"What madness, then, stirs thee now, breaking through all alliance, treading under foot all friendship, transgressing all right, to invade his land as an enemy without having been by him or his in any way injured, irritated, or provoked? Where is faith? Where is law? Where is reason? Where is humanity? Where is the fear of God? Thinkest thou that these wrongs are hidden from the eternal spirits and from the Supreme God who is the just rewarder of all our undertakings? If thou dost so think, thou deceivest thyself, for all things will come before His judgment."

Eloquence naturally loses a good deal when it is translated, but even in the above version we can feel the vigour, the rapidity of movement, and the absence of bombast which mark the whole speech. It may be noted that both in speeches and in other passages of grave and formal eloquence Rabelais Latinises considerably, alike in vocabulary and in construction. This is especially the case with letters; indeed, in the letter which Pantagruel wrote from Medamothi to Gargantua this habit is carried to such a pitch that the result is hardly more like French than the utterances of the

Limousin student. On the other hand, it is possible that Rabelais is here deliberately imitating the epistolary style of his day, which was stilted and obscure beyond all conception.

Of Rabelais's most daring flights, when without thought of Latin models he trusts solely to his own art and inspiration, it is impossible to give any adequate idea in a translation. Some of the finest examples of these dithyrambic outbursts, in which Rabelais's prose acquires all the imaginative sweep, the emotional vibration, the sustained music of lyrical poetry, and yet remains true prose, will be found in Panurge's panegyric on debtors and in the account of the plant Pantagruelion, passages from both of which have already been quoted.

If these lyrical utterances best represent the idealistic side of Rabelais's genius, his realism finds no less consummate expression in his conversations. The "talk of the drinkers", the feast to which Gargantua invited Brother John, the dinner at which Bishop Homenaz entertained the travellers, the dialogue between Panurge and the sheep-dealer, and, in a more sober vein, the conversation on board the vessel during the calm—these have already been referred to as masterpieces in the art of conversational mimicry. But room must be found for part of Brother John's inimitable discourse at Gargantua's feast:

"We shall not have many goslings to eat this year. Ha, my friend, give me some of that pig. Diavolo! there is no more must: *Germinavit radix Jesse*. I renounce my life on it; I die of thirst. This wine is none of the worst. What wine did you drink in Paris? I give myself to the devil if I did not once keep open house to all comers. Do you know Brother Claude of the Haults Barrois? Oh, the jolly companion that he was! But what fly hath stung him? He doth nothing but study since I don't know when. I do not study, for my part. In our abbey we never studied for fear of the mumps. Our late abbot used to say that it was a monstrous thing to see a learned monk. Pardy, sir, my friend, *magis magnos clericos non sunt magis magnos sapientes*. You never saw so many hares as there are this year. I have not been able to come by a goshawk or a tassel-gentle anywhere in the world. My Lord de la Bellonière had promised me a lanner-hawk, but he wrote to me not long ago that he had become pursy. The partridges will eat up our ears this year. I take no pleasure in fowling with a tunnel-net, for I take cold at it. If I do not run, if I do not bustle about, I am not at ease. True it is that in jumping over the hedges and bushes my frock leaves some jags behind. I have got a rare greyhound; devil a bit a hare escapes him. A groom was leading him to my Lord Maulevrier, and I robbed him of him. Did I do wrong?"

The fun and humour of this speech are obvious; it is more important to notice that it is characteristic of the speaker. For it is one of the great excellences of Rabelais's art that his three principal characters are nearly always recognisable by their speeches. It is not merely that what they say is in keeping with their character, but each has his own characteristic mode of speech, from which he seldom, if ever, departs. Pantagruel is deliberate and to the point; his language is grave and sober, and his sentences are compact and well turned. Brother John is bluff, homely, and inconsequent. Panurge is far the greatest talker of the three. He talks for talking's sake. But he is never tedious or long-winded; when he is really in vein, he uses short, disconnected sentences, scintillating with gaiety and wit, like the rapid fire of a Maxim gun. His talk is the very essence of wit, for it is the natural expression of an abnormally quick and lively intellect. He is intoxicated by the rapidity with which his nimble and well-furnished mind pours forth argument and illustration. In his delight in the logic of words he is blind to the sterner logic of facts.

In spite of the gusto with which Rabelais portrays Panurge's delightful loquacity, he doubtless regarded it, and meant his readers to regard it, as one of the defects of Panurge's character. The famous panegyric on debts and debtors is no doubt in part intended as a satire on paradoxical utterance. "I understand," says Pantagruel, somewhat coldly, on its conclusion, "and you seem to me to be a good utterer of commonplaces and well affected to your cause. But should you preach and advocate it from now till Whitsuntide, in the end you will be astonished to find how you have persuaded me not a jot."

In the prologue to *Gargantua* Rabelais tells us that he never employed more time on the composition of his book than that which was appointed for his "bodily refection, to wit, whilst eating and drinking". M. Faguet takes this remark seriously, but we may remember that Montaigne makes somewhat similar disclaimers of literary ambition, whereas, in fact, as he grew interested in his work he lavished on it all the loving care of a conscientious craftsman. So, too, it would be difficult to believe that Rabelais, with all his delight in language and his keen perception of its capabilities, did not bring to his task the same artistic spirit. It is true that he often seems to pour forth his words with careless profusion, but there are those who paint with a full brush and there are those who paint with a thin one, and the former are not less true artists than the latter.

But to say that Rabelais is an artist is not to imply that he has the faculty of self-criticism. That was wanting to his art, as to most of the literary art of France in the sixteenth century. Hence we find in him, as in nearly all his contemporaries, stretches of dull flat and barren waste interspersed between the green pastures and purple mountains. "He is unequal, and wanting in measure; he lacks taste; . . . he forgets himself, he is negligent. . . . He has all the characteristics of natural genius; he has spontaneity, imperturbability, and an art which is in a manner unconscious of itself, and which is certainly uncritical. . . . He accepts herculean tasks, and triumphs over them. He stops his work, abandons it, forgets it. He returns to it as if he had not left it for an hour." These are the words in which a great critic of painting, himself a painter, Eugène Fromentin, sums up the art of Rubens. Might they not be applied, with hardly the change of a word, to the art of Rabelais?

CHAPTER XI

WE saw that in the prologue to *Gargantua*
Rabelais urges his readers not to regard his book
simply as a story of mirth and adventure, but
to penetrate beneath the surface and, like a
dog with a marrow-bone, get at the "substantial marrow". "For you will find," he says,
"another taste and a more abstruse learning,
which will reveal to you very high sacraments
and dread mysteries, as much in that which
concerns our religion as also the public polity
and domestic economy." According to M.
Faguet, Rabelais is here only laughing at his
readers, and there is nothing in his book either
abstruse or enigmatic. It is simply an amusing book, written at his odd moments to divert
himself and his patients. His philosophy is
merely the expression of ordinary common
sense, but it is "neither original nor profound,
nor even very useful". If this view be correct,
the title of this chapter is a misnomer. But
for the majority of those who have read Rabelais with some attention. he is something more
than a story-teller of genius, and there is much

in his book which invites that closer study recommended by the author, and from which we may extract to our profit the "substantial marrow". Only we must not fall into an error similar to that of the commentators of the earlier part of the last century, who saw in every character some historical personage, and in every trivial incident some historical event. We must not expect from Rabelais, any more than from Shakespeare or Montaigne, a complete system of philosophy. We must remember that during the twenty years which elapsed from the time when he began to write his book his opinions must have undergone considerable modification. We must remember that he is essentially a lover of laughter, and that it is often difficult to say whether he is simply amusing himself or whether his outward buffoonery conceals an inner meaning. There can be no doubt that the censorship of the Sorbonne and the Parliament and the ever impending danger of prosecution for heresy made it impossible for him, a martyr "to the stake exclusively", to speak out openly and boldly on religious subjects. In one of the dialogues of Des Periers's *Cymbalum Mundi* the speakers are two dogs, Hylactor and Pamphagus, who have recently acquired the faculty of speech, by which the writer evidently

FRANÇOIS RABELAIS

signifies freedom of thought, emancipation
from authority and tradition. Hylactor is
represented as anxious to show off his new
accomplishment. "What," he says to his
companion, "have you not yet made known
to people that you can speak?" "No," replies Pamphagus. "And why?" "Because I
don't care to; I prefer to keep silence." M.
Frank has ingeniously conjectured that Hylactor, or the Barker, stands for Étienne Dolet,
and Pamphagus, the All-devourer, that is to
say, the devourer of all knowledge, for Rabelais.
Whether this be correct or not, the prudent
attitude of Pamphagus certainly bears some
resemblance to that of Rabelais. We must
remember, too, that Rabelais is an imaginative
writer, a poet in all but "the accomplishment of
verse", and that his deepest thoughts often find
expression in lyrical outbursts, which, height-
ened as they are by the artist's delight in the
exercise of his faculty, do not necessarily represent a reasoned or abiding view of life. Finally,
we must remember that much of Rabelais's
book is cast in a dramatic form, and that
though his characters, sometimes one and sometimes another, are undoubtedly at times the
mouthpieces of his own experiences and his
own opinions, we can as a rule only conjecture
when this is the case. He might fairly have

defended the irreverent remarks of Panurge and Brother John, or the unorthodox views of some of his other characters, on the plea of dramatic necessity.

With this much by way of proviso, we may now proceed to consider Rabelais's views, first on matters connected with the "public polity", and then on religion and the destiny of man. As regards the constitution of the state, he seems to have regarded monarchy as practically the best form of government, but he had no belief in the divine right of the monarch. He held that kings, like other members of the body politic, have duties to perform, and that the neglect of them ought in extreme cases to be punished with deposition. Picrochole and Anarchus, the two bad rulers of his book, end their days the one as a day-labourer, the other as a hawker of green sauce. He would certainly have answered in the affirmative the question which was so hotly discussed in France after the massacre of St. Bartholomew, as to whether it is ever lawful to depose an unjust ruler.

His idea of a just ruler is partly set forth in the first chapter of the Third Book, where he controverts "the erroneous opinion of certain tyrannical spirits" (alluding, doubtless, to Machiavelli, whose *Prince*, dedicated to the father of Catherine de' Medici, had been published in 1532) "that the proper manner of retaining newly conquered countries is to pillage the people, racking them with taxes and ruling them with rods of iron". Then, after citing instances to the contrary, he goes on to say that "a conqueror cannot reign more happily, be he king, prince, or philosopher, than by making justice second his valour. . . . His justice will appear in that by the good-will and affection of the people he will give laws, publish edicts, establish religion, and do right to every one." In the characters of Grandgousier, Gargantua, and Pantagruel we have a more complete expression of his ideas in a concrete shape. They are just, merciful, and tolerant. They are lovers of peace, and for the sake of peace are ready to make large concessions to neighbouring monarchs. But they are versed in the whole art of war, and when their peaceful overtures have been rejected, they carry war into the enemy's territory, and do not stay their hand till they have brought him to his knees. It is from Pantagruel, though except during his father's mysterious sojourn in the Land of the Fairies he is only the heir apparent, not the reigning monarch, that we best learn Rabelais's conception of the perfect ruler. He is not only the most virtuous man in his kingdom, but he is also the best informed, the wisest, and the most enlightened. He has studied every branch of learning, has made himself acquainted with every kind of art and handicraft, and has become proficient in every accomplishment, in order that he may fit himself for his high position. He will bring to the throne not only philosophy, thus realising Plato's idea that philosophers should be kings, but a practical knowledge of affairs. Half a century later Rabelais might have found a monarch approaching in some respects to his ideal. Henri IV. had the capacity, the tolerance, the endurance, the kindliness, the care for his subjects' welfare which Rabelais demanded, but he had not Pantagruel's learning and cultivation, and in one respect, at least, nothing of his self-control. With his more ambitious projects Rabelais would have had little sympathy. He strongly disapproves of wars undertaken for the sake of conquest. In the days of the long rivalry between Charles V. and François I., he could boldly say that "the time has gone by for conquering kingdoms to the loss of our nearest Christian brother; this imitation of the Alexanders, Hannibals, and Cæsars of old is contrary to the profession of the Gospel". As we have seen, the whole of chapter xxxiii of *Gargantua* is an exquisite satire on the schemes of universal conquest. There is, of course, nothing strikingly original in these views. They may have been inspired, as has been suggested, by passages in the writings of More and Erasmus, or, as seems equally possible, they may have been held by Rabelais in common with these enlightened thinkers. In either case it is not surprising that Rabelais should have identified himself with the best thought of his age.

As time went on, Rabelais seems to have become more conservative in his political attitude, more inclined to acquiesce in the existing order of things. This may be ascribed partly to a natural tendency to become more conservative with advancing years and partly to his close intercourse with statesmen like Guillaume and Jean du Bellay, who were actively engaged in the work of constructive government. Or perhaps the true explanation is rather that his interest was now given to deeper and more abstruse questions, and that in order to gain a hearing for their discussion it was necessary to propitiate the ruling powers. Thus we find him, in the Fourth Book, as has been already pointed out, paying dexterous compliments to Henri II. and the Duke of Guise and generally supporting the policy of the government.

When we turn to the consideration of Rabelais's views on religion and philosophy, a more difficult task confronts us. It is here especially that we need the premonitory caution given above. We must also be on our guard against certain prejudices which may tend to warp our judgment. Especially must we bear in mind that irreverence does not necessarily imply either disbelief or impiety. Men often laugh at what they love, and make jests on what they reverence. "The man doth fear God," says Don Pedro, of Benedick, "howsoever it seems not in him by some large jests he will make." Rabelais certainly "feared God". In one place he speaks of the "unique and supreme affection which man owes to God". In the Third Book he cites the famous definition of God as "an infinite and intellectual sphere of which the centre is everywhere and the circumference nowhere". But he finely supplements the definition with the words, "to whom no new thing happeneth, whom nothing escapeth, from whom nothing falleth away, to whom all time is present". It is, however, in the *Prognostication* that we find the most striking passage on God's relation to the world and to human affairs.

"Believe that in this year there will be no other governor of the world than God the Creator, who rules and orders everything by His Divine word (by which all

things exist in their nature, property, and condition), and
without whose maintenance and government all things
would be reduced in a moment to nothing, as from nothing
all things have by Him been brought into being. For
from Him proceeds, in Him exists, and through Him is
perfected all Being, all Good, all Life, all Motion. . . .
And neither Saturn, nor Mars, nor Jupiter, nor any other
planet, nor angels, nor saints, nor men, nor devils will have
any virtue, efficacy, power, or influence unless God give it
to them of His good pleasure; according to the saying of
Avicenna, that secondary causes have no influence or
action at all unless the First Cause influence them
thereto."

Rabelais believes, too, in the efficacy of
prayer. "All true Christians," says Gargantua,
"of all conditions, in all places, and at all times
pray to God, and the Spirit prays and inter-
cedes for them, and God is gracious to them."
And again, "I have hope in God that He will
hear our prayers, seeing the firm faith in which
we make them, and that He will accomplish
our wishes, provided they be moderate."
But we must not only pray to God; we must
coöperate with Him. God helps those who
help themselves. This view is set forth by
Epistemon, immediately after the storm, in
the Fourth Book: "We ought without ceasing
to implore, invoke, pray, beseech, and sup-
plicate Him, but not make an end there; we
ought on our part likewise to do our endeavour
and, as the holy apostle saith, to be workers

together with Him." Friar John agrees, in his own fashion: "I give myself to the devil if the close at Seuilly would not have been quite stripped of its grapes and destroyed if I had done nothing but sing a psalm, as did the other monks, and had not succoured the vine with blows of my cross-staff against the marauders of Lerné."

With regard to immortality, he represents the old poet Raminagrobis declaring, as he lay on his death-bed, with "a joyous, open countenance and bright look", that he was already contemplating and tasting "the happiness and felicity which the good God has prepared for His faithful and elect in the other life, which is eternal". In the Fourth Book there is a remark on the same subject which has sometimes been misunderstood. "I believe," says Pantagruel, in the course of the discussion on the demons or heroes who inhabit the Isle of the Macræons, "that all intellectual souls (*âmes intellectives*) are exempt from the scissors of Atropos. All are immortal, whether they be of angels, demons, or men." It has been suggested that by "intellectual souls" Rabelais means those that have freed themselves from the domination of the flesh, and that he is expressing here a belief in the immortality of a select few. But there is no reason for attribu-

ting to him so aristocratic and so unphilo-
sophical a doctrine. The term "intellectual
souls" is one invented by Aristotle to denote
the quality in the soul or vital principle of
man which distinguishes it from that of beasts
and that of plants. Thus Pantagruel's remark is
a simple affirmation of the immortality of man.

It was the above remark which led Pantagruel to relate the story of the death of Pan,
taken from Plutarch's *On the Cessation of
Oracles*, and to follow Eusebius in referring it
to the death of "the great Saviour of the faithful . . . seeing that He is our All, all that we
are, all our life, all that we have. . . . He is
the good Pan, the Great Shepherd." And
then we are told that Pantagruel "having
ended this discourse remained in silence and
profound meditation. A little while after we
saw the tears run down from his eyes as large as
ostrich-eggs." From this as from all Rabelais's
references to Christ, notably in the almanacs
and in the letters of Grandgousier and Gargantua, it is difficult to avoid drawing the conclusion that he not only held the character of
Christ in the highest reverence, but that he
believed in His divinity. Finally, the more
one reads in his book, the more one is impressed
by the essentially Christian note of many of
its passages.

But what were his relations to the Church,
and especially what was his attitude in the great
controversy which began to divide Christen-
dom during the last years of his residence at
Fontenay-le-Comte? Like the great majority of
his fellow-humanists, he saw clearly the evils
from which the Church was suffering in France
—a materialised and mechanical ritual, an idle
and ignorant clergy, a secularised and non-
resident episcopate. He hated the monks, and
he hated that pillar of orthodoxy, the Sorbonne.
He therefore naturally welcomed the first signs
of reform—the early writings of Luther, the
preaching of Lefèvre d'Étaples and his friends,
the favour shown to the movement by the
King's sister, Margaret of Angoulême, and
more fitfully by the King himself. Did he go
further than this? A little, perhaps. According to Calvin, "he heard the Gospel gladly"
(*gustavit Evangelium*), and these words must
be taken in conjunction with the fact that
the Protestant movement in France began
with the work of Lefèvre d'Étaples and his
friends at Meaux, and that this work chiefly
consisted in preaching the Gospel, or, in their
own words, in "preaching Christ from the
sources". It was this side of the movement
that appealed most strongly to Rabelais. Just
as he saw in Alciati the purifier of Roman law

from the embroidery of the glossators, so he welcomed the Meaux preachers as purgers of the primitive text of the Gospel from the glosses and interpretations of the canonists. This view is clearly set forth in the remarkable prayer uttered by Pantagruel, just before his combat with the giant Loupgarou. It concludes with the following words:

"Therefore if it should please Thee at this hour to come to my help, as in Thee is my whole trust and hope, I make a vow unto Thee that through all countries, whether in this land of Utopia or elsewhere, wherein I shall have power and authority, I will cause Thy Holy Gospel to be preached, purely, simply, and entirely; so that the deceits of a rabble of popelings and false prophets, who have by human constitutions and depraved inventions poisoned the whole world, shall be exterminated from about me."

The most Protestant in tone of the five books is *Gargantua*. Thus Grandgousier, in his letter to his son, says that the human will and understanding "cannot choose but be wicked if they be not continually guided by Divine grace"—which is the very essence of Protestant theology; and at the close of the same letter he adopts the Protestant usage of the name of Christ, without the definite article. At the famous dinner to which Friar John is invited, Gargantua contrasts the lazy monk with the good Evangelical doctor. In the inscription over the great gate of the abbey of Thelema, among those who are invited to enter are those "who preach the Holy Gospel".

"Here you shall find a tower of refuge against the error of your foes, who with their glosses and false language seek to poison the world. Enter, then, that here we may establish our profound faith, and then confound by speech and writing the enemies of the Holy Word."

It must be remembered that *Gargantua* was written during the years 1533 and 1534, when the prospect of a peaceful reform of the Church in France was at its highest point. During the whole of Lent, 1533, Gérard Roussel, one of Lefèvre's friends, was preaching daily in the Louvre to large congregations, with the open support of Margaret of Angoulême, now Queen of Navarre, and with the favour, it was said, of Jean du Bellay, the new Bishop of Paris; and when Noel Beda and some other doctors of the Sorbonne began to stir up the populace to sedition, and even ventured to accuse the King and Queen of Navarre of heresy, François I., on hearing of the matter, banished them from the city. Though the scandal caused by Cop's Latin oration, coinciding as it did with the conference held between the French King and the Pope, provoked a sharp attack on the Protestants towards the close of the year, it did not go beyond imprisonment, or last be-

yond the first month of the new year. During
Lent of 1534 Evangelical doctrines were again
preached in the Louvre, and to congregations
that were even larger than those of the preceding year. Many members of the humanist
circle attended the sermons. Then came the
mission of Guillaume du Bellay to Germany,
with the object of concerting with the German
theologians some *via media* of reconciliation.
He was so far successful that when he returned
to France at the beginning of the autumn, he
brought with him a paper drawn up by Melanchthon, in which the various points in dispute
were discussed and means of arranging them
were suggested. It was no wonder, then, if
Rabelais, who, it will be recollected, paid his
first visit to Rome in the early part of 1534,
in the company of Jean du Bellay, shared to
the full the sympathies of his humanist friends
with the reform movement.

Then came the Affair of the Placards (October, 1534), and with it the downfall of the
hopes of those who looked to a peaceful settlement of the great controversy. Rabelais,
suspected as he was of Protestant sympathies,
had to go into hiding for eight months, and
then accompanied Jean du Bellay on a second
visit to Rome, from which he did not return
till March, 1536. Calvin's *Institution* had just

been published. In place of the somewhat
nebulous and inconsistent teaching of Lefèvre
d'Étaples and his friends, Rabelais now found
a body of clearly defined doctrines, linked
together with logical precision and set forth
with a lucidity of reasoning hitherto unknown
in French literature. Before long the irrecon-
cilable cleavage that had taken place between
the two parties was evident. Moderate men
could no longer hope to reform the Church
from within. They had come to the parting
of the ways; they must choose between the
two alternatives, between their political and
their religious sympathies, between the un-
reformed Church of the majority of the nation
and the reformed Church of a fragment.

Rabelais, who was primarily a humanist, and
to whom the unity of the nation seemed of
greater importance than any particular form of
creed or ritual, chose, like the majority of his
fellow-humanists, to adhere to the Church of
his forefathers. And in this choice he must
have been confirmed by Calvin's *Institution*. A
perusal of it, or even a knowledge of its leading
features, must have convinced him how profoundly their views differed. In spite of what
he says, in the passage quoted above, as to the
necessity of Divine grace, and without laying
too much stress on the belief in the natural vir-

tue of well-bred and well-educated men and women which appears in his picture of the abbey of Thelema, we may confidently say that he was very far from sharing Calvin's belief in the innate corruption of man. Rather, like the other leaders of the Renaissance, he had a firm conviction of man's virtue and dignity. Secondly, he must have been alienated from Calvin by the divergence of their views on the question of religious tolerance. Rabelais, as a humanist, had welcomed Protestantism as a vindication of the principles of free inquiry and individualism. In the abbey of Thelema there was no place of common worship, but each member of the community worshipped in his private chapel according to his own pleasure and free will. To Rabelais, therefore, Calvin's intolerance must have seemed a violation of the right of free inquiry equally unjustifiable with that of the Catholic Church. He must also have regarded with peculiar repugnance the rigid discipline in morals which Calvin had imposed upon pleasure-loving Geneva. For, like the whole Renaissance, Rabelais underrated the value and importance of moral sternness; he forgot that by self-restraint and self-discipline are built up the characters of strong men and strong nations. Though Pantagruel himself is strictly virtuous alike in word and in deed, he allows too much license to Panurge.

While, however, Rabelais rejected French Protestantism as a creed, he continued to regard with favour some of its practices. M. Lefranc has noticed that the religious service which Pantagruel held on board his vessel at the beginning of the voyage is entirely Protestant in character, consisting as it does of a brief exhortation, a prayer, and a favourite Protestant psalm. Moreover, Pantagruel himself, without the help of any priest, read the exhortation, and possibly also, though this is left doubtful, offered up the prayer. Later on in the same book, in the story of the little devil and the labourer of Popefig-land, the little devil complains that students have recently added the *Bible* to their studies, and that "for this reason we cannot draw one of them to the devil, and I believe that if the hypocrite monks do not help us by taking their St. Paul from their hands by threats, violence, and burnings, we shall get no more to nibble at down below". Thus Rabelais retained to the end of his life his belief in the importance of the study of the *Bible*, differing from Montaigne, who regarded the diffusion of the Holy Scriptures by means of a translation into the vernacular as "more dangerous than helpful". Montaigne, too, objected to the promiscuous singing of psalms, and would certainly not have approved of Pantagruel's service.

There was nothing in these views to prevent Rabelais from being a loyal son of the Church. And indeed, nowhere in his book is there any satire, open or covert, on the principal doctrines of the Roman Catholic Church, on the worship of the Virgin and the saints, on Purgatory or confession or the mass. Moreover, even when he was leading a wandering life from university to university, he occasionally celebrated mass and performed other offices of the Church, while for two years he held a permanent cure as a parish priest. It may be said that the orthodoxy of his book, such as it is, was dictated by prudence, and that it implies at the most an outward conformity to the doctrines of the Church of Rome. It may be so; but Rabelais actually administered the rites of that Church, and to accuse him of not believing in its main doctrines is to bring against him a charge of hypocrisy and dishonourable conduct for which there is no evidence, and which is wholly foreign to what we know of his character.

When, however, Rabelais asserts, in the letter to the Cardinal de Châtillon prefixed to the Fourth Book, that there is not a word of heresy in it, we must remember that such was not the view taken either by the Sorbonne, which censured it within a month of its publication, or by the Paris Parliament, which prohibited its sale. Their action is hardly surprising, for it is in this very book that we have the violent onslaught on Lent and fasting, the observance of which was accounted in those days one of the surest tests of orthodoxy. To a breach of it Clément Marot owed his first imprisonment; and when at the beginning of the reign of Charles IX. Catherine de' Medici and her Court wished to display their Protestant sympathies, they not only listened to sermons during Lent—a most un-Catholic proceeding, in the eyes of the orthodox—but they ostentatiously abstained from fasting. On the other hand, there is nothing in Rabelais's satire on the more extravagant pretensions of the Papacy or the warlike character of some of the previous popes which does not accord with the attitude of France towards the Vatican at the time of the publication of the book. It is merely the protest of a good Gallican against Ultramontanism. It gives the same support to Henri II. in his quarrel with Julius III. that Pierre Gringore gave to Louis XII. in his quarrel with Julius II. forty years before.

Rabelais, then, if we go by the plain evidence before us, was what he professed to be:

FRANÇOIS RABELAIS

a loyal servant of the Church, not over-sub-
missive to authority, holding his own opinions
on less essential matters, but, as to the central
doctrines of the Faith, a true Catholic. But
can we penetrate further into his beliefs and
hopes? Can we follow him into regions beyond
the limits of the Church's teaching, and discover his opinions on topics about which she is
silent or has given vague and unsatisfying answers? It is in the quest of Panurge that some
commentators have claimed to find the key to
Rabelais's philosophy, and it is certainly here,
if anywhere, that we may hope for success.
But before making the attempt it is essential to
bear in mind once more the caution given at
the beginning of this chapter. Rabelais is not
a systematic philosopher. His speculations do
not profess to have any logical cohesion, or to
lead up to any definite and sure conclusion.
They are merely the inspired utterances of an
imaginative writer, all the more valuable, all
the more suggestive, because in matters which
lie beyond the ken of human knowledge they
claim neither consistency nor finality.

Let us recall the object of Panurge's quest.
He was anxious to marry, without having any
particular woman in view. But before taking
any further steps he wanted to be assured on
three points. Would his wife, whoever she was,

be faithful to him? Would she beat him? Would she rob him? Now, apart from their connection with the controversy as to the character of women which at that time was occupying public attention, these questions have no particular interest. We may therefore fairly assume, without being accused of looking for allegory where none is intended, that they are symbolical of some larger inquiry. First, can man foretell the future? and then, as corollaries to this, what are the relations between man and the unseen world, and what is man's destiny?

In his search for a definite answer to his questions, Panurge resorts to various methods of foretelling the future, and consults various classes of men. But all his methods may be included in two categories, supernatural and natural. Under the first come different forms of divination, such as dice, Virgilian lots, dreams, and the utterances of those who are supposed to have the faculty of second sight. The second category is formed by the opinions of those who seem particularly qualified to form a judgment on such a subject: a philosopher, a theologian, a doctor, and a lawyer. Now, the first class of answers are invariably unfavourable to Panurge, while the second agree in making the result depend partly upon the character and upbringing of the lady chosen by Panurge, and partly upon Panurge's own conduct after marriage. In other words, Panurge must be the arbiter of his own destiny. But Panurge is equally dissatisfied with both kinds of answers, with the former because they are unfavourable, and with the latter because they are contingent on his own actions. His refusal to accept an answer unless it is favourable is an illustration of the words in the parable of the rich man and Lazarus: "If they hear not Moses and the prophets, neither will they be persuaded, though one rose from the dead." For in the majority of the cases the answer given to Panurge is perfectly unambiguous, and he rejects it, not because he questions the prophetic powers of the person whom he has consulted, but because he insists on interpreting the answer in a sense contrary to the obvious one. Men ask for an authoritative revelation—this, at least, seems to be Rabelais's meaning—but if they had one, would they necessarily believe it? However incontestable the demonstration of truth might seem to the majority, there would always be found a Panurge to contest it. "If Heaven gives me a warning," says Don Juan, in Molière's play, when the spectre appears to him, "it must speak a little more clearly, if it wishes me to understand the warning."

Moreover, Panurge is not satisfied with a conditional promise, the fulfilment of which depends on his own conduct. "Marry a virtuous woman," says, in effect, the theologian, "live virtuously and chastely yourself, and she will be faithful to you." But this does not suit Panurge. He does not believe in the existence of a virtuous woman, and he does not wish to live virtuously himself. To interpret the allegory, he wants to lead a sinful life in this world, and then to enter on eternal bliss. His religion—and it must be remembered that he is scrupulously orthodox—is the ordinary religion of his day. It is purely mechanical, and has no connection with morality. To sin, to confess, to be absolved, and then to sin again, and so on till the final scene, with the last confession, the last absolution, the last rites of the Church, the devil cheated and heaven won—that is Panurge's religion.

The first part of the quest furnishes Rabelais with an opportunity of pouring forth his learning on the various methods of ascertaining the future that have been practised in ancient and modern times, and of satirising the credulity of those who believed in them. Much of this has mainly an antiquarian interest, but it must be remembered that all the methods employed by Panurge still found favour in

Rabelais's day. Even the Sibyl of Panzoust, in spite of her classical title, is only an ordinary witch; and, indeed, there is a tradition that an old woman who was reputed to be a witch lived at Panzoust, seven miles east of Chinon. The use of Virgilian lots, as they were called, was common in the sixteenth century, and like the casting of dice, another form of the lot, was a favourite means of ascertaining the will of God.

On the subject of divination by dreams Pantagruel is full of learning. He begins his exposition with a list of the ancient authorities on the subject, of whom the principal is Artemidorus Daldianus, a Greek writer who lived at Rome under Antoninus Pius and Marcus Aurelius, when the belief in dreams was at its height. Rabelais's attitude towards this method of divination is much more sympathetic than towards any of the others. His explanation of the matter is as follows:

"When the body sleeps and the digestion is in all parts completed, nothing being necessary till the waking up, our soul takes its pastime and revisits its native country, which is heaven. From there it receives a notable participation of its first divine origin, and in contemplation of God . . . [here occurs the famous definition referred to above] notes not only what has passed in things moving here below, but also things to come, and then by means of the body's senses and organs setting them forth to its friends, that soul is termed vaticinating and prophetic."

As regards all the other methods of divination experimented with by Panurge, Rabelais's standpoint is purely rationalistic. Especially noteworthy is his disbelief in astrology. Already, in his Second Book, he had by the mouth of Gargantua stigmatised it as "a cheat and a vanity", and now he turns his satire against Her Trippa (evidently Cornelius Agrippa), who is represented as an expert in astrology, chiromancy, geomancy (or divination from earthquakes), and other similar arts. This attitude towards astrology is remarkable, because not only did there exist a wide-spread belief in it in Rabelais's day, but the belief was shared by men of real intellectual eminence. Agrippa himself was astrologer to Louise of Savoy, the mother of François I. Nostradamus, the famous astrologer of Catherine de' Medici, who had begun to write his famous prophecies in Rabelais's lifetime, was a physician of considerable skill and distinction. Jerome Cardan, also a physician, but more famous as a mathematician, believed firmly in astrology and wrote treatises on the subject. Jean Bodin, who in spite of his belief in witchcraft was one of the ablest thinkers of the sixteenth century, has a long chapter in his great work *On the State* (*Six Livres de la République*) in which, though he points out the defects in the astrological schemes of Cardan and other writers on the subject, he fully admits the theoretical possibility of an astrological science. Servetus, the forerunner of Harvey, gave public lectures on astrology at Paris, till he was stopped by a decree of the Parliament. In fact, almost the only scientific contemporary of Rabelais who rejected the current belief in astrology was Paracelsus.

Panurge, having failed to obtain satisfactory answers to his questions in his own country, determines to consult the oracle of the Bottle. During the voyage the object of his quest remains in abeyance, and we hear nothing more of it till the travellers arrive at their destination. This does not happen till the Fifth Book, the genuineness of which is, as we have seen, still under controversy. Those, however, who regard the concluding chapters of this book not only as Rabelais's genuine work, but as bearing the stamp of his genius in a remarkable degree, will find the answer of the Bottle and the ensuing explanation of the priestess Bacbuc of great importance for the determination of Rabelais's philosophy.

It will be remembered that the answer of the Bottle is simply the word "Drink", and that when Panurge, who is no wiser than he was before, asks for the interpretation, the only one vouchsafed to him is a draught of Falernian wine. Then the priestess takes up her parable, and after some remarks, to which reference will be made later, proceeds as follows:

" 'We maintain that not laughing but drinking is the special property of man. I do not say drinking, simply and absolutely, for so also the beasts drink; I mean drinking wine, delicious, fresh wine. Note, my friends, that by wine man becomes divine, and there is no argument so sure, no art of divination less fallacious. Your academics assert this when they give the etymology of wine, the Greek word for which they say is like *Vis*, strength, power, because it fills the soul with all truth, all knowledge, and all philosophy. If you have noticed what is written in Ionic letters over the gate of the temple, you may have understood that in wine is truth hidden. The Holy Bottle sends you thither; be yourselves the interpreters of your undertaking.'

" ' 'Tis impossible,' said Pantagruel, 'to speak better than does the venerable Pontiff. This much I told you when you spoke to me of it at the beginning.' "

Now, at the very outset of the inquiry Pantagruel had said to Panurge, "Are you not assured of your own will? The chief point lies in that; all the rest is a matter of chance, and depends upon the predestined dispositions of Heaven." And again later, with reference to the reply of Raminagrobis to Panurge's questions: "I have not seen an answer which pleases me more. He means to say briefly that in the enterprise of marriage every man must be arbiter of his own thoughts and take counsel of himself." Thus Panurge receives no specific answer to his questions. His success in matrimony must depend on his own choice and his own conduct. He must be "the interpreter of his own undertaking". In other words, he must act for himself.

But the lesson is of larger application. We learn from it that no authoritative revelation is possible for man, none that will convince his reason. He must work out his own destiny; at every step he must make his own choice; he must act for himself. Drinking, not laughing, is declared to be the special property of man, and by drinking the priestess primarily means acting. "To will is the principal thing," says Pantagruel; "all the rest depends upon the predestined dispositions of Heaven." Rabelais believes firmly in the free will of man, as a matter of practical ethics. But he believes equally in the government of the world by an all-powerful and all-wise God, working by fixed laws and predetermined dispositions. On either side of the entrance doors of the temple there was a table let into the wall, and on one of these tables was inscribed a Latin verse, signifying,

"Fate leads him who consents, and drags him who refuses";

while the other bore the words,

"All things move to their end".

Thus Rabelais makes no attempt to solve the mysterious and insoluble problem of fate and free will. But he realises that it is upon man's practical belief in his own power to will that human endeavour largely depends. And he further realises that this belief does not necessarily exclude a conviction in some men that they are the chosen agents of God's immutable decrees. It was, indeed, the combination of these two contradictory theories which gave strength to Calvinism, and made it so powerful as a militant and progressive force; and though Rabelais, with his inborn dislike of Calvin's hard and narrow creed, overlooked this aspect of what may be called supernatural determinism, he must have been familiar with historical examples of men who, like Julius Cæsar, were encouraged and strengthened in their task of reshaping the world by the conviction that they were working with Destiny.

But the answer of the Bottle suggests yet another line of thought. Had a definite answer been made to Panurge's questions, had the veil of the future been lifted, one of two results would inevitably have followed. If the answer had been favourable, Panurge would have married the first woman who took his fancy, and would have continued in his evil ways, secure of happiness. If the answer had been unfavourable, he would have abstained from matrimony. In either case action, in the proper sense of the word, that is to say, action as the result of a free choice, would have been paralysed. Similarly, if a clear revelation of his future destiny had been granted to man, if a sign, as has been said, had been written across the sky, all progress, material, intellectual, or moral, would have come to an end; all human endeavour would have been dried up at its source. "Man errs," says Goethe, in a famous line, "so long as he strives"; but the moral of *Faust* is that man by striving at last attains to happiness. Rabelais would have agreed with Goethe that to strive is the proper function of man. But to strive after what? The priestess gives us the clue to the answer. "I do not say drinking, simply," she explains to the travellers, "but drinking wine"; and then she goes on to remind them of the inscription in Greek characters over the gate of the temple. It was the old saying, "In wine is truth", but she interprets it in a novel fashion, as meaning that "wine fills the soul with all truth, all knowledge, and all philosophy". Thus the word of the Bottle, the "most joyous, most

divine, most certain word" that the priestess
had yet heard, is a command to strive after
truth. "Not by the possession but by the
investigation of truth," says Lessing, "are the
powers of man expanded, and therein alone
consists his ever-growing perfection. If God
held all truth shut in his right hand, and in
his left nothing but the ever restless instinct
for truth, though with the condition of for
ever and ever erring, and should say to me,
'Choose', I should humbly bow to his left
hand, and say, 'Father, give. Pure truth is
for Thee alone.' " *

But after what sort of truth is man to strive?
Scientific truth? This, no doubt, is part of
Rabelais's meaning. We know how keen was
his interest in scientific discovery and in every
form of human progress. He was a humanist,
in the widest sense of the word, eager for everything which might extend the limits of human
knowledge and add fresh dignity to the microcosm, man. We have seen him carrying his
studies in botany, anatomy, and physiology
almost to the furthest point reached in his day;
we have seen him foreshadowing, by the help of
imaginative insight rather than as the result of

---

* Quoted by Bayard Taylor, *Studies in German Literature*.

actual experiment, some of the discoveries of
modern science. Everything goes to show that
his vision of the future was cheered and illu-
mined by the thought of scientific progress.
"When you come to your world," says the priestess, in her parting speech to Pantagruel and
his companions, "bear witness that under the
earth are great treasures and wonderful things.
. . . Your philosophers who complain that
all things have been described by the ancients,
and that nothing new has been left to them to
invent, are very clearly in the wrong. All
that appears to you from heaven, and that
you call phenomena, all that the earth has
produced for you, all that the sea and the
rivers contain, is not comparable to that which
is concealed in the earth." There is a somewhat
similar passage in the panegyric on the herb
Pantagruelion. The gods are represented as
being greatly alarmed by Pantagruel's invention. They fear that "by his children may be
invented an herb of like energy, by means of
which mortals will be able to visit the sources of
the hailstorms, the floodgates of the rains,
and the forge of the thunderbolts, to invade
the regions of the moon, to enter the territory
of the celestial signs, to sit at table with us,
and take our goddesses for wives". So, too,
Messer Gaster is praised as the author of every

kind of invention, from the rudest forms of agriculture to gunpowder.

But the word of the Bottle is a command to strive not only after scientific truth, but after absolute truth. "That which you call phenomena," says the priestess, "is not comparable to that which is concealed in the earth." This surely means that Rabelais is thinking not only of future scientific discoveries, but of absolute truth, or, as he presently calls it, the veiled, the secret, the hidden. And then the priestess gives directions as to how the search for this truth is to be conducted. "All philosophers and ancient sages have esteemed two things necessary in order to follow safely and pleasantly the road of divine knowledge and the search for wisdom, namely, the guidance of God and the company of man." Of Rabelais's belief in God's guidance of human affairs enough has been said already, but the second requirement, "the company of man", needs some further explanation. This is in part given by the priestess, who points out that many of the ancient philosophers took some friend as the companion of their search. She had already expressed the same thought, pointing out, by reference to a fable of Æsop, that all men have need of one another; "that there is no king under heaven so powerful that he can do without the help of others, no poor man so proud that he can do without the rich man". A somewhat similar idea is expressed in the words she uttered just before making the travellers write their names in the book of ritual. "We place," she says, "supreme good, not in taking and receiving, but in imparting and giving, and we count ourselves happy, not if we take and receive much from others, as perhaps the sects of your world decree, but if we are always imparting and giving much to others." This is in accord with Rabelais's teaching elsewhere, especially as expressed in the discussion on debts and debtors between Pantagruel and Panurge, where Panurge breaks forth into a magnificent pæan in praise of human fellowship, painting an ideal world in which all are debtors and all are lenders. It may be said that this latter passage occurs in a chapter which is more or less meant to be paradoxical, and that Panurge's ideas on the subject of debts are expressly repudiated by Pantagruel. But the paradox is surely meant to contain a serious element, and on the whole we are justified in regarding Rabelais, typical representative of the Renaissance though he is, as introducing a distinctly social element into the exaggerated individualism of Renaissance thought. It is, he believes, by the help of our fellow-men, and by helping our fellow-men, that we can most securely tread the path of wisdom, and finally attain to the truth that is hidden beneath the earth.

But here it is well to bear in mind the allegory of the fountain. It will be remembered that when the travellers first drank of it, they believed it to be pure water. Thereupon the priestess put before them viands to prepare their palates, and bade them drink again. "Imagine," she said, "and drink, and you will have the taste of whatever wine you imagine." This they did, and to one it tasted like Beaune, to another like Graves, and to a third like Mirevaux. So with the interpretation of the answer of the Bottle. To one man it may seem to bear one meaning, to another man another; each interprets according to his own imagination. In any case, however, the message is one of hope: "Good hope lies at the bottom of it." Rabelais's philosophy, however much we may be mistaken as to its exact import, is essentially an optimistic one. It leads us to that excellent state of mind to which he has given the name of Pantagruelism, and which he defines as "a certain gaiety of spirit built up of disregard of things fortuitous", adding, in another place, that "its possessors will never take in bad part anything that they recognise to spring from a good, frank, and loyal courage". It is of this philosophy that Pantagruel is the living embodiment. "He took everything in good part, he put a good interpretation on every act, he never tormented himself, and was never scandalised . . . for all the treasures that the heaven covereth and the earth containeth, in all their height, depth, length, and breadth, are not worthy to stir our affections or trouble our senses and spirits."

With this note of unworldliness and optimism we may leave Rabelais. It is one of his greatest merits, as it is one of his greatest charms, that, having a clear insight into the social and political evils of his day, he looks forward to the future with a calm and robust confidence. "*Bon espoir y gist au fond.*"

ARTHUR TILLEY.

BIBLIOGRAPHY

PRINCIPAL EDITIONS OF RABELAIS'S WORKS

(*a*) Principal early editions of *Gargantua* and *Pantagruel*.

1.	*Pantagruel*	Lyons	[1532]
2.	*Pantagruel*	Lyons	1533
3.	*Pantagruel*	[Lyons]	1534
4.	*Gargantua*	[Lyons]	[1534]
5.	*Gargantua*	Lyons	1535
6.	*Pantagruel* and *Gargantua* ...	Lyons	1537
7.	*Pantagruel* and *Gargantua* ...	Lyons	1542
8.	Third Book	Paris	1546
9.	Fourth Book (in eleven chapters)	Lyons	1548
10.	The Four Books	Lyons	?
11.	Third Book	Paris	1552
12.	Fourth Book (complete)	Paris	1552
13.	Fourth Book	Lyons	1552
14.	The Four Books	?	1553
15.	*The Ringing Island*..........	?	1562
16.	Fifth Book	[Lyons]	1564
17.	The Five Books	Lyons	1565

(*b*) Principal later editions of Rabelais's works.

1. With notes by J. Le Duchat and B. de La Monnoye. Amsterdam, 1711, 5 vols.
2. With notes by J. Le Duchat and P. Motteux. Amsterdam, 1741, 3 vols.
3. Ed. Esmangart and Éloi Johanneau (variorum edition). Paris, 1823–1826, 9 vols.

BIBLIOGRAPHY

4. Ed. Burgaud des Marets and E. J. Rathery. Paris, 1857–1858, 2 vols; second ed., 1870.
5. Ed. P. Jannet. Paris, 1867–1868, 6 vols.; second ed., 1873–1874, 7 vols.
6. Ed. A. Montaiglon and L. Lacour. Paris, 1868–1872, 3 vols. The Fifth Book is printed from the MS. in the Bibliothèque Nationale.
7. Ed. C. Marty-Laveaux. Paris, 1868–1903, 6 vols. With notes, life, glossary, and bibliography.
8. Ed. L. Moland. Paris, 1881, 1 vol.
9. With a notice by Maxime Formont. Paris, 1906, 4 vols. Without notes. Text of Marty-Laveaux.

TRANSLATIONS

1. The first and second books of Sir Thomas Urquhart's famous translation of Rabelais were published in 1653. The third book did not appear till 1693, more than thirty years after his death. It was edited by Pierre Motteux, who in the following year reprinted the first two books and added a translation of the fourth and fifth books, by himself. This joint translation was republished under the title of *The Whole Works of Francis Rabelais*, *M. D.*, London, 1708, 2 vols. It has been several times reprinted in recent years, notably in the series of *Tudor Translations*, with an excellent introduction* by Charles Whibley, London, 1900, 3 vols.

---

* Republished in *Literary Portraits* (see page 364 following).

BIBLIOGRAPHY

2. *Rabelais, the Five Books and Minor Writings, together with Letters and Documents Illustrating his Life*, a new translation, with notes, by W. F. Smith. London, 1893, 2 vols. The translation, which is far more faithful than Urquhart's, is excellent, and the notes are helpful and judicious.

3. The German translation by Gottlob Regis, 2 parts, Leipsic, 1832–1841, is furnished with a good bibliography and a very full and learned commentary. A reprint is announced.

See, for the early editions, J. C. Brunet, *Recherches bibliographiques et critiques sur les Éditions originales de Rabelais*, 1852, and, for a full and elaborate bibliography of all Rabelais's works, P. Plan, *Bibliographie rabelaisienne, les Éditions de Rabelais de 1532–1711*, Paris, 1894.

It may be useful to mention here the following selections:

BESANT (W.). *Readings in Rabelais*. Edinburgh and London, 1883.
STOKES (F. G.). *Hours with Rabelais*. London, 1905.
WRIGHT (C. H. C.). *Selections from Rabelais's Gargantua*. New York, 1904.

AUTHORITIES ON RABELAIS

In what follows I have only attempted to give a select bibliography. It comprises,

BIBLIOGRAPHY

I hope, all that is of first-rate importance for the study of Rabelais.

ABEL (C.). *Rabelais, Salaried Physician to the City of Metz* (*Rabelais, Médecin stipendié de la Cité de Metz*). Metz, 1870.

ALBÉNAS (G. D'). *Portraits of Rabelais* (*Les Portraits de Rabelais*). Montpellier, 1880.

ARNSTÄDT (F. A.). *François Rabelais and his Treatise on Education* (*François Rabelais und sein Traité d'Éducation*). Leipsic, 1877.

BESANT (WALTER). *Rabelais.* Edinburgh and London, 1879. In *Foreign Classics for English Readers.*

BESANT (WALTER). *The French Humourists from the 12th to the 19th Century.* London, 1873. (Rabelais, pp. 91–121.)

BRUNETIÈRE (F.). *History of French Classical Literature* (*Histoire de la Littérature française classique*). Paris, 1904. (Rabelais, vol. I, part i, pp. 105–164.)

COLLETET (GUILLAUME). *François Rabelais,* an extract from the *Lives of French Poets,* published by Philomneste Junior (Gustave Brunet). Geneva, 1867.

COMPAYRÉ (G.). *A Critical History of the Doctrines of Education in France* (*Histoire critique des Doctrines de l'Éducation en France*). Paris, 1879, 2 vols. (Rabelais, vol. I, pp. 55–82.)

COUTANS (A.). *The Pedagogy of Rabelais* (*La Pédagogie de Rabelais*). Paris, 1899.

DELARUELLE (L.). *Rabelais's Debt to Erasmus and Budé* (*Ce que Rabelais doit à Érasme et à Budé*). From the *Revue d'Histoire littéraire,* vol. XI, pp. 220–262. Paris, 1904.

DUBOUCHET (A.). *François Rabelais at Montpellier, 1530–1538* (*François Rabelais à Montpellier, 1530–1538*). Montpellier, 1887.

FAGUET (ÉMILE). *The Sixteenth Century* (*Seizième Siècle*). Paris, 1894. (Rabelais, pp. 77–126.)

BIBLIOGRAPHY

FLEURY (J.). *Rabelais and his Works* (*Rabelais et ses Œuvres*). Paris, 1877, 2 vols. A useful introduction to the study of Rabelais, as it contains a careful analysis and exposition, chapter by chapter, of his book.

FLINT (AUSTIN). *Rabelais as a Physiologist*. New York, 1901.

GEBHART (E.). *Rabelais, the Renaissance, and the Reformation* (*Rabelais, la Renaissance, et la Réforme*). Paris, 1877. Republished with alterations in 1897 as a volume of the *Classiques populaires*. An excellent criticism, especially the chapter on Rabelais's religion.

GORDON (R.). *François Rabelais and the Faculty of Medicine at Montpellier* (*François Rabelais et la Faculté de Médecine de Montpellier*). Montpellier, 1876.

HEULHARD (A.). *Rabelais, his Travels in Italy, his Exile at Metz* (*Rabelais, ses Voyages en Italie, son Exil à Metz*). Paris, 1891. Illustrated. Elucidates several obscure points in Rabelais's life.

LE DOUBLE (A. F.). *Rabelais, Anatomist and Physiologist* (*Rabelais, Anatomiste et Physiologiste*). Paris, 1899. With admirable illustrations. Important.

LEFRANC (ABEL). *The Voyages of Pantagruel* (*Les Navigations de Pantagruel*). Paris, 1904. Throws a new and important light on Rabelais's interest in geographical discovery.

LENORMANT (C.). *Rabelais and the Architecture of the Renaissance* (*Rabelais et l'Architecture de la Renaissance*). Paris, 1840.

LIGIER (H.). *The Political Ideas of Rabelais* (*La Politique de Rabelais*). Paris, 1880.

MARTINOZZI (G.). *The Pantagruel of François Rabelais* (*Il Pantagruele di Francesco Rabelais*). Città di Castello, 1885.

MARTY-LAVEAUX (C.). *Rabelais*, in L. Petit de Julleville, *Histoire de la Langue et de la Littérature française*, vol. III, pp. 29-72. Paris, 1897.

BIBLIOGRAPHY

MILLET (R.). *Rabelais*. Paris, 1892. A volume of *Les Grands Écrivains français* series.

NICERON (J. P.). *Memoirs to Serve for the History of Men Illustrious in the Republic of Letters, with the Catalogue Raisonné of their Works* (*Mémoires pour servir à l'Histoire des Hommes illustres dans la République des Lettres, avec le Catalogue raisonné de leurs Ouvrages*). Paris, 1729-1745, 43 vols. (Rabelais, vol. XXXII, 337 ff.)

PAGE (C. H.). *François Rabelais*. Introduction to *Rabelais* volume of *French Classics for Englis'. Readers* series. New York and London, 1905.

QUICK (R. H.). *Educational Reformers* (No. 5, Rabelais). New York, 1890.

REVILLOUT (C.). *The Promoters of the Renaissance at Montpellier* (*Les Promoteurs de la Renaissance à Montpellier*), in *Mémoires de la Société archéologique de Montpellier*, series II, vol. II, pp. 209-383. Montpellier, 1902.

SCHNEEGANS (H.). *History of Grotesque Satire* (*Geschichte der grotesken Satire*). Strasburg, 1894.

SÉBILLOT (PAUL). *Gargantua in Popular Tradition* (*Gargantua dans les Traditions populaires*). Paris, 1883.

STAPFER (PAUL). *Rabelais, his Personality, his Genius, and his Work* (*Rabelais, sa Personne, son Génie, et son Œuvre*). Paris, 1889. The best biographical and critical work on Rabelais; distinguished by good sense and appreciation of Rabelais's humour.

THUASNE (L.). *Studies in Rabelais* (*Études sur Rabelais*). Paris, 1904.

TILLEY (ARTHUR). *The Literature of the French Renaissance*. Cambridge, 1904, 2 vols. (Rabelais, vol. I, pp. 165-223, and pp. 262-267 for the bibliography.)

WHIBLEY (CHARLES). *Literary Portraits*. London, 1904. (Rabelais, pp. 1-108.)

ZIESING (T.). *Erasmus or Salignac? a Study of the Letter*

BIBLIOGRAPHY

of François Rabelais (Érasme ou Salignac? Étude sur la Lettre de François Rabelais). Paris, 1887.

The *Revue des Études rabelaisiennes*, a quarterly the publication of which was begun in Paris in 1903, is of first-rate importance for the study of Rabelais, and contains numerous articles which have added considerably to our knowledge of the subject.

Finally should be mentioned *Rabelais, his Life and Work, by the Light of Recent Research (Rabelais, sa Vie et son Œuvre, d'après des Travaux récents)*, by V. L. Bourrilly, an extract from the *Revue d'Histoire moderne et contemporaine*, Paris, 1905–1906, and a similar account by J. Boulenger in the *Revue critique* for July 9, 1906.

A. T.

INDEX

Names containing *de* are, for convenience of reference, entered under the last portion of the name. Names containing *le*, *la*, *du*, or *des* are entered under these elements.

INDEX

INDEX

INDEX

INDEX

INDEX

INDEX

INDEX

INDEX

INDEX

INDEX

INDEX

379

INDEX

INDEX

381

INDEX

INDEX

INDEX

INDEX

Rouen, 41
Rousseau, 160
Roussel, Gérard, 335
Rovigo, 282
Royal Chapel (Paris), 121
Ruach, Island of, 221, 232, 280
Rubens, 311, 321
Rue des Jardins (Paris), 114
Rue du Fouarre (Paris), 170
Ruel, Jean, 22, 31
Russia, 144
Russians, 240
Ruzé, Louis de, 22

Sacramentarians, 59
Sagres, 207
Saguenay, the, 213, 218
Saint-Aignan, bell of (Orléans), 42
Saint-Ay, 88, 89, 91; Seigneur of (Étienne Lorens), 89, 96
St. Babolin, 92, 184
St. Bartholomew, massacre of, 325
St. Benet, boot of, 146
St. Brandan, 252
St. Brandan's Isle, 250
Saint-Christophe du Jambet, 105, 106
St. Clement, 98
Saint-Cloud, 134
Sainte-Chapelle (Paris), 121, 259
Sainte-Croix, bell-tower of (Orléans), 42
Sainte-Marthe, Charles de, 141
Sainte-Marthe, Gaucher de, 141, 142 n, 149, 150
Sainte-Marthe, Gaucher (Scévole) de, 141
Sainte-Marthe, the brothers (Louis and Scévole), 141
Saintes, 25
Saint-Gelais, Mellin (Merlin) de, 160, 161, 216, 289
Saint-Germain, 79, 98
St. Hilaire the Great, church of (Poitiers), 37
St. Jerome, 263
St. John, Knights of, 239

St. Lawrence, Gulf of, 209
St. Lawrence, the, 209, 213, 218
Saint-Malo, 122, 123, 208, 210, 214, 215
St. Mark's (Venice), 121
St. Martin, church of (Tours), 12
St. Martin of Tours, 19
Saint-Maur-des-Fossés, 92, 106, 183; abbey of, 67, 79, 92, 189
Saint-Mesmin, monastery of, 27
Saintonge, 214, 215, 217, 223
St. Paul, 148, 339
Saint-Paul, cemetery of (Paris), 114
St. Paul the Hermit, 252
St. Peter's (Rome), 310
St. Pierre, cathedral of (Poitiers), 37
St. Porchaire, church of (Poitiers), 37
St. Quenet, 128
St. Radegonde, church of (Poitiers), 37
Saint-Symphorien, 90
St. Victor, abbey of (Paris), 164
Salignac, Bernard, 53
Salle des Pas Perdus, la (Poitiers), 37
Salmigondin, 183, 217
Salmon, Jean (Macrin), 68–71, 115
Sancho Panza, 293
Sandals, Island of, 264
Sandy Sea, 144
Sangallo, Antonio da, 64
Sansay, 33
Santa Maria del Fiore, cathedral of (Florence), 63
Sardanapalus, 178
Sark, 122, 215
Sarmatians, 144
Satin, Land of, 265, 266
Satire, 144, 172, 179, 219, 253, 255, 259, 265, 275–278, 286, 319, 328, 341
Saverne, 97
Savoy, 47, 81, 82, 144
Scaliger, 54, 117, 164

385

INDEX

INDEX

387

INDEX

THE END